P9-DKD-473

DATE DUE

Changing Youth
in a
Changing Society

PATTERNS OF ADOLESCENT
DEVELOPMENT AND DISORDER

CHANGING YOUTH
IN A
CHANGING SOCIETY

PATTERNS OF ADOLESCENT
DEVELOPMENT AND DISORDER

Michael Rutter

HARVARD UNIVERSITY PRESS
CAMBRIDGE, MASSACHUSETTS
1980

Library of Congress Cataloging in Publication Data

Rutter, Michael.
  Changing youth in a changing society.

  Bibliography: p.
  1. Adolescence.   2. Adolescent psychology.
I. Title.
HQ796.R88   305.2'3   80-146
ISBN 0-674-10875-2

CONTENTS

v

Contents

PREFACE

I feel deeply honoured to have been elected to the Rock Carling Fellowship of 1979 but I was considerably daunted by the topic assigned to me—that of reviewing the field of psychosocial problems of adolescents in society today, with particular reference to whether there are definable problems specifically associated with the adolescent age period, whether the problems are increasing or changing in character, and how the health and social services should be geared to cope with them. The subject indeed proved to be both complex and far-reaching and it was rapidly clear that some constraints would have to be imposed if the review was not to become unmanageably large and cumbersome. Accordingly, I have considered adolescence in terms of the circumstances of present-day U.K. and the U.S.A. and I have approached the topic from the two perspectives with which I am most familiar—the developmental and the epidemiological.

It seemed imperative first to survey the developmental changes which occur during adolescence if there was to be any hope of considering the difficult question of how far there are definable adolescent problems. These issues constitute the basis of the first chapter of the monograph. In that section of the review I pay particular attention to the changing pattern of psychosocial disorders during the teenage years but there has been no attempt to provide a clinical account of the numerous syndromes which arise during that age period, as details of these are readily obtainable from standard text books. The second chapter considers the issue of whether problems are increasing or changing in character and for this purpose I have focussed on those problems most typical of adolescence. However, I have also been constrained here by the very patchy nature of the available evidence on secular or historical trends. In the third chapter I have tried to provide an overview of some of the main influences on adolescent behaviour. Throughout the monograph, but especially in this chapter and the final one, I have given most space to those topics where the findings are novel or are likely to be least familiar.

vii

Where there has been little new to say and where the evidence has been well reviewed before I have simply referred to the relevant sources and have given only a brief summary of the main points. In the fourth chapter I note some of the main changes which have taken place or are taking place in society and which might be relevant to the theme of adolescence. Of course, this topic potentially covers the whole of life and inevitably I have had to be highly selective.

The final chapter deals with the question of services and here I have followed the instructions to Rock Carling Fellows to speculate about the future and to consider practical possibilities in the development and implementation of ideas likely to lead to progress and improvement. Because it has tended to receive less attention in the past, I have given most extensive coverage to the difficult field of prevention. As with the whole of the review, I have placed emphasis on empirical research findings but I have attempted to go beyond what is proven (as that is very little) in order to suggest the leads which may be worth following in the future. Lastly, this monograph is perhaps most different from its predecessors in extending well beyond the traditional medical domain into fields of delinquency, sexuality, and social behaviour more generally. I make no apologies for having done this as I believe that there are many useful parallels to be drawn between them and that the ideas for effective services which stem from one area of interest could often be usefully applied in others.

ACKNOWLEDGEMENTS

Necessarily in a review of this kind I have had to rely heavily on the ideas and findings of many colleagues in different disciplines and I am extremely grateful to everyone who helped me in this way. However, I am especially indebted to those who most generously provided me with unpublished data and allowed me to include figures based on their material. In this connection very special thanks are due to James Douglas, David Galloway, Patrick Ivin, the Inner London Education Authority, the Home Office Research Unit, Post Office Telecommunications, British Transport Police, and the Department of Education and Science, all of whom went out of their way to provide the material I asked for. I am also most grateful to colleagues on collaborative projects who undertook further analyses to answer questions I raised, and particularly to Oliver Chadwick, Russell Schachar, David Quinton, Bridget Yule, Maggie Winkworth, Grace Gray, Daphne Holbrook, and Janet Ouston. Throughout the first chapter I have made extensive use of unpublished material from the Isle of Wight epidemiological study of adolescents and I am most grateful to my colleagues Philip Graham and Oliver Chadwick for generously allowing me to use data for which they were jointly responsible.

James Tanner kindly gave permission to reproduce two figures from *Arch. Dis. Child.,* 1966. In several places I have utilized material of my own included in earlier publications and I am grateful to the *Journal of Child Psychology and Psychiatry, Psychological Medicine, Proceedings of the Royal Society of Medicine,* Penguin Books, Heinemann Medical, Open Books, and Blackwell Scientific for permission to do so.

Ideas and leads to useful sources of material came from many people but I would particularly like to thank Ron Clarke, Pat Mayhew, F. W. Solley, Patrick Fallon, Henri Giller, Jean Davies, Elizabeth Jay, Timothy Hope, Chief Constable E. Haslam, Chief-Inspector A. D. Thompson, Eric Bolton, Peter Sainsbury, Peter Mortimore, A. M. Sutherland, and my wife, Marjorie. Barbara

Maughan, Janet Ouston, Eric Taylor, Lionel Hersov, and Marjorie Rutter all read earlier drafts of various chapters and made extremely helpful comments; however, they should not be held responsible for the views expressed or any errors of fact or interpretation which may remain. Finally, I am particularly grateful to Joy Maxwell, who prepared almost all of the figures and checked the bibliography as well as typing the manuscript.

I

Patterns of
Adolescent Development
and Disorder

INTRODUCTION

As defined by the *Shorter Oxford English Dictionary*, adolescence simply refers to the process of growing up or to the period between childhood and maturity, which is said to extend from 14 to 25 years in males and from 12 to 21 in females. That there is (and must be) this phase of transition from immaturity to maturity, from childhood to adulthood, has been recognized from at least the time of Aristotle onwards (Muuss, 1975). However, the notion that adolescence is in some way very different from the whole of development which precedes and which follows it, is a relatively modern notion first clearly conceptualized by G. Stanley Hall (1904) in his major treatise on the subject published just after the turn of the century. He put forward the view of adolescence as a time of 'storm and stress' characterized by an inherent instability, emotional turmoil and psychic disturbance.

Psychoanalytic theorists have supported this concept of adolescence as a period of great upheaval and disturbance (see Rutter et al, 1976). Thus, Blos (1970) asserted that: 'The more or less orderly course of development during latency is thrown into disarray with the child's entry into adolescence ... adolescence cannot take its normal course without regression'. Similarly, Anna Freud (1958) maintained that:

> Adolescence is by its nature an interruption of peaceful growth, and ... the upholding of a steady equilibrium during the adolescent process is in itself abnormal ... adolescence resembles in appearance a variety of other emotional upsets and structural upheavals. The adolescent manifestations come close to symptom formation of the neurotic, psychotic or

dissocial order and merge almost imperceptibly into ...
almost all the mental illnesses.

Eissler (1958) saw adolescence as predominantly 'stormy and
unpredictable behaviour marked by mood swings between
elation and melancholy'.

However, the supposed uniqueness of adolescence has not only
concerned the extent of storm and stress. At least three other concepts have been put forward: the lability and unpredictability of
adolescent behaviour, the distinctly different nature of the psychological tasks and issues during adolescence, and the separateness of
the adolescent peer group culture. Thus, with regard to the essential variability of adolescent behaviour, Josselyn (1954) suggested
that: 'A typical adolescent may present a picture today of hysteria
while the history indicates that a month ago his behaviour
appeared typically impulsive'. In the same vein, Eissler (1958)
stated that:

> ... (adolescent) psychopathology switches from one form
> to another, sometimes in the course of weeks or months, but
> also from one day to another. ... The symptoms manifested
> by such patients maybe neurotic at one time and almost
> psychotic at another. Then sudden acts of delinquency may
> occur, only to be followed by a phase of perverted sexual
> activity.

The view that psychiatric disorders arising in adolescence are
different from those in either childhood or adult life in being largely reactive to the stresses of that developmental phase is reflected
in clinicians' diagnostic habits. Among adolescents seen at American outpatient clinics in the 1960s 'transient situational disorder'
constituted much the commonest diagnostic category (Rosen et
al, 1965) and even among inpatients the diagnosis was made
in nearly a quarter of all cases (U.S. Department of Health,
Education and Welfare, 1966). The implication is that psychiatric
problems beginning in adolescence should have a particularly
good prognosis.

The view that the psychological tasks of adolescence are quali-
tatively different from those in other age periods has been argued
most systematically by Erikson (1955 and 1968). He sees the

2

psychosocial crisis of adolescence as the need to put aside childhood identifications and to develop a new personality configura-
tion. The crisis at this point may lead to 'role confusion' or
'identity diffusion'. He writes:

> ... in spite of the similarity of adolescent 'symptoms' and
> episodes to neurotic and psychotic symptoms and episodes,
> adolescence is not an affliction, but a normative crisis, i.e. a
> normal phase of increased conflict characterized by a seeming
> fluctuation in ego strength ... what under prejudiced
> scrutiny may appear to be the onset of a neurosis, often is
> but an aggravated crisis which might prove to be self-
> liquidating and, in fact, contributive to the process of identity
> formation.

The essential task of adolescence is thought to be the establishment of a sense of one's own identity as a unique person and the
avoidance of role confusion. The development of identity refers
to the basic core of a person's character, and identity is thought
to be a necessary precursor to true intimacy—the reciprocal
personal sharing of deep relationships, considered to be the stage
following adolescence.

While Erikson has been the most seminal writer on the emotional and social issues distinctively associated with adolescence,
Piaget (1970) has been even more influential in postulating discrete
stages of cognitive development, which are invariant in the order
in which they occur (although the timing varies from individual
to individual). About the age of 12 years, young people first become capable of 'formal operations'—that is the ability to mani-
pulate hypotheses or propositions in the absence of concrete or
tangible referents, in other words, systematic and rational abstract
thinking. Kohlberg (1969), similarly, has suggested distinct and
invariant stages of moral development which correspond to the
cognitive processes. Adolescence is characterized by the beginnings
of a shift from a 'conventional' morality with internal motivations
based on a duty to maintain the given social order to a 'post-
conventional' level in which standards conform to personal inner
processes of thought and judgement which reflect ethical principles independent of the reactions of other people.

3

The separateness of the adolescent peer group culture has been most forcefully argued by Riesman (1950) and Coleman (1961). Riesman maintained that middle-class parents were abdicating their responsibilities and authority to their children's peer group which had come to occupy a predominant role in terms of both models of behaviour and group pressures for conformity. Coleman, in reporting a study of high school students, similarly concluded that peers were relatively more influential than parents for this age group and that there was a cultural cleavage between adolescent and adult communities. According to Coleman (1961), the adolescent:

> ... is cut off from the rest of society, forced inward toward his own age group, made to carry out his whole social life with others his own age. With his fellows he comes to constitute a small society, one that has most of its important connections *within* itself, and maintains only a few threads of connection with the outside adult society.

Adolescence, then, is seen as a period during which young people become alienated from their parents and during which the 'generation gap' widens and becomes associated with negative feelings.

A further point which derives from some of these views is that things are getting worse. Thus, Bronfenbrenner (1970) has suggested that in the U.K. and the U.S.A. there has been a decline in the amount of time parents and children spend together and a disengagement from the responsibilities of parenthood. It is thought that adolescents are being increasingly pressed into a peer group culture with a loss of family ties and family influences. The argument is that there has been a progressive disintegration of the family with an accompanying marked increase in adolescent suicide, juvenile delinquency, and educational failure (Bronfenbrenner, 1976).

As we shall see, each of these views has been subjected to considerable criticism and there have been forceful attempts at refutation with respect to all of them (see e.g. Elkin and Westley, 1955; Jahoda and Warren, 1965; Masterson, 1967; Weiner, 1970; Rutter et al, 1976). However, as John Coleman (1978) has pointed

4

out, a rejection of the 'storm and stress' view of adolescence and an acceptance of the polar opposite—that adolescence is peaceful and harmonious—leaves unexplained how young people cope with the major adaptations required of them as they pass through puberty, leave school, take up employment, and move from home.

My main aim in this monograph is to review the evidence on each of these issues and in doing so to speculate on the implications for services. However, first it is necessary to consider a little further what is meant by adolescence and what is distinctive about the adolescent age period.

Psychosocial adolescence

Several writers have emphasized that adolescence is a socially created category (e.g. Campbell, 1969; Baumrind, 1975; Sommer, 1978a). It is, of course, connected with puberty which is a biologically determined phenomenon, but the roles and expectations of that age period are determined by society. Rites of passage or ceremonies in which the child or adolescent is initiated into adulthood take place in many different cultures but, for males, physiological and social puberty are essentially different and only rarely converge (see Sommer, 1978a). The event of menstruation in girls provides a pressure for a recognition of a change of status so that where specific rituals occur they tend to be more closely tied to physical development in females. Moreover, psychosocial concepts of adolescence have varied greatly over time (Ariès, 1962; Kett, 1977). The term adolescence was rarely used prior to the eighteenth century and although the characteristics of puberty were well recognized, little psychological significance was attached to them. The reaching of adulthood was determined by the acquisition of independence, a point having no direct connection with physiological maturity. During the eighteenth and nineteenth centuries children often left school and started work well before reaching puberty. Clearly adolescence then meant something very different from its meaning now when most young people reach sexual maturity several years, and often many years, before completing their schooling. Modern concepts of adolescence were shaped to a considerable extent by the introduction and extension of compulsory education, by the laws prohibiting the employment of juveniles and by the development of laws and services differentiating juvenile from adult offenders (Sommer, 1978a). These changes coincided in time with the emergence of views about the pubescent years as tumultuous, hazardous and in need of adult guidance. Adolescence was not discovered in the sense that anyone studied the behaviour of young people and noted its distinctive character. Rather, the teenage years came to constitute an age period of interest and concern and it was decided that adolescence, in the psychosocial sense, *should* be a universal experience.

Commercial interests added their effect following the Second World War. As Baumrind (1975) has put it, psychosocial adolescence is a luxury afforded only by the affluent. As young people came to be financially better off they came to be a market worth fostering. As a consequence, since the 1950s there has been an explosion of spending by adolescents on clothes, on records, and on entertainment. To a considerable extent, adolescence has been identified as a meaningful age period because it constitutes a rich source of potential customers. The youth 'pop' culture has been shaped in considerable part by commercial market forces.

In the eyes of the public, the youth culture has also been identified with radical social movements. Although often thought of as a new phenomenon of the 1960s, such movements are as old as history (see Braungart, 1975). Thus, in more recent times, the youth culture challenged Victorian social and sexual mores in the 1920s and became involved in anti-war movements in the 1930s. Awareness and concern with the sociopolitical world increases during adolescence and it is during this age period that young people search for a congruence in ideals, beliefs and actions. That has been so for a long time. Nevertheless, there can be little doubt that the extent and force of the youth movement in the U.K. and the U.S.A. did increase markedly during the last 25 years. A possible explanation lies in the changes in education (Braungart, 1975) as radical ideas tend to be most prominent in college student groups (Yankelovich, 1972). First, far more young people are attending colleges of further education—a threefold increase over two decades in the U.S.A. Second, not only do colleges provide a 'city of youth' and hence centres of critical thinking and

6

discussion on sociopolitical issues, but also more minority groups (both ethnic minorities and also women) have gone on to further education. Hence, colleges may have come to include more individuals who feel discriminated against or alienated. Thirdly, colleges provide an international medium for the rapid dissemination of 'new' ideas and the spread of ideological values. Similar conditions throughout much of the world provide the opportunity for a 'critical mass' of youth who actively participate in social and political activities. Fourthly, the increase of studies in social sciences have meant that more people have been likely to become knowledgeable about society's problems and concerned with theories dealing with society's ills. For these and other reasons (Braungart, 1975), there has been an increasing involvement of young people in various social or political 'protest' groups or movements. Nevertheless, political activists today, as in days gone by, constitute a tiny minority of young people.

It is clear then that to a considerable extent the youth 'phenomenon' and the current concepts of 'psychosocial adolescence' are products of the prevailing western culture. Adolescence is recognized and treated as a distinct stage of development because the coincidence of extended education and early sexual maturation have meant a prolonged phase of physical maturity associated with economic and psychosocial dependence; because many of the widely held psychological theories specify that adolescence *should* be different; because commercial interests demanded a youth culture; and because schools and colleges have ensured that large numbers of young people are kept together in an age-segregated social group. To that extent, psychosocial adolescence is created by society and has no necessary connection with the developmental process. However, the shaping of adolescence by social forces does not mean that there are no inherent developmental changes which occur during the teenage years. In order to examine that issue we need first to consider the evidence on the physical changes associated with adolescence and their psychological consequences.

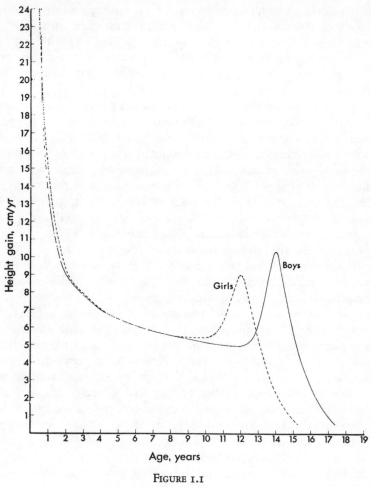

FIGURE 1.1

(Data from Tanner et al, 1966)

PHYSICAL CHANGES DURING ADOLESCENCE

Height and physique

Longitudinal studies of physical growth clearly show that adolescence is associated both with marked changes in the *tempo* of development and *alterations* in its character (Tanner, 1970, 1971).

8

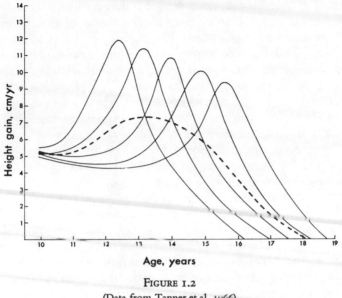

FIGURE 1.2
(Data from Tanner et al, 1966)

In general, the velocity of physical growth progressively decreases from the fourth month of foetal life onwards until there is a marked acceleration during adolescence—the so-called adolescent growth spurt. In the U.K. the typical girl begins the adolescent height spurt at about $10\frac{1}{2}$ years and reaches peak height velocity at approximately 12 years; the boy begins his spurt and reaches his peak just 2 years later, the boys' peak being higher than the girls' (Tanner, 1970).

However, it is important to recognize that there is huge individual variation in the age when this growth spurt occurs. This is illustrated in fig. 1.2 in connection with five boys in the Harpenden Growth Study (see Tanner et al, 1966) who reached their peak height velocity at different times with four years between the earliest and latest. The dotted line shows the 'average' figures obtained by treating the values cross-sectionally and so deriving a mean height for each age. The effect of averaging gravely distorts the shape and greatly diminishes the height of the growth

9

spurt. The lesson is that cross-sectional data are likely seriously to misrepresent the course of individual patterns of development. This is an important issue with respect to the psychological changes of adolescence where most of the available data stem from cross-sectional studies or from longitudinal studies analysed in cross-sectional fashion. The linking of physiological and psychological changes is further hampered by the fact that nearly all psychological data are reported in terms of chronological age rather than in terms of stage of puberty.

The growth spurt is accompanied by marked changes in physique, the changes being different in the two sexes in a way not apparent before puberty (Tanner, 1970). Girls have a particularly large spurt in hip width whereas boys increase most in shoulder breadth. Both sexes show an increase in muscle bulk but this increase is much more marked in boys than girls. Boys show a very marked strength increase whereas this is scarcely apparent in girls. The bones thicken and widen, and the dimensions and shape of the face alter—more so in males than females. The head, hands, and feet reach their adult size earliest so that some adolescents complain of having large hands or feet. Shortsightedness increases throughout childhood from age 6 years onwards but there is a particularly rapid increase at puberty. Boys on average lose fat at adolescence with a further gain as height velocity slows down. Girls show a similar curve but there is only a temporary go-slow (rather than a loss) in limb fat accumulation, and a steady rise in body fat, together with a general tendency for the laying down of fat as they cease to gain height.

In keeping with these changes in the deposition of adipose tissue, the period of adolescence is accompanied by a marked increase in the proportions of girls who feel fat and who diet (Nylander, 1971). Thus, Nylander found that the proportion of girls who felt fat rose from 26 per cent at 14 years to 50 per cent at 18 years, and the proportion who had dieted (of those who felt fat) from 8 per cent at 14 years to 44 per cent at 18. Neither was at all common in boys and the proportion did not rise during adolescence. The more extensive data from Huenemann's longitudinal study of teenage girls in California (Huenemann et al, 1966) showed similar patterns. More than half the girls (56 per cent of twelfth-graders and 43 per cent of ninth-graders) described themselves as fat, compared with less than a quarter of the boys. Boys tended to want to gain in weight, size, or strength whereas girls usually wanted to lose weight—the boys generally responded to these wishes with exercise and the girls with diet. It was noticeable, too, that many of the girls had unrealistic ideas of their own fatness and that very few of their dieting efforts proved successful (indeed as many gained weight as lost it!). How far this concern with being slim is a modern phenomenon is uncertain but it appears that over the last 50 years female models and 'pin-ups' (who may be taken as representing popular views of the 'ideal' shape) have become progressively thinner, so that it may well be so.

Puberty

Considerable changes in hormone secretion occur during adolescence (Tanner, 1970; Marshall and Tanner, 1974). The first event in puberty is an increased secretion of gonadotrophic hormones by the pituitary which causes the follicles of the ovaries and the tubules of the testes to develop. Oestrogen production remains roughly constant in both sexes up to age 7 years and then rises gradually. As adolescence begins in girls, oestrogen production rises very sharply and becomes cyclic. Oestrogen production also increases slightly in boys during puberty, but the main change is a very large rise in testosterone secretion. In both boys and girls adrenal androgens also increase greatly at puberty, and these are responsible for the emergence of some of the secondary sexual characteristics—particularly pubic and axillary hair.

The first sign of puberty in boys is usually an acceleration of the growth of the testes and scrotum, associated often with the onset of sperm production before the acquisition of male secondary sex characteristics (Richardson and Short, 1978). Pubic hair growth and then the spurts in height and in penis growth follow. Axillary and facial hair appear on average some two years after the beginning of pubic hair growth; body hair growth begins a little later and continues until well after puberty. The breaking of the voice (which accompanies enlargement of the larynx) occurs relatively late in adolescence and is often a gradual process. There is a permanent increase in the breadth of the breast areola and sometimes a temporary enlargement of the underlying breast tissue which may cause discomfort or embarrassment.

There are two main points to note in relation to the physical changes shown by boys during adolescence. First, the development spans a period of at least 4 to $4\frac{1}{2}$ years; and second, there is immense individual variation in the age at which puberty occurs. For example, in the Kinsey study (Kinsey et al, 1948) the average age of first ejaculation was just under 14 years, but in 10 per cent of cases it occurred either before the eleventh or after the sixteenth birthday. A similar range is found if puberty is assessed by height spurt, pubic hair growth or gonadal development (Tanner, 1970). Thus, in normal boys there is roughly a 5-year range for the age at which puberty is reached.

In girls, puberty begins some two years earlier and extends over a slightly shorter period (3 to 4 years rather than 4 or 5). However, individual variation is equally great. The average age of menarche is about 13 years but the range extends from 10 to $16\frac{1}{2}$ years. Breast development, beginning between 8 and 13 years, is usually the first sign of pubescence. It is followed within a year or so by the appearance of pubic hair, a height spurt and changes in general physique. Once again, however, there is considerable individual variation in the ordering and timing of these physical changes.

The increased production of androgens during adolescence in both boys and girls leads to an increase in skin thickness and in oily secretion from the sebaceous glands, often with clogged pores and inflammation. As a consequence, over the course of the pubertal years there is a rapid rise in the proportion of young people reporting pimples, blackheads and acne—from a fifth of boys at age 12 years to two-thirds at 16 years, and from a quarter of girls at 12 years to a half at 15 years (see Sommer, 1978a). Boys tend to experience rather worse acne than girls but both are very common users of various sorts of acne medication.

Hormonal effects on emotional behaviour

The role of sex hormones in relation to physical maturation is clear, but their effects on emotions and behaviour are less so. It is evident from a variety of studies (see Money, 1961; Money and

Ehrhardt, 1972) that androgens have an important (but far from exclusive) controlling function on sex drive in the male. They probably have a similar effect in the female, the hormones being secreted by the adrenal. Thus, the rise in androgen production at puberty is responsible for the accompanying marked increase in eroticism and sex drive which is such an obvious feature of adolescence. However, it does not follow that differences in hormone level account for individual differences in libido after puberty and the evidence suggests that in fact the links are quite weak (see Rutter, 1979a). Androgens play a major role in the initiation of the rise in sex drive in puberty but thereafter normal variations in sex drive (either between individuals or within individuals over time) are not primarily determined by hormone level.

Animal studies indicate that androgens influence assertiveness and dominance, as well as sex drive, in both sexes. Thus, Joslyn (1973) reported that androgens injected into female rhesus monkeys between 6 and 14 months of age increased their aggressive behaviour so that they replaced males in the top positions of the social hierarchy. Evidently, high androgen levels may lead to an increase in social assertiveness but the association between testosterone levels and dominance is complex with two-way effects. Thus, Rose et al (1972) showed that when adult male rhesus monkeys were provided with individual access to a group of receptive females they became more dominant and their testosterone levels increased several-fold. Conversely, when these males were subjected to sudden and decisive defeat by an all male group their testosterone levels fell. Apparently, in humans too, stress may lead to lower levels of testosterone (Kreuz et al, 1972). It seems that not only can testosterone influence social behaviour but so also can social experiences influence testosterone level.

The differences between boys and girls in sex typed behaviour are not due to differences in post-natal hormone production (see Rutter, 1979a). Rather, they are established early in childhood and, insofar as hormones play a part, prenatal androgens appear to be responsible.

The emotional and behavioural consequences of the changes in oestrogen and progesterone levels which occur in adolescence are less well understood. However, several rather different sets of evidence suggest that there may be effects. First, there is good evidence that the puerperium is associated with a substantial increase in psychiatric disorder (Kendell et al, 1976) and it is generally thought that endocrine changes play a part in increasing women's vulnerability to emotional disturbance at that time. Secondly, irritability and depression are commonly reported as particularly frequent during the few days immediately preceding menstruation (Kessel and Coppen, 1963). The premenstrual phase also seems to be the time when a variety of emotional and behavioural disturbances and upsets are at their most common in women (Dalton, 1977). However, the findings here are open to more than one interpretation (Sommer, 1978b) in that there is some indication that severe stresses may bring on a period prematurely. Thirdly, it appears that in a minority of women (but not in most) oral contraceptives may predispose to depression, although again the findings are rather conflicting (see Weissman and Klerman, 1977) and in general it seems that they do not constitute a risk factor for depression (Fleming and Seager, 1978). It should be added that there is some weak evidence that prenatal oestrogens may have an effect on later personality functioning (Reinisch and Karow, 1977). We may conclude that it is likely that the hormonal changes experienced by girls at puberty may have emotional consequences but evidence is lacking both on how far this is the case and on the possible mechanisms involved.

Early and late maturers

The timing, as well as the nature, of physical maturation during adolescence has psychological significance (see Graham and Rutter, 1977). One of the most puzzling findings is the observation that, on average, early maturing boys and girls have a slightly higher level of intelligence than do late maturing children (see Tanner, 1966). The difference is not great but it is evident long before puberty and it is *not* due to any pubertal spurt of intelligence (see e.g. Douglas et al, 1968). It is not known whether it continues into adult life. Similarly, on average, tall children achieve better scores than short children; and children from small families better than those from large (see Tanner, 1970). These three variables (early puberty, height and small family size) tend to be associated, and it is evident that, in part, the correlation between IQ and height is a consequence of family size. However, this is not the whole story as a reduced but positive correlation between IQ and height remains even after allowing for the number of sibs (Scott, 1962).

Of more direct psychiatric relevance is the finding from some U.S. studies that early maturing boys have a slight advantage in personality (see Graham and Rutter, 1977; Clausen, 1975). In general there was a tendency for them to be more popular, more relaxed, more good natured and generally more poised. In contrast, late maturers were found to feel somewhat less adequate, less self-confident and more anxious. The personality tests used in these studies were not very satisfactory and the differences found have usually been quite small. Nevertheless, rather similar differences have been shown by several tests in independent studies so that it is possible to place a limited confidence in the findings. It is also notable that one study (Jones, 1965) found that although the psychological differences associated with the timing of puberty diminished with age, some differences were still evident at age 30 years. The picture found in girls has been far less consistent; the differences between early and late maturers have been less marked and have varied according to age and to study, with early maturation sometimes an advantage and sometimes a disadvantage.

It is relevant that the associations with age at puberty are paralleled by similar associations with physique (Clausen, 1975). Mesomorphic boys tend to be rated as more assertive, more popular, less introspective and more socially mature. Fat boys tend to be seen as having most difficulty in peer relationships, and thin boys as somewhat submissive. There is an association between mesomorphy and early maturation.

The explanation for both sets of associations are almost certainly social and psychological rather than directly biological. The correlations between physique or age of maturation and personality variables have usually been stronger in working-class boys than in middle-class boys (Clausen, 1975), and the extent to which late puberty is a handicap varies between different cultures, emphasizing that the disadvantages are largely due to society's reaction to continuing physical immaturity or to different physiques (Mussen and Bouterline-Young, 1964). The world of adolescent boys is one where physical prowess brings prestige as well as athletic success. Early maturing boys tend to be more intelligent and more muscular and part of their advantage may lie in the social benefits within the peer group of being strong and good at sport. The intelligent athletically-built boy not only tends to dominate his fellows in early adolescence but by getting an early start he is in a good position to continue his leadership. That strength and athletic prowess are not so important in determining a girl's popularity may explain why early puberty does not carry the same psychological advantage for females. A child's physique plays an active part in determining how other people will react to him and the mature boy of manly appearance may be better accepted by adults too than his childish looking companion who has yet to reach puberty. In this connection, it is relevant that in western societies the cultural sex role prescription for males is more clear-cut than that for females.

Sexuality is very important to adolescents and much talk centres around the topic. Early puberty tends to be associated with both earlier and greater sexual experience (Schofield, 1965) and boys who have still not reached puberty by 16 years or so may well begin to doubt their masculinity and become anxious and introspective about their development. However, there are also disadvantages to early maturity, especially in girls. In both sexes, the very early maturer may not yet be emotionally prepared for sexuality as psychosexual interests are influenced by age and cognitive level as well as by physiological maturity (Rutter, 1979a). Sexuality is not as accepted a part of the world of primary school girls as it is of those at secondary school, and very early maturing may sometimes be associated with undue self-consciousness and anxiety together with an attempt to conceal breast development through altered posture. The early maturer also either has a longer period of frustration of sex drive or has to start sexual activities before others of the same age. The early onset of sexual experience is not without its consequences—at least up to the recent past the earlier girls started sexual relationships the more likely they were to have a premarital pregnancy (Schofield,

Late Puberty and Psychiatric Disorder

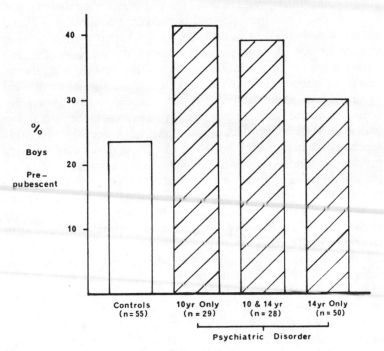

FIGURE I.3

1973). Early maturing boys also tend to marry early (Clausen, 1975).

Clear-cut relationships between age at puberty and psychiatric disorder have not been demonstrated (see Graham and Rutter, 1977). However, the few studies which have been done have mainly focussed on girls or on delinquents rather than on older emotionally disturbed boys where the greatest efforts might be expected. Nevertheless, Littlemore et al (1974) did find that older adolescents (over 14 years) with severe psychiatric disorder did show skeletal immaturity, as assessed by wrist X-ray; this was not found with younger adolescents.

The Isle of Wight findings indicate some of the complexities

17

involved in the interpretation of associations between age at puberty and either psychiatric disorder or personality functioning. Scarcely any girls were pre-pubescent (i.e. no signs of pubertal development) at age 14 to 15 years, but perhaps it is worth noting that three out of four showed emotional disturbance arising during adolescence and none was without disorder. There were more pre-pubescent boys (as expected from the later physical maturation of males) and late puberty showed some association with psychiatric disorder (see fig. 1.3). However, the association was mainly with disorders already present at age 10 years (irrespective of whether they persisted to 14 years), rather than with psychiatric conditions arising *de novo* during adolescence. As no boys had reached puberty by 10 years, it is clear that the association could not reflect any psychological response to late puberty as such. Rather the association is likely to reflect the lower intelligence, less muscular physiques or larger families found with late maturing boys.

Somewhat similar findings have been found with respect to delinquency. Thus, Wadsworth (1979) found that boys in the U.K. National Survey who were still pre-pubescent at 15 years were significantly more likely to be delinquent than boys who were by then pubescent or fully mature. Of the sexually infantile boys only a quarter had scores of 0 or 1 on the crime scale (meaning that they were non-delinquent or had engaged only in trivial offences) compared with half of those who were fully mature and more than three quarters of those in an advanced stage of puberty. However, this association was lost once social group, birth order, and height had been taken into account, suggesting once more that late puberty *per se* was not directly responsible.

Moreover, the interpretation of these trends is complicated by a rather different effect associated with puberty. Adolescence is associated with a marked rise in depressive disorders (see below) and it appears that this may be associated more with puberty than with chronological age. Figure 1.4 shows the findings for boys from the Isle of Wight study of adolescents (no analysis was possible for girls as virtually all girls were pubertal). Among the 19 pre-pubescent boys from the randomly selected general population sample, scarcely any showed depressive feelings, whereas

Depressive Feelings and Stage of Puberty

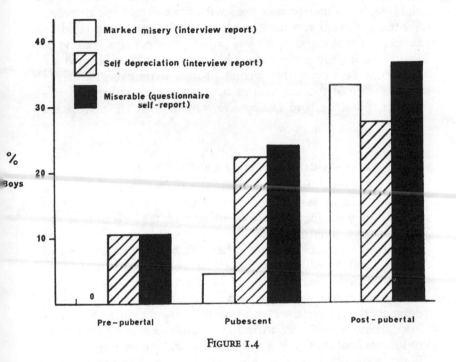

FIGURE I.4

of the 19 post-pubertal boys, a quarter to a third did so, as assessed from either the 'malaise inventory', self-report of 'often feeling miserable or depressed', or the adolescents' description at interview of self-depreciatory feelings or severe misery. The findings for the 45 pubescent boys were intermediate on all measures. The results using teacher or parent ratings were less clear-cut; far fewer noted depressive feelings and the association with puberty (although present) was less marked—in keeping with other findings from the same study (Rutter et al, 1976) that adults frequently failed to notice adolescents' depression.

Thus, it seems that two rather different processes may be at work. Firstly, the one study with evidence on the matter shows a tendency for puberty to herald a sharp increase in depressive feelings. Most of these feelings occur in normal well-adjusted children, but some are associated with frank psychiatric disorder. Secondly, there is also some tendency for late-maturing children to feel less secure and to be less popular and perhaps because of that to be slightly more vulnerable to emotional or behavioural problems. However, this second process is probably largely a consequence of the associations between age at puberty, intelligence, physique, and family size, rather than late maturation *per se.*

PSYCHO-SOCIAL DEVELOPMENT AND BEHAVIOUR

There are many difficulties in the study of developmental change but two stand out as particularly important. The first is that longitudinal study findings necessarily reflect both the increasing age of the subjects and historical changes in the population as a whole as a result of socio-cultural and other influences (Nesselroade and Baltes, 1974). If only longitudinal data are available it is not possible to separate these two effects. Ideally a combination of longitudinal and repeated cross-sectional data are required. The second difficulty stems from the common happening that there is a heavy loss of subjects and hence attrition of sample size during the course of longitudinal studies. It is usual for the missing subjects to differ in many respects from those that remain (Cox et al, 1977) so that this constitutes an important potential source of bias. Cross-sectional data have even more serious limitations for the study of the process of development because of uncertainties on whether the two age groups are comparable but more importantly because it is not possible to examine links within individuals between the two age periods. One or other of the various longitudinal strategies is essential for this purpose (Farrington, 1979; Robins, 1979; Rutter, 1979d). Inevitably, few of the studies to be discussed adequately deal with all these difficulties but in considering the weight to be attached to the evidence in the sections that follow I have borne these problems in mind and have tried to deal with the issue by seeing how far different types of studies with different limitations agree in their conclusions.

Psychosexual development

Although psychoanalytic theories have maintained that the middle childhood years are sexually 'latent' with a real break in the course of sexual development up to the point in adolescence when there is a resurgence of sexuality (Fries, 1959), it is now clear that this is far from the case (see Rutter, 1979a). Anthropologists first pointed out that whatever happened in western societies, in sexually permissive cultures sex play and love making were common during middle childhood. In recent years, a number of U.S. studies have produced somewhat similar findings. Although there may well be some greater concealment of sex interests during middle childhood than either before or after, nevertheless overt sex activities and interests are common and widespread (references in Rutter, 1979a). The findings leave no doubt that sexuality is manifest during the so-called latency years, but it should not be concluded from these figures that there is necessarily a continuity between pre-pubertal sex play and adult sexual relationships. In the early school years sexual activity is a much more sporadic activity than it is later and it has neither the intensity nor the complexity of later sexual behaviour.

Homosexual play in boys (which mostly consists of mutual handling of genitals) also shows a gradual rise during childhood, reaching perhaps 25- to 30 per cent at 13 years—the figures for girls are somewhat similar. However, the emergence of homosexual activities is probably much influenced by the social setting and by the presence or absence of heterosexual opportunities; whether this transient phase of homosexual activity has any bearing at all on persisting adult homosexuality is doubtful.

The rates of various sexual activities, in themselves, are of very limited interest in view of the known marked differences between different societies. What is more important is the light thrown on the process of psychosexual development by the pattern of age differences. In this connection it is relevant that Broderick (Broderick and Fowler, 1961; Broderick and Rowe, 1968) showed that in the pre-adolescent period there was a gradual progression from generally wanting to marry someone, to having a particular girl-friend, to being 'in love' with this particular

21

girl-friend and finally to social activities in the company of this friend. Similarly, Schoof-Tams et al (1976) found that although most 11-year-olds were still pre-pubertal, two-thirds reported having been 'in love' and half had kissed; by 16 years nearly all of them had had both experiences. Of course, the meaning of these experiences changes with maturity and during adolescence young people's views about the meaning of sexuality also alter. Thus, the traditional concept of sex as mainly for the purpose of pro-creation, held by most pre-pubertal children, becomes superseded by the view that the main function of sex is to strengthen and deepen affectionate relationships.

Up to the age of about 7 or 8 years children play with boys and girls, then during the pre-pubescent years there is a phase of playing mainly or only with children of the same sex as themselves, followed at about puberty by increasing social interaction with the opposite sex (Campbell, 1939). However, as already noted, while same-sex friendships are a feature of middle childhood they are accompanied by considerable heterosexual interest and some sexual activity.

During and after adolescence, however, there is a very marked upsurge in sexual activity in both sexes. In Schofield's (1965) U.K. study of teenagers during the early 1960s, he found that by the age of 13 years, a quarter of the boys and almost a third of the girls had had their first date. During the next two years there was a rapid rise in the incidence of dating so that by 16 years over 70 per cent of the boys and over 85 per cent of the girls had experienced dating. The figures for kissing were closely paralleled and again boys lagged behind girls in the age when they started. Between 15 and 18 years the curve for sexual experience rises fast with deep kissing, breast fondling and then genital contact becoming increasingly prevalent. Thus, at 15 less than a fifth of the boys had touched a girl's genitals but by 17 nearly half had done so. By the age of 18 a third of the boys and about a sixth of the girls had had sexual intercourse. More recent data (see chapter 2) suggest that today's teenagers start sexual activities rather earlier but the pattern of development remains much the same.

In keeping with their slower physical development, boys begin sexual activities later than girls, but by 17 years there is no longer any difference. Young people of both sexes who start dating and kissing at an early age are more likely to have early sexual intercourse; however there are differences between boys and girls in the pattern of sexual activities. Fewer girls have intercourse but once they have started they are more active sexually. The boys have more sexual partners (implying a small core of promiscuous girls) but the girls more often have an enduring sexual association. There are also differences in attitudes; girls tend to look for a romantic relationship while boys seek a sexual adventure. This is reflected, for example, in the findings from Sorensen's (1973) survey of personal values and sexual behaviour among American teenagers. Among sexually active girls four-fifths engaged in 'serial monogamy' (that is they had sexual relationships of some lasting quality, generally remaining faithful to that one partner so long as the relationship lasted). This was so for less than two-fifths of boys, over half of whom were 'sexual adventurers', moving freely from one sex partner to the next without feeling any obligation to remain faithful to any one person. Like most studies of this kind, there was a rather high proportion of eligible subjects who could not be interviewed for one reason or another (just over half), but there was no sex difference in non-interview rate and it seems unlikely that the loss of subjects influenced this particular finding.

At the time of Schofield's survey in the early 1960s most adolescents were not using birth control although nearly all had some knowledge of it. Contraceptive techniques are now much more widely employed (Farrell and Kellaher, 1978) but still most teenagers (especially in working-class groups) do not use efficient birth control methods at all consistently (Ryde-Blomqvist, 1978). Sorensen's (1973) U.S. study showed that nearly half of sexually active teenagers sometimes 'just trusted to luck' that the girl would not become pregnant, and a fifth always did so.

It is sometimes thought that sexual competence somehow 'comes naturally' and that sexual experience is necessarily pleasurable by some innate mechanism, but it is evident that neither is the case. Sexual behaviour includes many learned components and depending on whether a person's first sexual experience is enjoyable or unpleasant he may not try again for many years or he may

23

have intercourse again within a few days and continue to have sex regularly and frequently (Schofield, 1965). Sexual intercourse tends to be most pleasurable within the context of a long relationship, emphasizing that sexuality and socialization are linked. The development of a harmonious sexual relationship is often associated with tensions and Schofield (1973) found that a fifth of young adults expressed anxiety over their sexual performance and a half had a sexual problem of one kind or another.

Now, as in the past, young people are most likely to receive information on sexual behaviour, on reproduction, and on birth control, from their friends rather than from parents or school teachers (Schofield, 1965; Farrell and Kellaher, 1978). This is particularly so in the case of working-class children, many of whose parents seem to regard sexual curiosity as suspect and open discussion of these personal matters as undesirable. However, there is some indication that parents and teachers are somewhat more often the first course of sexual information now than they were a dozen years ago (Farrell and Kellaher, 1978).

Friendships and social relationships

Although friendships are characteristic of children of all ages, the characteristics of friendship alter with age (Douvan and Gold, 1966; Hartup, 1975, 1979). The main changes from childhood to adolescence may be summarized as follows: in younger children friendships tend to constitute a partnership focussed on a common activity whereas in adolescents there is a mutuality which is inherent in the relationship itself; adolescence is associated with an increasingly intense emotional interaction involving understanding, self-disclosure, and the sharing of deeper feelings; friendships during the teenage years come to be able to tolerate conflict in a way that was not possible when younger; and friendships become more stable and long-lasting during adolescence. It is also the case that children's concepts of friendship and the language they use to describe friendships becomes more complex and well-differentiated during adolescence. Group interactions also change in quality. Younger children's groups appear more like aggregates of individuals sharing a game or activity whereas older children show more reciprocity and synchrony in their social relations.

Interactions among adolescents are more finely tuned with the use of acknowledgements, the requesting of opinions, and the giving of social signals to indicate that communications have been understood.

Although adolescents continue to identify with their parents and to rely on them for guidance (see below), there tends to be a decreasing involvement in family leisure activities during the teenage years and an increasing engagement in activities with friends and with groups of peers. Thus, Bowerman and Kinch, (1959) found that whereas the great majority of fourth-graders preferred family activities over activities with friends, this was so for only a small minority of tenth-graders. On the other hand, at all ages young people were more likely to *identify* with parents than with friends. The tendency to identify mainly with peers rose during the teenage years (from 5 per cent in the fourth grade to 27 per cent in the tenth grade) but remained well below that with parents.

Similarly, in the Isle of Wight study of 14- to 15-year olds, only 9 per cent of boys and 11 per cent of girls went out with their parents as often as once per week; whereas nearly all of them saw their friends that often. Of those who had gone away on holiday in the previous year, 38 per cent of the boys and 32 per cent of the girls had gone away with friends rather than family, and a further 13 per cent of boys and 12 per cent of girls had either had joint holidays with friends and family or separate holidays with both. It should also be noted, however, that most adolescents have contact with younger children as well as those in their own age group. Thus, in the National Child Development Study (Fogelman, 1976), three-fifths of 16-year-olds did babysitting for other families and one in nine had helped to run a playgroup.

The teenage years are also a time of an increasing amount of responsible independent activities outside the home. Among 14- to 15-year-old boys on the Isle of Wight, over half (52 per cent) had a paid job during term time but among girls the proportion was considerably lower (27 per cent). This sex difference may simply reflect the types of job opportunities in the area as almost as many girls as boys (63 per cent vs 71 per cent) had held paid holiday jobs. The National Child Development Study (Fogelman,

1976) also showed that half 16-year-olds had a paid job during term time.

Informal peer groups and cliques become more prominent during the early part of adolescence and there is a marked tendency for the formation of cohesive social groups whenever young people come together to share a common purpose or activity (Sherif et al, 1961). At first the groups tend to be all of the same sex but these then often coalesce to form larger mixed 'sets' of young people who do things together. Usually the structure is informal and changing so that, at least in the U.K., only occasionally is there a more regular gang with an accepted leader. Nevertheless, these groups can assume an important role in the life of adolescents, asserting influence through group norms of behaviour and through claims on loyalty. At the same ages as these informal peer groups are tending to increase, adolescents' membership of traditional organized groups (such as Scouts and Girl Guides) tends to fall off (Burk et al, 1973). In later adolescence there is an increased pairing off so that the crowd comes to consist of only loosely associated groups of couples.

Sex differences in friendship patterns are also evident during adolescence. Friendship patterns among boys tend to be scattered across many individuals whereas in girls the networks tend to be more intensive and concentrated. In general, girls' friendships tend to be more fervent and demanding of strong loyalty and security with a pressure to spend great amounts of time together. However, the desperate feverish quality of girls' friendships during the mid-teens tends to give way to calmer more modulated friendships during the later teens. Boys, in contrast, are more likely to have a looser (but often more stable and less conflicting) pattern of friendships with the camaraderie of a larger group. In line with their greater physical maturity, girls develop heterosexual friendships and become members of mixed sex social groups earlier than do boys.

These differences are illustrated by the Isle of Wight findings shown in fig. 1.5. Whereas 29 per cent of girls reported having a special boyfriend, only 14 per cent of boys said that they had a special girlfriend. Similarly, a quarter of girls but only 7 per cent of boys were members of mixed sex groups or gangs. There were

Friendships of Adolescent Boys and Girls

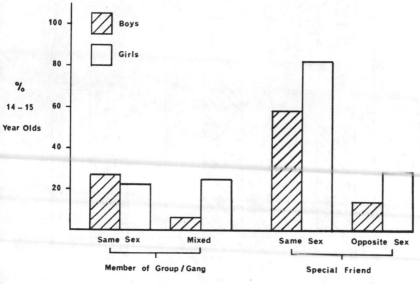

FIGURE 1.5

fewer differences with the same sex friendships but considerably more girls (82 per cent vs 59 per cent) reported having a special friend of the same sex.

Over a quarter of adolescent boys (28·3 per cent) on the Isle of Wight engaged in team games compared with a mere $4\frac{1}{2}$ per cent of girls—emphasizing the much greater male involvement in sport (see fig. 1.6). Over two-fifths of both boys and girls attended youth clubs of one kind or another but Church attendance was nearly twice as common among girls. Most adolescents were regular readers. While comics predominated (79 per cent of boys and 94 per cent of girls read them), two-thirds (64 per cent of boys and 74 per cent of girls) had read a book during the month preceding the interview and about the same proportion read the news section of a daily paper—a third of both sexes did so regularly at least 5 times per week.

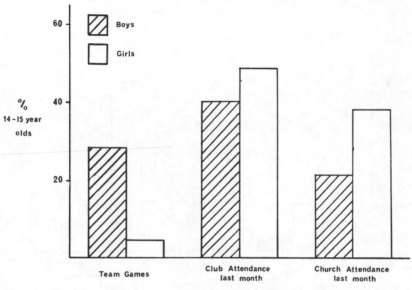

FIGURE 1.6

Parent–adolescent relationships

Although it has been customary to assume that adolescents usually become increasingly estranged from their families so that parental influences on teenagers greatly diminish and parents feel that they can no longer 'get through' to their children, the empirical evidence is consistent in denying that stereotype (Rutter et al, 1976; Graham and Rutter, 1977; Coleman, 1978). Thus, although Coleman (1961) interpreted his results differently, his findings (based on interviews with some 7000 U.S. adolescents) showed that just over half the high school students felt that parental disapproval would be harder to take than breaking with a friend (this was in spite of the fact that breaking with someone is of obvious greater emotional importance than incurring their disapproval—Epperson, 1964); that the majority would follow parental suggestions regarding club membership; that only a few felt that teachers were not interested in them; and that pleasing

28

their parents, learning as much as possible at school and living up
to their religious ideals were all felt to be more important than
being accepted and liked by other students. Epperson (1964) took
the issue further, in a smaller scale survey of American high school
students, by directly comparing parental disapproval and friends'
disapproval. It was found that 80 per cent of adolescents would be
made more unhappy by parental disapproval than by the disapproval of friends. Furthermore, secondary school students were
if anything more concerned about parental disapproval than were
younger children.

Douvan and Adelson (1966) studied the attitudes of 14- to 16-
year-olds in a questionnaire survey of over 3000 U.S. adolescents.
They found that of all other people parents were most admired;
helping at home was a major source of self-esteem; that most were
honest and trusting with their parents; and that over half had
some part in rule-making at home. Where moral or religious or
political beliefs were concerned, adolescents not only tended to
agree with their parents but also looked to them for advice. The
findings from other studies are closely similar. For example,
Meissner (1965) in a questionnaire study of the same age-group
found that over half thought that their parents understood them,
the great majority were satisfied and happy at home and three-
quarters generally approved of their parents' discipline. Offer
(1969), in a study of 'modal' U.S. adolescents (in effect the most
normal and least atypical), reported that most got on well with
their parents and shared their values. Similarly, in Sweden,
Gustafson's (1972) study of over a 1000 students found that
the majority accepted the conventional values of the communities in which they had been raised; most had faith in their parents
and marital satisfaction was very high on their list of priorities.
Adolescents and their parents tend to agree on the important
issues and moreover tend to do so to a greater extent than do
their parents and grandparents (Bengtson, 1970; Jennings and
Niemi, 1975). The impression is of the generations moving together rather than drawing apart. Of course, during adolescence
peer group influences do increase with respect to some things.
Brittain (1963, 1967) suggested that peers acted more as guides in
current situational dilemmas while parents did so more in *future*

29

oriented situations. Larson's more recent study (1972) has cast some doubt on the validity of this distinction. He found that the majority of adolescents were generally pro-parent in their orientations but decisions were influenced more by situational context than by either parental or peer approval. Taken together, the findings from all studies seem to indicate that adolescents still tend to turn to their parents for guidance on principles and on major values but look more to their peers in terms of interests and fashions in clothes, in leisure activities and other youth-oriented pursuits.

In the Isle of Wight study (Rutter et al, 1976) of 14- to 15-year-olds in the general population, both the adolescents themselves and their parents were separately interviewed. The great majority of parents had approved of their children's friends and nearly all had discussed with their children what they might do when they left school. In order to assess the extent to which the adolescents had become alienated or had withdrawn from their families, parents were first asked if the teenager tended to withdraw by going off to his room, or staying out of the house, or just not doing things with the rest of the family.

Only a tiny minority (12 per cent of boys and 7 per cent of girls) did any of these things and in half the cases the withdrawal was a continuation of pre-adolescent behaviour. Parents were also asked if they had any difficulties 'getting through' to their child, and how much the young person discussed with his parents how he was feeling and what were his plans. Nearly a quarter of the parents reported some emotional withdrawal or communication difficulty with their sons but in the great majority of cases this difficulty had always been present and in only 4 per cent of cases had difficulties increased during adolescence. Communication difficulties were reported with only 9 per cent of girls and in only 6 per cent had these increased during adolescence.

The reports from the adolescents themselves gave much the same picture—very few rejected their parents and most continued to go on family outings with them. Figure 1.7 illustrates the contrast between the predominant continuing harmony between parent and adolescent and the infrequency of alienation or rejection. Other U.K. studies have found much the same. The National

Parent – Adolescent Relationships
(Isle of Wight Study)

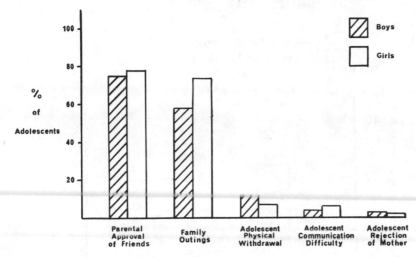

FIGURE 1.7

Child Development Study found that 89 per cent of 16-year-old boys and 87 per cent of girls said they got on well with their mothers, and only slightly fewer (74 per cent and 80 per cent respectively) reported that they got on well with their fathers (Ghodsian and Lambert, 1978). Only about a quarter of parents ever disapproved of their children's friends and disagreements over choice of friends, over smoking or over drinking were all quite infrequent (Fogelman, 1976).

The overall conclusion must be that although young people's leisure activities with their peers increase during adolescence and although their shared activities with parents decrease, nevertheless in the great majority of cases parent–adolescent relationships remain generally harmonious, communication between the generations continues and young people tend both to share their parents' values on the major issues of life and also to turn to them for guidance on most major concerns. The concept of parent–child alienation as a usual feature of adolescence is a myth.

31

PARENT-CHILD ALIENATION AND
PSYCHIATRIC DISORDER AT 14 YEARS

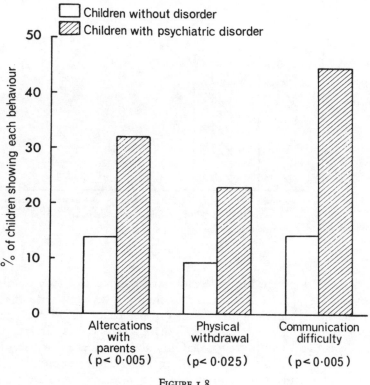

☐ Children without disorder

▨ Children with psychiatric disorder

FIGURE 1.8

(Data from Rutter *et al*, 1976)

Why then has this view come to be so widely accepted? Three main reasons may be put forward: firstly, the findings with respect to teenagers with psychiatric problems are rather different; secondly, altercations between parent and teenager on the minor issues of day-to-day life are rather common; and, thirdly, moodiness, depression, and irritability become more common during adolescence (see section on emotional development below).

32

Psycho-social development and behaviour

The first point is relevant because most of the clinical descriptions of stormy adolescence derive from studies of patient groups. The Isle of Wight findings (Rutter et al, 1976) clearly show that parent–adolescent alienation is very much more common among adolescents with psychiatric disorder. Figure 1.8 compares altercations, physical withdrawal, and communication difficulties in the control group children who showed no form of psychiatric disorder together with the total sample with some socially handicapping psychiatric condition. These indications of alienation were two- or three-times as frequent in the psychiatric group. Thus, opinions based on psychiatric patients are confirmed in so much as alienation was found to be much more frequent in adolescents with psychiatric problems. Even so, alienation was found in less than a half. However, it is relevant that the Isle of Wight teenagers were not patients and other studies have shown that psychiatric clinic referral is related to stresses in the parent–child relationship as well as to disorder in the child (Shepherd et al, 1971). In short, alienation is more common in adolescents with psychiatric disorder, but this association may be exaggerated in clinic samples because the very presence of alienation probably predisposes to clinic referral.

The relative frequency of minor disagreements or clashes between parents and adolescents on mundane day-to-day issues involving hair length, clothes, music, and the time to be in at night have been shown in numerous studies. For example, the National Child Development Study (Fogelman, 1976) found that 46 per cent of 16-year-olds had disagreements with their parents over dress or hairstyle and 34 per cent did so over the time of coming in at night or going to bed. Similarly, the Isle of Wight study showed that 24 per cent of the parents of adolescent boys and 34 per cent of the parents of girls disapproved of their children's clothing; and 46 per cent and 29 per cent respectively disapproved of hairstyles. On the other hand, disagreements over major issues were much less common and altercations were fairly infrequent. Thus, the parents of only 11 per cent of Isle of Wight boys and 7 per cent of girls had altercations as often as once per month. But of those who did have altercations a substantial proportion had them very frequently (4 per cent of families had daily altercations).

The findings from other investigations are in agreement with this general pattern of reasonable harmony on major issues, infrequent altercations on any issue, but rather common parental disapproval of superficial aspects of adolescent culture.

Self-image

Erikson's notions about the universality of identity crises in adolescence are difficult to test directly. However, some indication of possible difficulties in the establishment of personal identity may be obtained through measures of self-image, self-esteem, and self-concepts. The evidence casts considerable doubt on the concept of adolescent identity crises as a usual phenomenon. Thus, for example, Engel (1959) used 'Q sorts' to study the stability of self-concepts between eighth-grade and twelfth-grade (roughly 14 to 18 years). Most adolescents had a positive self-concept, there were no differences according to age or sex, and the general pattern was one of stability over time. The few subjects with a negative self-concept tended to be more maladjusted on the MMPI scales. Monge (1973) used semantic differential scales applied cross-sectionally to examine the same issue in sixth- to twelfth-grade children. The factor structure was similar at all ages for both sexes, but with consistency particularly strong in the case of boys. Older adolescent boys tended to score more highly on achievement/ leadership and older adolescents of both sexes did so on congeniality/sociability. On the other hand, both sexes became more maladjusted with increasing age. Moreover, it seems that where there are changes in self-image these may be related more to external circumstances than to maturation *per se*. Simmons et al (1973) using self-rating scales, found little change in self-image between 12 and 15 years, but the shift from elementary school to high school at 12 years tended to be accompanied by heightened self-consciousness, lowered self-esteem and greater instability of the self-image. Depressive feelings were also more frequent in older adolescents. Bachman (1970) conducted a longitudinal study of American high school students followed from tenth- to twelfth-grade. Self-esteem scores showed a moderate degree of stability ($r=0.49$) over the 30 month period, with similar mean scores at each age. John Coleman (Coleman, 1974; Coleman et al, 1977b)

34

used projective techniques to study adolescents' self-image. The
young people's responses suggested that there were no changes
between 11 and 17 years in the extent to which they maintained
a positive or negative view of themselves as they were at the
present time; on the other hand, older adolescents were considerably more likely to express negative feelings or worries about how
they would be in the future. We may conclude that identity
crises are not a usual feature of adolescence, but there is some
suggestion that anxieties about the future may increase during
the teenage period.

In contrast to the concept of adolescence as a time of identity
confusion and uncertainty about the self, there is also the opposing
view that adolescents tend to have unrealistically high opinions
of themselves. This view, too, seems to be mistaken as apparently,
if anything, adolescents tend unduly to idealize adults compared
with themselves. Thus, Hess and Goldblatt (1957) in a small scale
study of 32 U.S. teenagers and their parents found that parents
and adolescents were in general agreement in their mildly favourable evaluation of teenagers, but that relative to their parents,
adolescents tended to over-estimate the attributes of adults. In a
small sample of 24 U.K. parent–adolescent pairs, Coleman et al
(1977a) found that parents and adolescents were agreed that
teenagers tended to be rather lazy, noisy, and untidy, but that on
other traits (such as honesty and reliability) adolescents tended to
give adults more positive ratings than the adults gave themselves.
It seems then that adolescents tend to be slightly unsure of themselves and to see adults as more competent than the adults feel
they are. However, in most respects adolescents have a fairly
realistic view of themselves.

Of course, these findings do not mean that there is no change
during adolescence in young people's ideas about themselves and
about the issues of life. As children pass through adolescence they
become strikingly more able to generate and explore hypotheses,
to make deductions and to derive higher order abstractions.
Adolescents' questioning and criticism of established views and
their idealism is probably as much a function of their greater
cognitive capability as a response to their social situation or
pattern of upbringing (Adelson, 1975). Between the ages of 12 to

35

18 years it appears that there is a gradual replacement of ingenuousness and naïve moralism by more complex attitudes founded on an augmented realism. This involves an increase in both a degree of cynicism and also a more pragmatic activist approach.

Although manifest in different ways at different ages and although influenced greatly by cultural pressures and expectations, adolescence is often a period of intense idealism and occasionally this may include a rejection of society's norms and standards. In some cases the idealism may include an element of rebellion against home, but more frequently the socio-political activism of youth is rather an extension and development of their parents' own idealism (Graham and Rutter, 1977). Studies of U.S. 'hippies' and student activists in the 1960s (Brown, 1967; Flacks, 1967; Keniston, 1967) showed that they tended to come from privileged professional families in which the parents have presented permissive, liberal, or socialist views with a strong humanitarian concern for the plight of others, but with less emphasis on personal self-control. In short, it appears that the activists were often implementing the values of their socially conscious parents, even though they often did so in ways of which their parents would not approve. Although political activism and involvement in 'protest' movements tends to be a phenomenon particularly characteristic of youth, it should not be thought that it constitutes just a passing adolescent 'phase'. Follow-up studies show that activists may change their activities as they move into adult life, but still they are more likely than other adults to be involved in service occupations and to hold radical political views (Fendrich, 1974). In addition to the activists, there are also socially alienated youngsters who have rejected society's values on a much more widespread scale—they are more likely to show personal psychological disturbance. While this idealism is a prominent feature in some adolescents it is necessary to recognize that only a tiny minority are activists and protesters; like their parents, most are rather conforming. Indeed, Logan and Goldberg (1953) in their study of London 18-year-olds in 1950 comment on their apparent lack of interest in the life of the community and their lack of satisfaction in either work or leisure—features, however, by no means confined to the adolescent age group (Rowntree and Lavers, 1951).

Emotions

Although data are rather sparse, it seems that as children grow older they become progressively more understanding of other people's emotions, more aware of the emotional connotations of social situations and better able to utilize emotional concepts (see Chandler, 1977). These changes mainly take place during early and middle childhood but they continue into adolescence, in keeping with the development of powers of abstract thought.

One aspect of this developmental change may be reflected in young people's responses to bereavement (Rutter, 1979b). Few data are available but what little evidence there is suggests that the grief of younger children tends to be milder and of shorter duration than that of adolescents or adults. In part this may be a consequence of the younger child's imperfect concept of death but in part, too, it may reflect their less well developed ability to express depressive feelings. Whatever the explanation, it seems that things change in later childhood and adolescence so that immediate grief reactions become more common (Rutter, 1966).

Many studies have shown that there is a general tendency for specific fears to become less frequent as children grow older (see Rutter, 1979b). Thus, the fears of animals or of the dark which are common in young children are quite uncommon in adolescents. However, there are some fears which show no particular tendency to increase or decrease with age. These include fears of snakes which are fairly widespread at all ages and fears of meeting people which are perhaps more closely associated with temperamental features. In addition, there are several fears which are infrequent in younger children and which tend to arise mainly in later childhood or adolescence. These include social anxieties and a fear of open or closed spaces (Marks and Gelder, 1966). Also, during adolescence a particular type of anxiety state taking the form of school refusal becomes much more common (Rutter et al, 1976). Thus, in the Isle of Wight study of 14- to 15-year-olds there were 15 cases of school refusal whereas there had been none in the same population at age 10 years. Many normal young children show initial anxieties in a new situation or when separating from their parents and because of this may be fearful of

37

nursery school or infants school. In most cases those fears rapidly diminish during the first few weeks. In contrast, the school refusal arising in adolescence tends to be much more persistent and more often it is part of a generalized emotional disorder.

On the whole, irritability, anger, and temper tantrums get progressively less frequent as children grow older (see Rutter, 1979b). However, Shepherd et al (1971) in their large scale U.K. epidemiological study found a tendency for a slight further increase in their prevalence among girls aged 14 to 15 years.

The understanding of all emotions necessarily depends to a considerable extent on people's reports of the feelings they are experiencing. The feeling state and its personal meaning to the individual are essential components of emotion. This is particularly the case with depression which involves not only misery and unhappiness but also a lowering of vigour and energy, a sense of rejection and a negative self-image. Hence, assessments of depressive feelings are heavily dependent on self-reports, but by the same token age trends in depression may be influenced by age differences in young people's ability to *express* their feelings.

Nevertheless, even taking this into account, it·seems clear that although feelings of misery and upset are fairly common in middle childhood (some 12 per cent of 10-year-olds on the Isle of Wight were said to have these feelings), there is a marked increase in moodiness, misery, depression, and ideas of self-depreciation during adolescence. Shepherd et al (1971) found this only in girls but in the Isle of Wight study it was evident in both sexes (Rutter et al, 1976). Over two-fifths of personally interviewed 14- to 15-year-old girls and boys reported substantial feelings of misery or depression; a fifth said that they felt that what happened to them was less important than what happened to other people, that they didn't matter very much (feelings of self-depreciation); 7 to 8 per cent reported they had suicidal ideas, and a quarter said that they sometimes got the feeling that people were looking at them, or talking about them, or laughing at them (ideas of reference). The findings for studies of self-esteem (discussed above) are in line with this general tendency. Furthermore, a U.S. study by Masterson (1967) also found that anxiety and depression were common in ordinary adolescents but no data were available on age trends.

38

The self-ratings based on the 'malaise' inventory completed by the adolescents themselves gave the same picture. More than a fifth of the adolescents reported that they felt miserable or depressed, and the same proportion reported great difficulties in sleeping and in waking unnecessarily early in the morning. All these figures are substantially higher than the equivalent figures for parents. It seems that feelings of misery and depression are particularly common during adolescence and are more frequent during this age period than during either earlier childhood or adult life. However, the same study also showed that in many cases the teachers and parents of the adolescents were unaware of the young people's inner turmoil. The feelings cause appreciable suffering but often they remain unnoticed by adults.

The extent to which this increase in depressive feelings is related to puberty rather than chronological age is unknown so far as girls are concerned. However, the Isle of Wight findings for boys, considered earlier in this chapter, clearly show that in them it is linked with puberty. Depressive affect is uncommon in prepubescent 14- to 15-year-olds and much commoner in those who have reached puberty.

Of course, it is important to keep the picture in perspective. Although the *rate* of feelings of misery and self-depreciation reaches a peak during adolescence, nevertheless it is also the case that *most* teenagers remain happy and confident without experiencing significant depression. An increase in depressive feelings is characteristic of the adolescent age period but such feelings are marked in only a minority of boys and girls in this age group.

Schooling

Finally, with respect to children's psychosocial development, it is obvious that schooling plays a major role in the life of adolescents —not only because a large proportion of their waking hours are spent at school and because their behaviour and attainments are influenced by the characteristics of the school attended (see Rutter et al, 1979, and also further discussion in chapter 3), but also because the teenage years in many countries are a period of public examinations, the results of which are crucial to career possibilities, and because for some there is the critical transition from school to

39

Patterns of adolescent development and disorder

institutions of further education and for others the equally critical hurdle of starting employment for the first time.

In Britain, children pass from primary school to secondary school at the age of 11 to 12 years. This move involves far more than just a change of school. In the first place, in most areas there is a need for the children (in conjunction with their parents) to choose which secondary school they wish to go to. For a proportion (perhaps one-in-five to one-in-ten) this means the demoralization of not being accepted at the school of their choice. Secondly, the transition means going from being the most senior and responsible pupils at primary school to being the youngest and most junior pupils at secondary school. Thirdly, virtually all state primary schools are co-educational whereas many (probably a majority) of secondary schools are single sex. Fourthly, an even greater change concerns the organization of classes. Primary schools are generally run on the lines of children remaining in their own classroom with their own class teacher—an arrangement by which the children have a stable familiar environment with a teacher whom they come to know well. In sharp contrast, in many secondary schools each child is likely to have a dozen different teachers for different school subjects, and the need to move from room to room for some of the lessons—a much more complex and bewildering environment. For some children these changes can be quite anxiety-provoking and secondary transfer tends to be followed by an increase in school refusal resulting from emotional disturbance (Hersov, 1977a). The pattern of transition in the U.S.A. is rather different and tends to involve far fewer changes. Nevertheless, from the study by Simmons et al (1973) there is some suggestion that there may be a drop in self-esteem following children's admission to junior high school.

Public examinations at 16 years mark the next major crisis. The GCE 'O' levels constitute the first hurdle on the way to possible further education for the 20 per cent or so most academic pupils. The less academic 'CSE' exams involve the 40 per cent of pupils in the middle of the ability range. For both these groups there is the challenge and stress of examinations which are felt to have career implications. For the 40 per cent of adolescents in the lowest ability group there is the different stress of having to remain at

Psycho-social development and behaviour

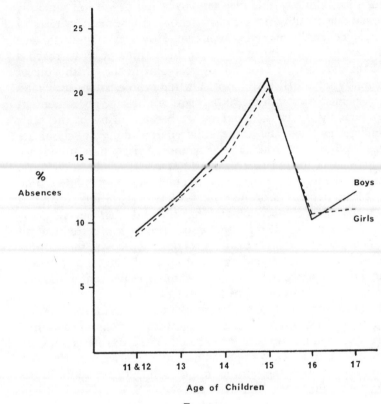

ILEA Secondary School Attendance Rates
by Age of Child in April, 1975

FIGURE 1.9
(Data from Inner London Education Authority, 1975)

school until 16 years (the lowest age at which pupils may now leave) without there being any very obvious purpose to being there. It is a period when some teenagers see little point in continuing to attend school, feeling that the curriculum has little to offer them and that the discipline is irksome and more appropriate to younger children. Perhaps as a consequence, the non-attendance rates tend to rise sharply during the last year of compulsory

41

attendance. This is illustrated by the Inner London Education Authority figures for 1975 shown in fig. 1.9.

During the first two years of secondary school the attendance figures for both boys and girls tend to be quite high and generally comparable to those in primary school where average rates of attendance usually exceed 90 per cent. However, non-attendance increases gradually throughout the next three years to reach a peak of over 20 per cent for 15-year-olds in their fifth year of secondary school (ILEA, 1976). On the whole, attendance rates are very much better in the sixth form; not because poor attenders are attending better then but rather because many of the poor attenders have left and those children remaining at school are there by choice. A rather similar picture of rising non-attendance is obtained if, instead of considering average school attendance, there is a focus on the proportion of children not attending school for at least 50 per cent of the time. Galloway (1976 and 1979), in a study of Sheffield schoolchildren, showed that severe non-attendance of this degree was considerably more frequent in secondary schools than in primary schools. Moreover, the proportion of children not attending for at least half the time rose each year throughout secondary school—from 0·15 per cent in the first year to 3·5 per cent in the fifth.

The transition from school to work at 16 years (in the U.K.) is the next point of stress for the teenagers leaving school as soon as compulsory education comes to an end. The stress arises not only from having to adapt to the fresh demands of a work routine but even more so from the humiliation of failing to get a job. In the U.K., other European countries, and the U.S.A., unemployment is now at a particularly high level among school leavers (Central Statistical Office, 1978). For many teenagers, their first experience after leaving school is being out of work and unable to find employment.

For others (a higher proportion in the U.S.A. than in the U.K.) the transition comes at 18 years or so when the move is from school to college or some other form of higher education. While clearly this is likely to constitute a source of satisfaction and pleasure as well as providing potential entry to professional and managerial occupations, it also involves stresses. This is reflected perhaps in the finding that the suicide rate for undergraduates is considerably greater than for equivalent age groups of the population (Carpenter, 1959; Parnell, 1951).

CHANGING PATTERNS OF DISORDER DURING ADOLESCENCE

Delinquency

Of all behaviours, delinquency is perhaps the most striking as an adolescent phenomenon. It reaches its peak rates for males at 15 years and for females at 14 years. The rate remains high during the whole of the teenage period but then falls rapidly during early adult life. Figure 1.10 shows the picture for indictable offences in males for the year 1976. Cautioning and findings of guilty are shown separately as the police are much more inclined to use cautioning with young offenders (and probably also with first offenders). The figure indicates that cautions reach a peak at 14 years, fall precipitously during the later teenage period, and are negligible in number throughout the whole of adult life. Court findings of guilty also rise steadily during the early teens but do not reach a peak until 17 years. The summation of cautions and findings of guilty is shown in the thick solid line on the graph and shows a peak at 15 years. The overall rates of delinquency are very much lower in females but the age trends show much the same pattern with peaks of cautions at 14 years and of guilty findings at 17 years; however, the summed total peaks at 14 years instead of 15 as in boys.

The official statistics do not present data in terms of the peak age for individuals making their *first* court appearance. However, West and Farrington (1977) do present figures on this point for their sample of boys in inner London. The peak occurred at age 14 years, which was several years before the peak for all convictions in their sample.

It should be appreciated that the figures apply to persons but not to individuals so that anyone with two separate court appearances during the year will be counted twice. It also follows that the rates are not equivalent to the number of offences, both because one offence can involve several offenders and because one

Indictable Offences in Males, 1976
(England & Wales)

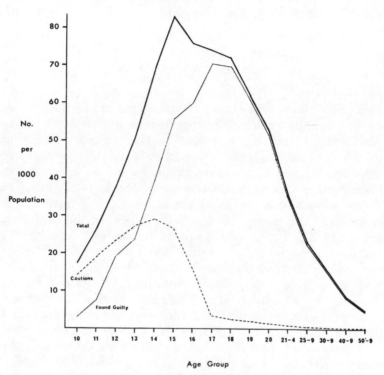

FIGURE I.IO
(Data from Home Office, 1977)

offender can appear in court for quite a list of offences all considered at the same time.

Even more importantly, however, the figures do not indicate
when the boys (or girls) started committing delinquent acts. It is
clear from self-reports of delinquent-type behaviour that many
young people are involved in delinquent acts for several years
before they receive a caution or are found guilty (West and
Farrington, 1973). Moreover, over half of inner city boys engage

44

Changing patterns of disorder during adolescence

in theft from shops and nearly all have committed offences such as deliberately travelling without a ticket or breaking the windows of empty houses—but many are never convicted.

Putting the various different sorts of findings together, it seems that delinquent acts probably most often begin in very *early* adolescence—the first offences may sometimes escape detection, others result in just a caution and frequently it is only after several delinquent acts that there is a court appearance. Nevertheless, however assessed, it is clear that delinquency is most common during the years of adolescence. It should be noted, however, that about half of juvenile delinquents only make one court appearance and are not convicted again (Rutter and Madge, 1976).

The vast majority of the offences in both boys and girls concern stealing of one form or another (Home Office, 1978a). In 1976, for both girls and boys in the adolescent age groups, over four-fifths of cases with a guilty finding involved theft, handling of stolen goods, burglary, or robbery. Criminal damage accounted for about 5 per cent of offences in girls under 17 years of age and for just over twice that proportion in boys. Violence against the person made up 2·8 per cent of cases with boys under 14 years and 4·7 per cent with girls in the same age group. It was rather more common in the 14- to 17-year-olds, accounting for 6·5 per cent of cases with boys and 9·6 per cent of cases with girls. This pattern is fairly similar to that seen with adults except that the proportion of aggressive crimes is higher in the 17 to 21 and 21 to 25 age groups (Home Office, 1977; West and Farrington, 1977).

Prevalence of psychiatric disorder

There have been only a few general population studies of the prevalence of psychiatric disorder specifically in adolescence (see Graham and Rutter, 1977). Kruspinski et al (1967; Henderson et al, 1971) used medical students to interview all families in an Australian town of some 2000 inhabitants in order to determine the prevalence of all forms of medical disability. Some 10 per cent of children, 10 per cent of adolescents, and 24 per cent of adults were diagnosed as showing some form of psychiatric disorder. The findings suggested a rate of disorder which increased during adolescence only to rise further still in adult life. However, the

45

criteria for disorder were not clearly specified and direct psychiatric assessments were not made so that age comparisons are problematic and of dubious validity.

Leslie (1974) surveyed some 1000 13- and 14-year-olds in Blackburn, an English industrial town. Diagnoses were based on extensive data for parents, teachers, and the children themselves. Psychiatric disorder of a severity thought to warrant clinic referral occurred in 21 per cent of boys and 14 per cent of girls; comparisons with other age groups were not possible.

Lavik (1977) used multiple sources of information to assess the psychiatric state of adolescents in Oslo and also in a rural area in south-east Norway. In Oslo, one-in-five adolescents showed psychiatric problems but in the rural area only 8 per cent did so. Disorders of all kinds (except psychosis) were more frequent in the city group but the area difference was most marked with respect to behaviour disorders in boys. No comparisons with other ages are possible but the findings are important in emphasizing the extent to which psychiatric disorders in adolescents are much commoner in city teenagers than in small town or rural youngsters—a difference which closely parallels that found for 10-year-olds (Rutter et al, 1975a).

In the Isle of Wight study (Graham and Rutter, 1973; Rutter et al, 1976) a total population of over 2000 14- to 15-year-olds were screened using parents' and teachers' questionnaires of known reliability and validity. Those with high scores (indicating the possibility of disorder), together with a randomly selected control group, were psychiatrically studied in detail by means of interviews with parents, teachers, and the adolescents themselves. Psychiatric assessments were also available on 10-year-old children and on the parents of the adolescents so that it was possible to examine age differences in prevalence. When like was compared with like it appeared that psychiatric disorders were slightly commoner in adolescence than at age 10 years, and possibly also slightly more common than in adult life (although this last difference may have been a consequence of the fact that the adult figures applied only to parents and so excluded single people who tend to have rather higher rates of disorder).

The precise prevalence figure for psychiatric disorder obviously

46

depends on the severity cut-off point used but putting all the information together the one year period prevalence of disorder was probably about 10- to 15-per cent for the 14- to 15-year age group. But, in addition to adolescents with generally recognizable psychiatric disorders, there was a further group of teenagers who reported marked suffering associated with psychiatric symptomatology but whose problems were not evident to parents and teachers. When these were included the prevalence rate rose to about 21 per cent. The clinical significance of this affective disturbance suffered by the adolescents but not obvious to others remains uncertain, but it was this phenomenon which was most characteristically different about the adolescent age period. The tentative conclusions from all the available epidemiological findings are that the great majority of adolescents are free of psychiatric disturbance but that disorders may be somewhat more frequent during the teens than during childhood, and possibly slightly more than during the middle adult life.

Questionnaire scores provide another index of age changes in the prevalence of psychiatric disorder. The 'malaise inventory', a screening questionnaire for emotional disturbance, showed that 17 per cent of adolescent girls had high scores indicative of possible disorder, compared with only 12 per cent of their mothers (Rutter et al, 1976). The 'neuroticism' scores on Eysenck's personality questionnaire (Eysenck and Eysenck, 1975) have been found to be higher in adolescence than in earlier childhood in girls (but not in boys). The data base is extremely limited but what little evidence there is suggests that emotional disturbance may be somewhat higher during adolescence than during either childhood or adult life. However, the differences are fairly small and once again it is clear that most adolescents show no disturbance.

Psychiatric clinic referrals are of limited value as an index of morbidity as they are heavily influenced by referral practices. Nevertheless, for what they are worth, U.K. figures indicate a rise of referrals between childhood and adolescence but a further rise to a peak in early adult life (Baldwin, 1968; Wing and Fryers, 1976). U.S. data shows a peak referral rate during adolescence (Rosen et al, 1965) but the rise from childhood is entirely due to

47

the increased referrals of girls; boys' rates remain fairly stable between 10 and 15 years.

In summary, it appears that there is a slight rise during adolescence in the overall rate of psychiatric disorder. However, the change in total prevalence is much less striking than the several changes evident in the pattern of disorders.

Types of psychiatric disorder in adolescence

Both the Blackburn (Leslie, 1974) and Isle of Wight (Graham and Rutter, 1973; Rutter et al, 1976) studies provide findings on the types of psychiatric disorder manifest during adolescence. About two-fifths of adolescents with a psychiatric condition showed some form of emotional disorder. Most of these consisted of anxiety states, depression, or some kind of affective disorder, obsessive-compulsive conditions, hysteria, circumscribed phobic states, and tics all affected a few individuals but were much less common. Conduct disorders occurred in about the same proportion—two-fifths of those with a psychiatric disability. In about half, this involved a widespread disorder of social relationships as well as disapproved conduct, but in the remaining half the adolescents appeared to have few problems with their own peer group. A substantial minority of teenagers, about a fifth, had disorders involving a mixture of antisocial behaviour and emotional disturbance. Enuresis, encopresis, and the hyperkinetic syndrome were only diagnosed in a handful of children and psychoses were quite rare. General practice figures (Office of Population Censuses and Surveys, 1974) also suggest a low rate of psychosis in mid adolescence—about 1 per 1000.

These data stem from general population epidemiological enquiries in which most of those with psychiatric disorder were not under hospital or clinic care. Obviously, in-patient figures show a different pattern simply because individuals with the most severe disorders are more likely to get admitted to hospital. Even so, Warren's figures (1965a and b) from an adolescent psychiatric in-patient unit showed that only 15 per cent of younger adolescents (below $14\frac{1}{2}$ years) and 25 per cent of older adolescents were psychotic.

48

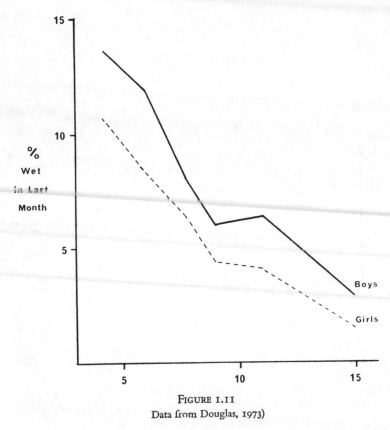

Age Trends for Nocturnal
Enuresis

FIGURE I.II
Data from Douglas, 1973)

Disorders decreasing or not changing in frequency during adolescence
Age trends in the pattern of disorders are most easily discussed in terms of individual conditions. First of all, there are those most characteristic of early childhood which show a sharply falling rate from childhood to adolescence. Nocturnal enuresis (shown in fig. 1.11) provides a good example of these. It still occurs in adolescence (2·9 per cent of 15-year-old boys and 1·5 per cent of girls had wet their bed in the previous month in Douglas' 1973

Suicide Rates by Age, 1966

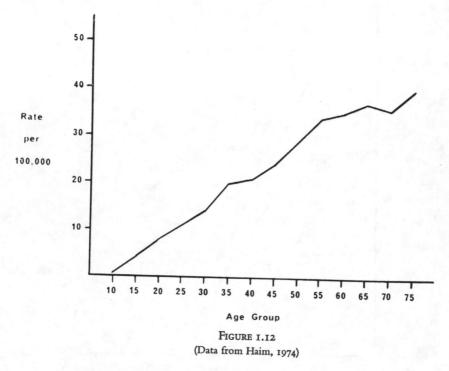

Age Group

FIGURE I.I2
(Data from Haim, 1974)

U.K. National Survey) but it is far less common than it is in younger children. The same applies to encopresis (Bellman, 1966).

Secondly, there are those conditions which show no particular age trend. This is the case, for example, with conduct disorders where the pattern at 14 to 15 years is much the same as that found at 10 to 11 years (Rutter, Tizard and Whitmore, 1970; Graham and Rutter, 1973). However, as discussed above, the official delinquency rate rises sharply during adolescence.

Disorders increasing in frequency

Thirdly, there are the larger group of disorders which (although accounting for only a small minority of psychiatric conditions

Changing patterns of disorder during adolescence

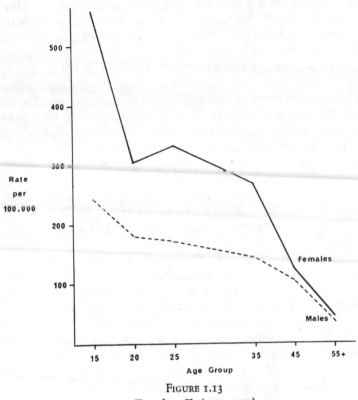

First-Ever Attempted Suicide Rates
in Edinburgh, by Age, 1974

FIGURE 1.13
(Date from Kreitman, 1977).

during adolescence) show a sharp rise in rate during the teenage
years. These include suicide and suicidal attempts, alcoholism,
drug dependency, schizophrenia, anorexia nervosa, and depression. Shaffer (1974) in a study of all reported suicides in children
under the age of 15 years in England and Wales between 1962 and
1968, found no cases in those below the age of 12 years, 2 in 12-
year-olds, 10 in 13-year-olds, and 18 in 14-year-olds—indicating
a sharp rise in early adolescence, but still a very low rate indeed.
National figures show that the rise becomes much more marked

51

in later adolescence but does not reach a peak until old age. Figure 1.12 illustrates this trend using French data but those from other countries show a very similar trend (Haim, 1974). It is clear that although the suicide rate begins to rise in adolescence it is far from a mainly adolescent phenomenon. To the contrary, the rate in the teens is but a tiny proportion of that in old age.

In contrast attempted suicide is specifically associated with later adolescence and early adult life as the Edinburgh figures (Kreitman, 1977) shown in fig. 1.13 demonstrate. The rates for females far exceed those for males but in both sexes the peak is in the 15- to 19-year age group. Comparable rates for children aged 10 to 14 years are not available but it is evident from other studies that attempted suicide is relatively infrequent in prepubescent children but becomes commoner during adolescence with the main rise about the age of 14 years (Connell, 1965; Toolan, 1962).

Alcohol use and abuse also increases markedly during the teenage ages. Jahoda and Crammond's (1972) Glasgow study indicated that children begin to learn about alcohol early in life, even before primary school. By age six a majority know the behavioural manifestations of drunkenness and by eight most have attained an understanding of the concept of alcohol. At first, drinking tends to be in the parental home on 'special occasions' but this then extends to other occasions, and between 14 and 17 years there is a transition from drinking in the streets and parks to drinking in the public house, although the latter is not legally allowed until 18 (Davies and Stacey, 1972). During this same period of development there is a massive rise in the frequency of drunkenness, so that for males in 1977 the rate of offences of drunkenness was less than 100 per 100,000, but for 18-year-olds it was nearly 1600 per 100,000 population (Home Office, 1978b).

Drug abuse is rare among primary school children, but it becomes increasingly more frequent during the course of adolescence tending to reach its peak in early adult life—although the age trend varies somewhat according both to the type of drug and to the culture. Figure 1.14 shows the figures for marihuana use in different age groups in the U.S.A. in 1972 as obtained from the National Survey undertaken by the Commission on Marihuana and Drug Abuse (1973). The rate of usage rises steeply

Changing patterns of disorder during adolescence

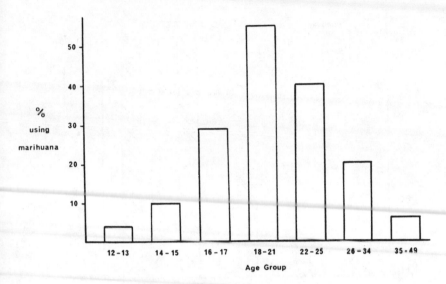

Incidence of Marihuana Use by Age, 1972

FIGURE I.14

(Data from US National Commission on Marihuana and Drug Abuse 1973)

during the mid-teens to reach a peak in the 18- to 21-year age group, with a steep fall off thereafter.

The pattern found with sedatives and stimulants was somewhat different in that there was only a relatively small increase in usage during the mid teens, a steep rise in the late teens and early 20s, and a continuing high rate of usage (especially for sedatives) into middle adulthood. With all these drugs the majority of young people tend to take them relatively infrequently and many give up using the drug after a year or so. Nevertheless, of those who take drugs about one-in-ten (one-in-three for marihuana) do so once a week or more.

Opiate usage and the taking of hallucinogens were somewhat less frequent in the U.S. Commission's surveys but nevertheless these drugs were used by a substantial proportion of senior high school students (5 per cent and 14 per cent respectively) and college

Sedative and Stimulant Drug Usage by Age

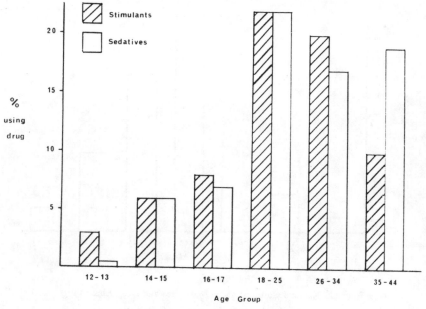

FIGURE 1.15

(Data from US National Commission on Marihuana and Drug Abuse 1973)

students (6 per cent and 15 per cent respectively) in 1972. But again, of those who did so most took the drugs only occasionally.

United Kingdom figures on the usage of all these drugs (see Blumberg, 1977) are all substantially lower—especially for opiates and hallucinogens but the pattern of an increasing rate of drug usage during the late teens and early 20s is much the same as in the U.S.A.

Figure 1.16 shows the age pattern of psychotic disorders in childhood and early adolescence. There is a first peak in the infancy period almost entirely made up of cases of infantile autism, a trough throughout middle childhood with a rather more varied group of psychoses, and then a further rise in later childhood and early adolescence made up of cases of schizophrenia

54

DISTRIBUTION OF CASES OF CHILD PSYCHOSIS BY AGE OF ONSET

(DATA FROM MAKITA, 1966 AND KOLVIN, 1971)

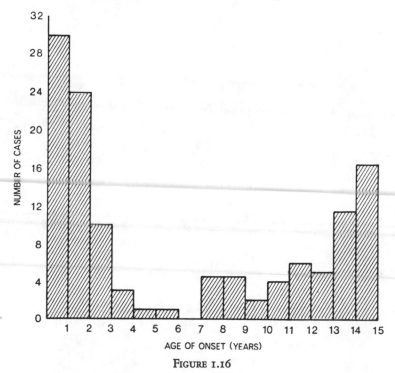

FIGURE 1.16

(Rutter, 1972a, 1974). Figure 1.17 shows the age trend for the whole adolescent age period with a steady increase throughout in the number of cases of schizophrenia. The data are based on the Monroe County register which covers individuals making either inpatient or outpatient contacts (Weiner and del Gaudio, 1976). Schizophrenia taking a form rather similar to that seen in adult life can occur in childhood (Eggers, 1978) but it remains a rather uncommon disorder until the mid teens. There is then a steep rise during the latter half of the teenage period with the peak not reached until early adult life. However, although schizophrenia most often becomes first manifest as a frank psychosis in the

Age Trend for Schizophenia during Adolescence
(Monroe County Register)

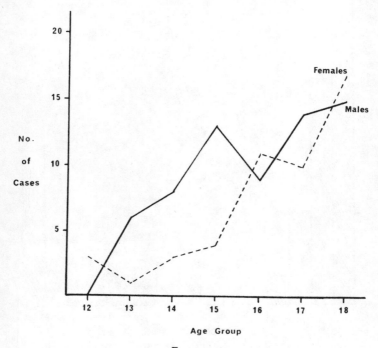

FIGURE I.17
(Data from Weiner and del Gaudio, 1976)

15- to 24-age period, in about half the cases non-psychotic abnormalities have been present from an earlier age. These do not take a particularly distinctive form and cannot usually be identified at the time as the beginnings of schizophrenia.

Anorexia nervosa can occur in the pre-pubertal period (Warren, 1968) but most characteristically it occurs during later adolescence. Crisp et al (1976) in their survey of girls at independent schools found an overall prevalence of 1·3 cases per 1000 girl-years for those aged 15 years and under and 3·9 per 1000 for those 16 years and over. Crisp's clinic series showed a mean age of onset of severe dieting at 17·6 years and a mean age of cessation of menstruation of 18·0 years. While the disorder can occur in both early adolescence and early adult life, most typically it is associated with the late teenage period.

Finally, the rate of depressive disorders increases sharply during adolescence. Thus, in the Isle of Wight survey of some 2000 10-year-olds (Rutter, Tizard and Whitmore, 1970) there were only three children with an overt depressive disorder. However, when the same children were studied again at 14 to 15 years (Rutter et al 1976) there were nine cases of depressive disorder plus another 26 with an affective disorder involving both depression and anxiety. While adolescence is certainly associated with a very marked increase in depressive conditions, it remains uncertain whether the peak for these disorders is in the teens or in early adult life. Comstock and Helsing (1976) studied two U.S. communities using a self-rating depressive scale; they found that high scores, indicating depressive symptomatology, were most frequently found in 18-year-olds (the youngest age group studied), with a decreasing frequency thereafter through the older age groups. On the other hand, hospital statistics suggest that the peak prevalence is not reached until the late 20s (Wing and Fryers, 1976). Either way it is clear that depression is particularly associated with later adolescence and early adult life.

Disorders with changing features

As well as disorders changing in frequency during adolescence there are a few important changes in pre-existing psychiatric conditions which occur at about the time of puberty. Most especially, this is the peak age period for the development of epileptic fits in autistic children (Rutter, 1970a). It is not known why this happens then but it is a most striking feature of the disorder. Earlier investigations indicated that fits were most likely to develop in mentally retarded autistic children (Bartak and Rutter, 1976). Subsequent experience has confirmed that this is indeed the case but the rate of development of fits in autistic children of normal non-verbal intelligence is probably rather higher than the published figures indicate.

Syndromes involving severe overactivity and difficulties in

attention usually begin in early childhood (Cantwell, 1977). The prognosis is not good and many children with these problems continue to present educational and behavioural difficulties in adolescence. However, the level of overactivity has usually diminished by the time the child has entered the teenage period. This is particularly the case when the hyperkinesis occurs in the context of infantile autism. During adolescence the severe over-activity of the early years is often replaced by marked *under* activity associated with lack of initiative and drive (Rutter, Greenfeld and Lockyer, 1967), which adds considerably to the teenage difficulties. While aggression does not usually increase appreciably in frequency, assertiveness, and disruptive behaviour sometimes gain in intensity about the time of puberty. The fact that the autistic adolescent is approaching adult stature makes this behaviour more difficult to deal with. A few autistic children also seem to generally deteriorate in adolescence—occasionally with a fall-off in cognitive performance (Rutter, 1970a).

Tics usually begin during the early school years and it is unusual for them to appear for the first time after late adolescence (Corbett, 1977a). Over half of cases treated at psychiatric clinics improve to some degree and two-fifths recover completely. This improvement most often takes place during late adolescence. However, adolescence (usually early adolescence) is also the age period when tics sometimes become more persistent and handicapping. In a few cases this takes the form of Tourette's syndrome with vocal utterances and then obscene words.

Finally, although their behaviour does not necessarily alter greatly, it is evident that severely retarded children often become more difficult for their families to manage at home as they reach adolescence, and rates of admission to hospitals for the mentally handicapped rise then.

Changing sex ratio of psychiatric disorders
During the course of adolescence there is a marked alteration in the sex ratio of psychiatric disorders, as shown by both general population epidemiological studies (Rutter et al, 1976) and the figures from psychiatric clinic and hospital referrals (Rosen et al, 1965; Baldwin, 1968). During childhood psychiatric disorders in

boys are much commoner than those in girls, whereas in adult life psychiatric disorder is much more frequent in women then men. Part of this change in sex ratio is due to the ways in which patterns of disorder alter with age. Thus, the developmental disorders and infantile autism which show a particularly marked male preponderance are essentially conditions of childhood, while puerperal psychoses which of course are confined to women only arise in adult life. Part of the change is also probably due to age-related referral practices. Boys with disturbances of conduct are likely to get referred to a psychiatrist whereas in adult life men with criminal behaviour or personality disorders are likely to be often dealt with in other ways. However, in very large part the altered sex ratio is real. It reflects the marked increase in emotional disorders in females as they pass from childhood to adult life (Rutter, 1979b).

During early and middle childhood there is little difference between the sexes in rates of emotional disturbance, however measured. In the preschool years there may be a slight tendency for boys to be more anxious and during the middle years of childhood there is a minor tendency for girls to show more emotional difficulties but the sex differences are very small in both cases. However, during adolescence this picture changes; mood disturbances become increasingly common in girls and in adult life depression is twice as common in women as in men. Whereas there is no sex difference on neuroticism up to age 10 years, thereafter there is an increasing sex differentiation because of an increasing neuroticism with age in females but not in males (Eysenck and Eysenck, 1975). Not only do depression and neuroticism show a female preponderance in adult life which they do not in childhood, but so also does hysteria (Caplan, 1970). Below puberty hysteria occurs with equal frequency in boys and girls, whereas after puberty females far exceed males. These findings on the quite different pattern of sex differences for emotional disturbance in children and in adults are well documented by both epidemiological and clinical studies and it is clear that the findings are not a consequence of any kind of reporting artefact (see Rutter, Tizard and Whitmore, 1970; Weissman and Klerman, 1977). Nor is it likely to be just a

59

consequence of differing life circumstances (with most men at work and many women housewives) as the sex difference in depression applies similarly to college students (Kidd and Caldbeck-Meenan, 1966).

Several attempts have been made to explore possible reasons for this marked shift in sex ratio which takes place during adolescence (Rutter, 1970c; Gove and Tudor, 1973; Radloff, 1975; Weissman and Klerman, 1977) .Various suggestions can be ruled out but no entirely satisfactory explanation is available (Rutter, 1979b). The findings can*not* be accounted for in terms of sex differences in 'conditionability', in physiological responses to stress, in frequency of acutely stressful life events, or in the perception of stress (although there is some suggestion that stress may be felt to be somewhat greater by adolescent girls—Burke and Weir, 1978). Endocrine changes (as in the premenstrual phase, in the puerperium or through the use of oral contraceptives) may influence mood but the differences are not such as to account entirely for the preponderance of depression in women. Genetic factors, too, may play a role but the evidence so far is insufficient to provide an explanation for the developmental course of sex differences in emotional disorder. It has been argued that the findings may reflect a different mode of *expression* of emotional disturbance in men and women (Dohrenwend and Dohrenwend, 1976 and 1977)—in women by depression and in men by alcoholism and personality disorders. However, this does not account for the *change* in sex ratio of emotional disturbance which takes place during adolescence. Moreover, the factors of possible aetiological importance associated with emotional disturbance are rather different from those connected with antisocial disorder or personality disturbance. There may be something in the idea but it fails to account for many of the findings.

Finally, it has been suggested that women are more prone to depression because they have a disadvantaged status in western societies (Gove and Tudor, 1973). If this hypothesis is to account for the findings it must explain why this applies to adult life and yet not to childhood. Four findings begin to provide pointers as to why this might be so (Rutter, 1979b). Firstly, marriage serves as a protective factor for men whereas it does not do so for women (see reviews by Rutter, 1970c and by Weissman and Klerman, 1977). Secondly, among working-class women depression appears particularly frequent among those with preschool children (Brown and Harris, 1978; Roy, 1978; Moss and Plewis, 1977). Thirdly, in the same group of women employment outside the home may serve as a protective factor (Brown and Harris, 1978; Roy, 1978; Fleming and Seager, 1978)—although this has not been found in all studies (e.g. Moss and Plewis, 1977) and presumably it depends on the nature of the work and the satisfaction it provides (Rutter, 1979b). All of these three variables, of course, apply to adults and not to children and so they may begin to indicate some of the relevant ways in which female roles change as girls become adult.

The fourth suggested reason for the change in sex ratio of depression during adolescence concerns the possible role of 'learned helplessness'. Whereas boys tend to respond with greater efforts when they receive feedback from adults that they are failing, girls are more likely to give up and attribute their failure to their own lack of ability (Dweck and Bush, 1976). One of the reasons for girls being more likely to give up seems to lie in the sex differentiated pattern of feedback from adults. Dweck et al (1978) found that teachers were more critical of boys than girls but also that they were more critical of boys in a diffuse way which could readily be perceived as irrelevant to their intellectual performance. In contrast, almost all criticisms of girls referred specifically to their intellectual failings. Conversely, positive feedback tended to be work-specific for boys but diffuse for girls. The pattern is one likely to increase girls' tendency to feel that they cannot succeed. It has been suggested that the increasing experience of feedback for adults during the school years may lead girls to show an increase in 'learned helplessness' during the later years of childhood and adolescence. The potential importance of this lies in the evidence that experience with events felt to be outside one's control (learned helplessness) may predispose a person to depression (Seligman, 1975 and 1976).

There is insufficient evidence at present to decide how far the disadvantaged status of women is a cause of their greater propensity to depression but it seems likely that this factor plays some part in the origin of sex differences. On the other hand, it is probable that other factors are also influential. Further investigation is especially necessary in the case of genetic and endocrine factors.

CONTINUITIES AND DISCONTINUITIES ACROSS THE ADOLESCENT YEARS

Several rather different questions arise with respect to the issue of behavioural continuities and discontinuities across the adolescent years and it is appropriate to discuss them separately. First, there is the question of how far there are links between behaviour in early or middle childhood and behaviour during adolescence. This has been studied with respect to both normal variations in behaviour and also problem behaviours of various kinds.

Child-adolescent links

Several longitudinal studies have looked at the intercorrelations between behavioural or personality ratings over the years (see Bloom, 1964; Dunn, 1979; Rutter, 1970b, 1977a; Robins, 1979). It has generally been found that measures during the preschool years have little predictive value for an individual's behaviour during adolescence; but that there is a moderate degree of consistency between the early school years (5 to 10 years) and adolescence. The Fels study found that passivity in the first three years had a zero correlation with passivity at 10 to 14 years in boys and a correlation of 0·36 for girls over the same age period; however, the correlations for dependency between the 6 to 10- and the 10- to 14-year age periods were 0·60 for boys and 0·76 for girls (Kagan and Moss, 1962). Similarly, 'behavioural disorganization' (destructive acts, rages and tantrums) in adolescence correlated only 0·12 (both sexes pooled) with the preschool period but 0·47 with the 6- to 10-year period.

Longitudinal investigations looking at disturbed behaviour have produced much the same picture. Thus, the Berkeley Guidance Study (Macfarlane et al, 1954) showed that if destructiveness, sombreness, jealousy or shyness were present at 6 to 7 years, similar features were likely also to be present during adolescence. More recent studies, too, have demonstrated moderate continuities

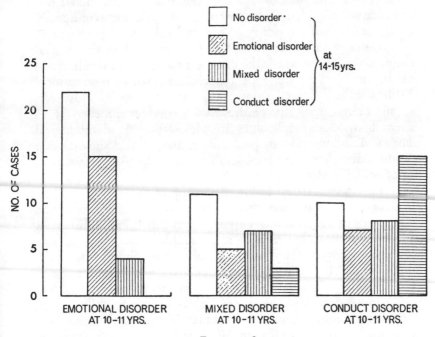

OUTCOME IN ADOLESCENCE ACCORDING TO DIAGNOSIS AT 10-11 YEARS

FIGURE 1.18
(Data from Graham and Rutter, 1973)

over this age period (references in reviews cited above). However, continuities differ with respect to both the *type* of behavioural disturbance and its *severity* (Rutter, 1972b; Cox, 1976). In general, severe disorders involving disruptive, aggressive or antisocial behaviour are those most likely to persist into adolescence.

This may be illustrated by the findings of the Isle of Wight follow-up study (Graham and Rutter, 1973) of a total population of children living in one area. Figure 1.18 shows the outcome at age 14 to 15 years of children diagnosed at 10 years as having a socially handicapping psychiatric disorder. The prognosis varied greatly by diagnostic group; those with conduct disorders fared

63

worst with three-quarters still showing a handicapping disorder in adolescence. The outlook for children with an emotional disturbance was considerably better but it was by no means uniformly good; nearly half (46 per cent) still had substantial problems in adolescence, a rate over twice that (21 per cent) in the general population. On the whole the disorders ran true to form in terms of diagnosis; thus, none of the children with an emotional disturbance at 10 years developed an antisocial disorder. However, an appreciable minority of those with conduct disorders at 10 showed emotional difficulties in adolescence. Epidemiological data on London children (see Rutter, 1977d) also showed that conduct disorders were considerably more likely to persist than emotional disorders.

Lefkowitz et al (1977) followed a group of New York children from age 8 to age 19 years, the study have a particular focus on the persistence of aggression. Aggression was much less common in girls than in boys but in both sexes, children who were highly aggressive at age eight years tended also to be unduly aggressive at 19 years (correlations of 0·38 for boys and 0·47 for girls). Unfortunately, half the subjects were lost to follow-up, the loss being much greater in the case of highly aggressive childrem, so introducing an important source of bias. However, the follow-up was much more complete in West and Farrington's study of London boys and again substantial continuity was shown (Farrington, 1978). Of the youths rated most aggressive at 8 to 10 years, 59 per cent were in the most aggressive group at 12 to 14 years (compared with 29 per cent of the remaining boys) and 40 per cent were so at 16 to 18 years (compared with 27 per cent of the remainder). The boys who were severely aggressive at 8 to 10 years were especially likely to become violent delinquents (14 per cent vs 4·5 per cent).

The same study demonstrated the very considerable extent to which troublesome, difficult and aggressive behaviour in young boys was associated with later juvenile delinquency. Figure 1.19 shows some of the findings relevant to this point. Both the measure at age 8 to 10 years of 'combined conduct disorder', which was based on combined ratings of teachers and social workers, and that of 'troublesomeness' at the same age, which was

64

Behaviour in Childhood and Later Delinquency

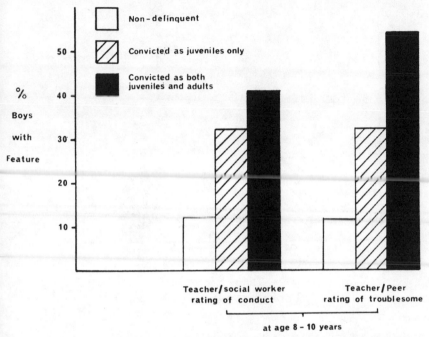

FIGURE 1.19
(Data from West and Farrington, 1973)

a combined rating of peers and teachers, proved to be powerful predictors of delinquency. This was especially so with respect to severe and persistent delinquency going on into adult life. Some half of such individuals showed deviant ratings on these measures compared with only one-in-six of non-delinquent boys. The Kauai study (Werner and Smith, 1977) also demonstrates the high persistence of the most severe disorders. Of the Hawaiian children, studied as part of an epidemiological investigation, who were thought to be in need of long-term mental health services at 10 years, three quarters (76 per cent) compared with only 12 per cent of controls were in contact with community agencies between 10

Overactivity and Behavioural Prognosis in Children
with Conduct Disturbance at 10 Years

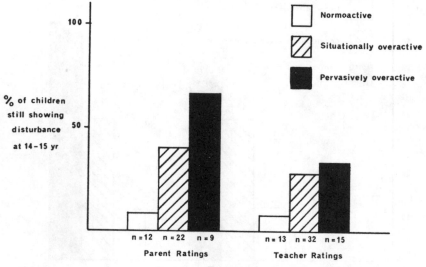

FIGURE I.20
(Data from Schachar *et al*, 1979)

and 18 years for severe and persistent behaviour problems. Interview measures at 18 years confirmed their poorer psychosocial
functioning compared with the rest of the population. It was also
noteworthy (although the number of subjects was tiny) that a
fifth of the girls considered to be in need of long term mental
health services at 10 had had teenage pregnancies (compared with
none of the controls). The children thought at 10 to be in need of
short-term mental health services had a slightly worse outcome
than controls but they had done much better than the first group.
Evidently, it was possible to make a reasonably valid appraisal at
10 years of the long-term seriousness of children's disturbed
behaviour.

In terms of the prognostic importance of particular behaviours,
two features stand out. First, several studies have shown that severe
difficulties in interpersonal relationships tend to be associated with

66

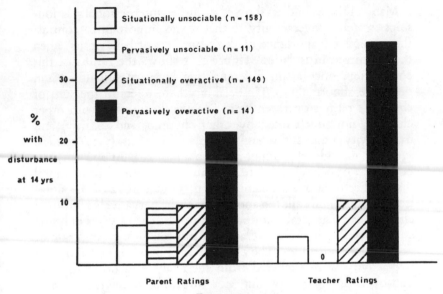

Unsociability and Overactivity at 10
and Behaviour at 14yrs

FIGURE 1.21
(Data from Schachar *et al*, 1979)

persistent psychosocial problems (Roff et al, 1972; Cowen et al, 1973). Secondly, a recent investigation by Schachar et al (1979) using the Isle of Wight data on children studied at both 10 and 14 to 15 years, has demonstrated the prognostic importance of overactivity and especially of pervasive overactivity (i.e. overactivity reported by *both* teachers and parents). Figure 1.20 gives the findings for all children who showed deviant scores on the behavioural questionnaires at age 10 years, according to whether they showed normal activity levels, or high scores on the overactivity factor on one questionnaire only (situationally overactive), or high scores on the overactivity factor on both the teacher and parent scales. Of the normoactive children with behavioural disturbance on the parental scale at 10 years only about 1 in 12 still showed disturbance at 14; in contrast two-fifths of those with situational overactivity and two-thirds of those with pervasive overactivity showed a disturbance which continued into adolescence.

Many of these children showed disturbed interpersonal relationships as well as overactivity so that it was important to contrast the predictive importance of these two sets of behaviours when they occurred in isolation. Figure 1.21 shows the results of this comparison, once again differentiating between situational and pervasive abnormalities. Unsociability here refers to the sum of children's ratings on three items (frequently fighting with other children, not much liked by other children, and solitary) and overactivity utilizes the same number of items (very restless, squirmy and fidgety, cannot settle to anything). At age 10 years both types of behaviour were associated with general behavioural disturbance to about the same extent (about 1 in 12 of the situationally abnormal children and a third of the pervasively abnormal children had a general disturbance at 10). But at 14 years only the children with pervasive overactivity showed an increased rate of behavioural difficulties. The children with both unsociability *and* overactivity were excluded from the analysis in order to have non-overlapping groups but, not surprisingly, this group also showed a large rate of difficulties at 14 years. In short, it seems that although both poor peer relationships and overactivity are associated with a relatively high rate of persistence of difficulties into adolescence, it is the presence of pervasive overactivity which is the most important factor. It should be noted, however, that this finding refers to the very small group of children with severe overactivity at both home and school. It would be wrong to extend it to the broad U.S. diagnostic concept of hyperkinetic syndrome which remains an entity of dubious validity without a prognosis which is demonstrably different from the general run of conduct disorders (Sandberg et al, 1978; Shaffer, 1978).

Psychiatric disorders during adolescence
The next issue concerns the characteristics of adolescent psychiatric disorders and particularly the extent to which these constitute continuations of pre-existing disorders rather than the emergence of new problems during the teenage years. The

FAMILY VARIABLES AND TIME OF ONSET OF DISORDER

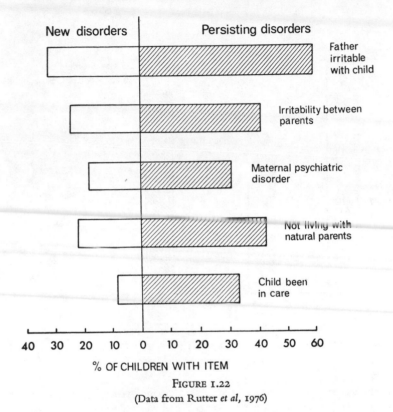

FIGURE 1.22
(Data from Rutter *et al*, 1976)

differences between these two groups are of especial interest. Clinic studies are in agreement that among adolescent psychiatric patients, the majority of disorders have been present from early or middle childhood (Warren, 1965; Capes et al, 1971). General population surveys show that just over half of adolescent disorders have an onset during adolescence (Rutter et al, 1976).

The Isle of Wight findings (Rutter et al, 1976) emphasize the major differences between the adolescent disorders persisting from childhood and those arising *de novo* after that age. The disorders beginning before age 10 years occurred predominantly

READING RETARDATION AND TIME OF
ONSET OF PSYCHIATRIC DISORDER

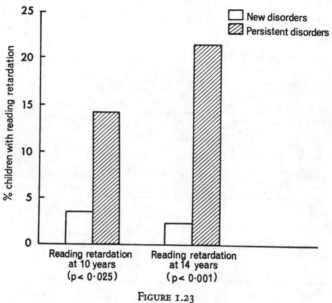

FIGURE I.23
(Data from Rutter *et al*, 1976)

in boys (sex ratio 2·3 to 1) whereas those arising in adolescence had a sex ratio nearer unity (1·3 to 1). However, the biggest group of differences concerned family and educational correlates of psychiatric disorder. The disorders beginning before 10 years but persisting into adolescence were strongly associated with indicators of family pathology such as break-up of the parents' marriage, the child going into care, marital discord, parental irritability toward the child, and mental disorder in the mother. In contrast, family difficulties were much less strongly associated with new disorders arising during adolescence (see fig. 1.22). This appears to be largely a function of chronicity, as family pathology was also not very strongly associated with psychiatric disorder arising before 10 years but not persisting to 14 years.

The differences with respect to reading retardation were even greater (see fig. 1.23). Children with psychiatric disorders persisting from earlier in childhood had a rate of specific reading retardation at 10 years far higher than that in the general population (14·3 per cent vs 4·1 per cent). The proportion was even higher and the difference from the general population even greater at 14 years. The picture with new disorders was quite different; these children had no more reading difficulties than children in the general population at age 10 years (3·3 per cent vs 4·1 per cent) or at age 14. This difference, unlike that for family pathology, was not a function of chronicity, as educational difficulties were as strongly associated with non-persistent disorders arising before 10 years as with persistent disorders. It is clear that the association with reading retardation is a characteristic of age of onset and not chronicity.

Very few other studies have compared these two groups of adolescent disorders but in so far as they have done so the results appear generally similar (Robins & Hill, 1966; Werner & Smith, 1977). We may conclude that conduct disorders in childhood are strongly associated with reading difficulties, but this is *not* the case with either conduct disorders or delinquency beginning in adolescence. Also, disorders beginning in childhood are strongly associated with family pathology whereas this is so to a much less extent in the case of disorders beginning in the teenage period. *Un*like the difference with respect to reading, the diminished association is at least partially a matter of chronicity. That is to say, gross family discord is most strongly associated with chronic psychiatric disorders and by definition these must have started before adolescence.

Of course, that leaves open the question of what *are* the causes of psychiatric disorder beginning for the first time in adolescence, if they do not mainly lie in either family discord or educational retardation? Unfortunately, very few data bear on this point. The Isle of Wight findings showed no features specifically linked with these new disorders. Parent-child alienation was fairly common in the children with new disorders but rather less so than in those with disorders persisting from earlier childhood (Rutter et al, 1976). It may be that deviant family relationships and

71

impaired communication patterns played a part in the aetiology of psychiatric problems beginning in adolescence but, if so, it seems that these family difficulties have usually been present for many years; alienation arising for the first time during the teenage period does *not* seem to be a common causal factor. Similarly, the misery and self-depreciation, or 'inner turmoil', sometimes characteristic of adolescence, was *no* more frequent in the disorders arising for the first time during adolescence than in those persisting from childhood. It seems to be a feature of the teenage years but does *not* seem to constitute a particular cause of new disorders. The findings for the Kauai study on psychosocial problems arising in adolescence also provide few clues as to the specific features leading to psychiatric disorders beginning at that time. The matter is one which warrants a particular focus in further investigations of adolescent disorders.

Course of adolescent psychiatric disorders

The main findings from follow-up studies of adolescent psychiatric disorders (reviewed in some detail by Robins, 1972, 1979; and Gossett et al, 1973) have been summarized by Graham and Rutter (1977) as follows. Firstly, most psychiatric disorders in adolescence run true to type; marked symptom fluctuation is not a common feature. There is no reason to suppose that symptoms are substantially more variable during adolescence than at any other age. Thus, Warren (1965a and b), whose study is in many ways the largest and most systematic, found that antisocial behaviour in the years after psychiatric treatment was almost entirely confined to those originally diagnosed as having a conduct disorder. Adolescents with an emotional disorder mostly continued to show similar problems if psychiatric disorder persisted or recurred. However, a few developed psychoses. Weiner and del Gaudio (1976) also found a tendency for schizophrenia to become apparent in some of the adolescents with mixed clinical pictures who originally had been variously diagnosed as having a neurotic personality or situational disorder.

Secondly, the prognosis varies markedly according to diagnosis. Pooling studies, about 83 per cent of adolescents with emotional or neurotic conditions improve, some 53 per cent of those with a character or conduct disorder do so, and about 45 per cent of psychotics make gains (Gossett et al, 1973). The U.K. studies show diagnostic differences of a similar kind but in general there has been a lower rate of improvement in the psychoses, presumably due to a more restricted diagnosis of schizophrenia (Cooper et al, 1972) compared with that in the U.S.A.

Thirdly, the prognosis for adolescent psychiatric disorders does not appear to be any different (neither better nor worse) from that for similar disorders in earlier childhood or adult life. On the basis of his own and other findings on this point, Masterson (1967) has argued that psychiatric disorders during adolescence should be taken just as seriously as those at other ages. Adolescence is a period of many psychological changes but psychiatric disorder is not a normal feature and most youngsters with psychiatric conditions cannot be expected to grow out of them.

Adolescent-adult links

The broader issue of the links between adolescence and adult life involve several further matters, including the persistence of personality traits as well as of disorder, and the question of how far adult psychiatric conditions are continuations of adolescent problems and how far they arise without any previous difficulties in the teens or in earlier childhood.

Surprisingly few data are available on the first question but the evidence indicates moderate, but only moderate, levels of continuity in behaviour. Figure 1.24, for example, provides the findings on the agreement between 'neuroticism' scores on the Eysenck scales as measured at 16 years and at 26 years (Douglas and Mann, 1979). It is clear that there is a highly significant agreement between the two measures (p <0·0001 for a sample of 1548), but the overall correlation (using Kendall's tau) was only 0·32, indicating that many individuals had altered considerably over the years in this personality trait—at least as measured by a self-rating questionnaire. Bronson (1967), using Q sort measures from the Berkeley Guidance Study, found correlations of much the same level between adolescence and adulthood (at age 30 years) for dimensions of expressive vs reserved and controlled vs explosive. Block (1971) combined data from the same study

73

Patterns of adolescent development and disorder

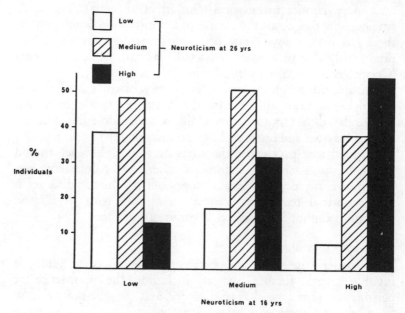

FIGURE I.24
(Data from Douglas and Mann, 1979)

with that from the Oakland Growth Study to examine the issue of coherence in personality development. The complex findings were not presented in a manner which makes for succinct conclusions but the main argument put forward was that it makes more sense to see development in terms of contrasting personality types rather than in terms of overall correlations for the population as a whole. When viewed in this way, both consistencies in personality pattern and changes in overt behaviour are evident.

On the question of the extent to which adult disorders begin in childhood, there are huge differences according to diagnosis. Robins (1978) has provided a most informative and useful summary of the findings on adult antisocial behaviour from her own four longitudinal studies of males. She concludes firstly, that, looking forwards, most antisocial children do *not* become antisocial adults. However, secondly, it appears equally strongly that most adult antisocial behaviour *was* preceded by similar behaviour in childhood. Only quite infrequently did antisocial behaviour begin for the first time in adult life. It follows from this finding that antisocial behaviour is much more frequent in childhood than in adult life. Thirdly, the severity and variety of antisocial behaviour in childhood is a better predictor of adult functioning than is any particular type of childhood behaviour. Fourthly, adult antisocial behaviour is better predicted by childhood *behaviour* than by family background or social class of rearing. The findings are impressive and convincing if only because of the remarkable degree of consistency in findings between four studies differing in both era and ethnic background. They are also broadly supported by West and Farrington's findings (1977) on London males. They showed not only a substantial degree of consistency between juvenile delinquency and adult crime, but also that persistent delinquency tended to be associated with a whole constellation of characteristics including aggressiveness, irregular work habits, immoderation in the pursuit of immediate pleasure, and lack of conventional social restraints. The concept of an antisocial personality first evident in childhood but persisting into adult life has extensive empirical support.

However, as shown by the West and Farrington study, as well as by others on both sides of the Atlantic (see Farrington, 1979, for an excellent review), continuities in antisocial behaviour are not the same thing as continuities in criminal record. About two-fifths of adult offenders have not been convicted as juveniles. Their characteristics are considered further below when discussing continuities in behaviour across adolescence.

The findings with respect to adult neurosis and depression are rather different, although it must be said that the evidence is less satisfactory (see Robins, 1972; Rutter, 1972b; Rutter and Madge, 1976; and Cox, 1976 for reviews—also Waldron, 1976 and Lewine et al, 1978). Data come from studies of child-patients followed into adult life; from studies of individuals experiencing psychiatric disorders both as children and as adults; and from retrospective studies of adult patients. It appears, firstly, that most

75

children with emotional disorders become normal adults (although this proportion varies considerably according to the severity of the childhood problems, being much lower with the more severe disorders), but that their risk of adult psychiatric disorder is substantially raised above that for individuals without disturbance in childhood. Secondly, if disorder persists into adult life it usually takes the form of neurosis or depression, but there is little continuity with respect to the particular types of emotional symptomatology. Thirdly, many adults develop emotional disorders for the first time in adult life, without ever having shown disturbance during childhood. Fourthly, but less certainly, an adult onset seems more frequent in the case of depressive disorders and especially manic-depressive psychosis than with neuroses.

As already discussed, schizophrenia usually does not become manifest until adult life. However, as a variety of different research strategies have shown (see Offord & Cross, 1969; Watt et al, 1970; Watt, 1976; Watt and Lubensky, 1976), about half of schizophrenic adults have shown behavioural abnormalities in childhood. Few of these abnormalities were evident in early childhood but most were manifest by early adolescence. No clear-cut syndrome identified pre-schizophrenic states but on the whole the pre-schizophrenic boys tended to become more irritable, aggressive, negativistic, and defiant, while the girls were more likely to become increasingly compliant, shy, and introverted.

Behavioural continuities across adolescence

It is clear then that, although the pattern and strength of the links vary with the type of behaviour or disorder being considered, there are significant continuities between childhood and adolescence and between adolescence and adult life. As already suggested in the earlier discussions (especially with respect to antisocial personalities) there are also links between childhood and adult life. This applies not only to people's behaviour but also to associations between childhood experiences and adult problems. Wadsworth (1979), for example, showed in relation to the National Survey data that 'broken homes' in the first four years of life were related to delinquency in early adult life. Similarly, with the same data, Douglas and Mann (1979) found that family

76

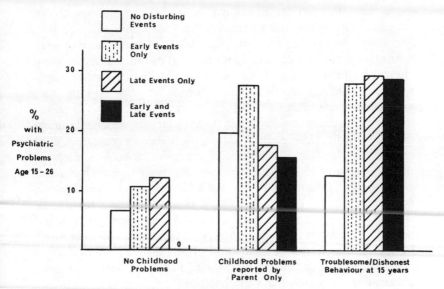

Disturbing Events, Childhood Problems and Adult Psychiatric Disorder

FIGURE 1.25
(Data from Douglas, 1979)

adversities during the first 15 years (divorce, sib death, parental death, parental illness, and parental remarriage) were associated with psychiatric problems in the 15- to 26-year age period. Of those with none of these adversities 8·5 per cent showed adolescent/adult psychiatric disorder, whereas of those with at least two adversities 18·9 per cent did so. These findings are interesting and important but they do not deal with the critical issue of how the associations are mediated and in particular with the question of whether the links between childhood and adult life require the presence of adolescent disorder. In other words, the issue is whether childhood experiences or behaviour are still associated with adult behaviour in individuals who have not shown problems during adolescence.

However, Douglas and Mann (1979) have recently undertaken some analyses of the National Survey data which deal with just these points, with some important and interesting findings (see fig.

77

1.25). The first point is that the rate of psychiatric difficulties during the 15- to 26-year age period is quite low (7·9 per cent) in individuals who showed no problems in childhood, irrespective of whether they experienced disturbing events either early or late. Secondly, the rate of psychiatric difficulties in adult life was very high (34·8 per cent) in the small number (43) of individuals showing childhood problems in both parent and teacher reports, irrespective of the presence or absence of disturbing events (in fig. 1.25 the data for this group are combined with those for individuals showing troublesome/dishonest behaviour on teacher reports only). Thirdly, late events (death, divorce, or remarriage of parents, death of sib, miscarriage or abortion, or broken marriage during the 15- to 20-year age period) were somewhat more common if there had been early disturbing events 'death, divorce, or remarriage of parents, death of sib, one parent family, or serious parental illness during the 0- to 15-year age period) than if there had not been any such events (37·6 per cent vs 27·9 per cent). Fourthly, the *presence* of disturbing events showed no association with psychiatric difficulties in early adult life in individuals who experienced no emotional or behavioural problems in childhood. Fifthly, however, there was some suggestion that the *absence* of disturbing events may have had some protective effect in individuals who showed troublesome or dishonest behaviour at 15 years. We may conclude that the main continuity between childhood and early adult life concerns emotional or behavioural disturbance; and that the effect of disturbing events in either childhood or adolescence with respect to psychiatric difficulties in the 15- to 26-year age period is rather marginal once the presence of childhood disturbance has been taken into account.

West and Farrington (1977) also have some data relevant to this point from their longitudinal study of London boys. Out of the total group of 389 there were 38 convicted for the first time as a young adult. Of these a quarter had high scores on self-reported delinquency at 14 and 16 years (compared with 10 per cent of non-delinquents) so that it could not be said that their antisocial behaviour did not start until adult life, even though their convictions did. Figure 1.26 shows the associations with earlier measures of behaviour at three ages. There was no significant association

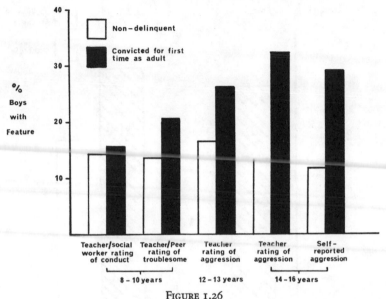

FIGURE 1.26
(Data from West and Farrington, 1973)

with the behavioural ratings at age 8 to 10 years (although, as shown in fig. 1.19, these were very strongly associated with juvenile delinquency which persisted into adult life), there was a weak non-significant association with the rating of aggression at 12 to 13 years but much stronger associations with measures at 14 to 16 years. In this case it seemed that it was only during adolescence that substantial behavioural continuity first appeared.

There were some associations between adult crime and a few of the early family measures (such as large family size, parental criminality, and low socio-economic status) but it was striking that these all referred to family characteristics likely to persist into adult life. Hence it may well be that the early features were related to adult behaviour simply because the families showed the same features years later. Delayed effects of early experiences can only

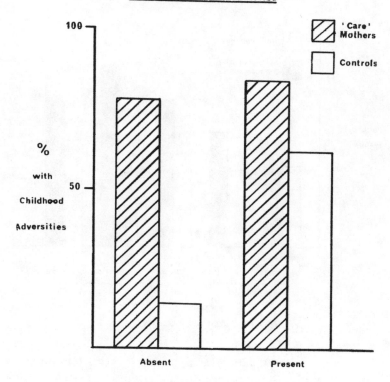

Associations between Teenage Difficulties and Childhood Adversities

FIGURE 1.27
(Data from Quinton and Rutter, 1979)

be studied with respect to experiences which are restricted to early childhood and do not continue throughout the whole of development. Unfortunately, childhood adversities tend to be very persistent and some of the continuities in people's behaviour may just mean that they are responding throughout to the same contemporaneous environmental stresses but that the stresses do not alter.

A further study to examine the question of whether adolescent difficulties necessarily serve as the mediating link between childhood stresses and adult disorder is Quinton and Rutter's (1979) investigation of child experiences and parenting behaviour. In the first retrospective part of the study, the parents of children admitted into the care of the local authority because of a breakdown in parenting were compared with a control group of parents living in a similar socially disadvantaged area. The 'in care' group of parents had had far more in the way of seriously adverse experiences, and this raised the issue of whether these early experiences could be linked with later parenting problems even in those individuals who had not shown teenage difficulties. Figure 1.27 shows the association between teenage difficulties and childhood adversities in the two groups. In the control group, the two were strongly associated; 62 per cent of those with teenage problems had had serious childhood adversities compared with only 14 per cent of mothers without teenage problems. However, this was not so in the 'in care' group where 78 per cent of mothers *without* teenage difficulties had experienced childhood adversities. The finding suggests that there may be important associations between childhood adversities and parental failure which are *not* mediated by teenage difficulties.

Figure 1.28 presents data relevant to that possibility. The pair of histograms on the left show the findings for the mothers in both groups who did *not* show teenage difficulties. It is obvious that there was a huge difference between the groups with respect to childhood adversity; very few control mothers *did* have childhood adversity whereas very few 'care' mothers did *not*. In short, even when there had been no substantial difficulties during adolescence, childhood experiences were associated with later parenting problems. The two pairs of histograms on the right refer to the mothers in both groups who showed teenage difficulties. Two findings stand out. Firstly, there was no difference between the groups with respect to teenage difficulties in the absence of childhood adversity, suggesting the lack of importance of teenage difficulties occurring on their own. On the other hand, within the group all of whom showed teenage difficulties, more of the 'care' mothers had had childhood adversities. Thus, childhood adversity

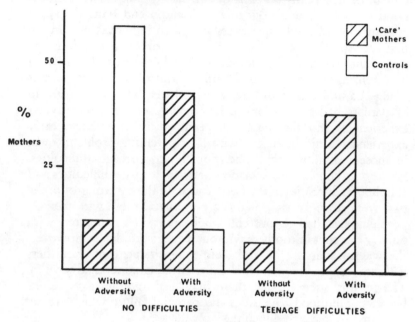

FIGURE I.28
(Data from Quinton and Rutter, 1979)

was still strongly associated with the 'care' families even after controlling for teenage difficulties.

The implication is that childhood experiences may be associated with later parental problems even when there are no gross overt problems evident during adolescence itself. However, the suggestion must remain very speculative at the moment in view of the reliance on retrospective data and the limited range of measures of adolescent behaviour. The second, prospective, part of the study, which is still in progress, should provide stronger data but certainly the possibility warrants further exploration and investigation.

The issue of the role of adolescence in the continuities between childhood and adult life is raised in a different way by the varying pattern of correlations across different time periods. For example, Bronson (1967) found that for females (but not males) the dimension of placidity vs explosiveness showed stronger correlations between early adolescence (11 to 13 years) and adult life (age 30) than between later adolescence (14 to 16 years) and adult life. The implication is that there may be temporary changes during late adolescence in this aspect of behaviour which are not of prognostic importance for adult functioning. Gersten et al (1976) showed something rather similar with respect to their 'mentation problems' variable (dealing with thought, speech and school achievement problems) and 'conflict with parents'. Both showed substantially lower correlations for the $14\frac{1}{2}$- to $19\frac{1}{3}$-age span than for either earlier or later five-year-periods. 'Isolation' showed a somewhat similar dip in stability during middle and later adolescence and 'regressive anxiety' did so for the $10\frac{1}{2}$- to $15\frac{1}{2}$-age span. The data are too few to warrant firm conclusions but there is some suggestion that behaviour may not always increase consistently in stability with increasing age—instead there may be a temporary period of transient fluctuations during adolescence which is not necessarily of great prognostic importance.

The issues of continuities in development between childhood and adult life were also examined by Elder in his use of the Berkeley and Oakland longitudinal data to examine the effects of growing up during the inter-war years of economic depression (Elder, 1974, 1979; Elder and Rockwell, 1979). Many findings of interest emerged but three points are particularly relevant here. First, many individuals who showed low self-esteem, indecision, and withdrawal from adversity during adolescence became confident and effective adults, in spite of some continuing disadvantages such as their lack of resilience in the face of criticism. The positive gains during early adult life were associated with occupational success and with the emotional support of a happy marriage. Clearly, development goes on well beyond the teenage years. Secondly, economic hardship seemed to have more deleterious effects on young children than on adolescents. Indeed, for some adolescents there were gains in terms of their being brought more into family activities through the need for them to take on both increased domestic chores and some kind of paid work outside the home. Dealing successfully with these responsibilities seemed both to develop their adaptive capacities and to provide them with the ambition to succeed by their own efforts. It may be that some of the apparent discontinuities between childhood and adult life are explicable in terms of the styles of adaptation during adolescence. Thirdly, the psychological ill-effects of the Depression were more evident in the middle-class sample than in the working-class group. Perhaps this was because the loss of status and the disparity between aspirations and current circumstances were greater in those who had most to lose, even though in absolute terms they were less handicapped. Evidently development has to be viewed in its social context; it cannot be considered in purely individual terms.

These themes are repeated in Vaillant's (1977) study of a very different group of individuals—the independent-minded college graduates in the Grant study. The findings suggested that isolated traumatic events rarely moulded individual lives but that a globally disturbed childhood was predictive of adult problems. There were substantial continuities in psychosocial adjustment between late adolescence and middle life but also there were some startling changes and evolutions during the adult years. Vaillant argued that although these were not necessarily predictable, nevertheless they were not chance happenings. Rather they seemed to be a function of styles of adaptation and of psychological defences which had been built up over the whole period of development.

CONCLUSIONS

Finally, we need to ask how these many research findings on patterns of adolescent development and disorder relate to the questions on adolescence with which we started: Is there anything distinctive about adolescence which separates it off from the rest of the developmental period of childhood?, Is normal adolescence characterized by storm, stress, and disturbance?, and are the disorders of adolescence meaningfully different from those arising in either childhood or adult life?

Conclusions

The data on physical growth alone mark adolescence as a period which stands out as different from earlier childhood. Firstly, growth is more rapid then than at any other time during development, apart from early infancy. Secondly, the hormonal changes during puberty are very considerable and, again, greater than at any other age period. Thirdly, puberty brings about the development of adult sexuality—a change in functioning of immense psychological importance. The findings suggest that all these biological changes have an important impact on psychosocial development.

However, it is not just the physical maturation which makes adolescence different; there are also crucial psychological hurdles erected at about the same time. Outside the home there is the important shift from elementary school to secondary school; public examinations involve stress a few years later at age 15 to 16 years; and these are then followed by the different stresses of the transitions to employment (or unemployment all too often) and to further education. Within the family there is the need for the adolescent to experience responsibilities and gain in autonomy and these may be associated with a fair amount of minor bickering with parents on everyday issues of hairstyle, clothing, and what time to be in at night. At the same time the coming of puberty is associated with a marked increase in feelings of misery, self-depreciation or 'inner turmoil'—an increase not seen at other age periods.

Moreover, adolescence is associated with a variety of important changes in the pattern of psychosocial disorders. Various problems reach peaks at this time which exceeds any occurring either before or after. Thus, delinquent behaviour is most common during the teenage period; and the late teens are also the years when anorexia nervosa, parasuicide, and depressive conditions, approach their peak. Drug abuse rises sharply during late adolescence although its peak is reached a little later, and it is during adolescence that there is the marked shift in the sex ratio of emotional disorders (from almost unity in childhood to a strong female preponderance in adult life). Adolescence is also a time when various psychiatric conditions somewhat change their manifestations; for example, it is the time when autistic children are most likely to develop

85

epileptic fits for the first time. For all these reasons, we may safely conclude that adolescence is indeed a meaningfully distinctive developmental period. In part, the special features are a function of the physical growth and development which takes place at that time and in part they relate to the environmental circumstances which surround the adolescent years in western cultures.

It also seems that the disorders arising for the first time during adolescence do differ in some respects from the psychiatric conditions of childhood. They tend *not* to be associated with educational retardation and are less likely to be associated with gross family discord and disruption. On the other hand, it is clear that it would be quite wrong to see most psychiatric disorders of adolescence as just transient reactions to the stresses of that age period. To the contrary, their diagnostic features, course and outcome follow much the same pattern as symptomatically similar disorders at other ages. As with children and adults, emotional disorders have a relatively good prognosis and antisocial problems a rather bad one. Psychotic conditions, similarly, carry much the same implications as those occurring in adult life.

It is also evident that normal adolescence is *not* characterized by storm, stress, and disturbance. Most young people go through their teenage years without significant emotional or behavioural problems. It is true, as already noted, that there is a substantial increase in depressive feelings during adolescence and there are challenges to be met, adaptations to be made, and stresses to be coped with. However, these do not all arise at the same time and most adolescents deal with these issues without undue disturbance. On the whole family influences remain powerful throughout adolescence and most teenagers continue both to have warm relationships with their parents and to rely on them for guidance on the major issues of life.

Although there are features which make adolescence a special period of development there is *not* a discontinuity in development then. There are major changes in adolescence in psychosexual functioning, in friendships, in the influence of peer groups, and in emotions, but all of these build on what has gone on before in development. Also, other aspects of psychosexual development show relatively few shifts during the teenage years and certainly it seems misleading to view adolescence as a time of identity crisis. Of course, the development of a personal identity is a crucial part of growing up and much of importance in this connection happens during adolescence, but so also it does earlier in childhood and later in adult life.

There are substantial continuities, although only moderate in strength, not only *between* adolescence and both childhood and adult life, but also *across* adolescence. To a considerable extent adolescence merely spans the period between childhood and adult life. However, although not well demonstrated as yet, there are some suggestions that not all the links between childhood and adolescence are mediated through adolescent behaviours, and also that at least for some behaviours adolescence may mark a period of relative instability with transient changes of little long-term significance. Of all the issues associated with adolescent development, those concerned with continuities and discontinuities across the adolescent years remain the least well documented and the most in need of further study.

2

Historical trends in adolescent behaviour

The question of whether patterns of adolescent behaviour have been changing over the years is both broad in its implications and methodologically difficult to answer. As indicated in the previous chapter, many changes take place during the course of the teenage years, and there are many different behaviours and disorders which could be included in a discussion of historical trends. However, rather than attempt a comprehensive coverage of all possible facets of adolescence, this chapter focuses on just five key areas which are particularly characteristic of this phase of development: the so-called 'generation gap', sexuality and marriage, scholastic achievement, delinquency and vandalism, and certain psychiatric disorders. Many of the methodological problems are inherent in the measurement of historical trends and apply to all five topics. However, as they are most easily illustrated through the use of specific examples, the methodological discussion is distributed across the five sections of the chapter.

THE GENERATION GAP

As already noted in the first chapter, the concept of a 'generation gap' which arises during adolescence is at most a half-truth. However, because it has often been supposed that the 'gap' has been widening, we need to examine the empirical evidence which might indicate how far this has been happening. For this purpose, we really need comparable assessments of the attitudes and feelings of parents and adolescents which are repeated over time with both the same cohort of individuals and with fresh samples of parent-adolescent pairs of the same ages as the initial group. It is also necessary to ensure that the measures have the same meaning for the subjects at each assessment. It is obvious that very frequently this will not be the case as issues such as the Vietnam war, the emergence of a drug culture, and rising unemployment are likely to alter the emotional content of questions on what is ostensibly the same topic. Moreover, findings may be affected by changes in the age difference between parents and their adolescent children. It will readily be appreciated that it is necessary to differentiate between a variety of patterns made up of permutations in life cycle effects (e.g. the younger generation may converge with the older as it ages), generation effects (i.e. stable differences between generations), and period effects (i.e. that over time both generations shift congruently). These methodological issues are well discussed and illustrated with empirical data by Jennings and Niemi (1975); and the conceptual viewpoints are outlined by Bengtson (1970). As no one study meets all requirements, we have to build up some kind of overall picture from rather disparate sets of data. Nevertheless, in spite of these limitations it is striking that the findings are generally in agreement in showing *no* widening of the generation gap.

For example, Aldous and Hill (1965; Hill and Aldous, 1969) interviewed a U.S. urban sample of grandparents, parents, and their married children, each generation maintaining a separate household. There was strong continuity over the three generations in religious affiliation (two-thirds of families), but more modest continuity in the division of marital household tasks (a third of families) and in decision-making (a sixth of families). In every area except economic planning there was greater similarity between parents and their married children than between grandparents and parents. Thus, for marital authority patterns there was parent-child continuity in 31 per cent of cases but grandparent-parent continuity in only 18 per cent. The comparable figures for marital task division were 24 per cent vs 20 per cent, and for sex role task allocation 37 per cent vs 19 per cent. The implication is that the generation gap has narrowed; but it could be that life cycle effects have influenced the findings in that the generations were of different ages.

Jennings and Niemi (1975) used a different research design in that they followed a sample of over a thousand high school seniors and their parents over an eight-year period between 1965 and

1973. Unfortunately, about a third of the sample were lost to follow-up. The questionnaire findings on a variety of attitudes and opinions regarding political issues showed little alteration in the generation gap over the eight years but on the whole a coming together of the generations. However, as a fresh sample of high school seniors was not obtained, it remains uncertain how far the gap at the *same* point in life cycles has widened or narrowed.

Various studies (see Bell, 1971; Reiss, 1976) have sought to assess generation differences in sexual behaviour. As discussed below, there has been an undoubted increase in sexual relationships involving intercourse among young adolescents. But, so far as can be judged from rather unsatisfactory data, the greatest change in premarital sexual behaviour occurred much earlier in this century with the cohort reaching adolescence and early adulthood after the First World War.

The findings on social mobility across the generations were reviewed by Rutter and Madge (1976), with the conclusion that during the last thirty years there has probably been little change in the extent of social mobility.

It is clear that the data to assess historical changes in the generation gap are less than adequate, but none of the studies provide any indication that the gap is widening and in some areas it may even be narrowing slightly.

SEXUALITY AND MARRIAGE

It is sometimes thought that teenagers today have become sexually promiscuous and have rejected the values of earlier generations on the importance of stable relationships. The available evidence suggest that this is *not* the case, although there have been real changes in young people's approach to sexuality and marriage. One of the difficulties in examining historical trends with respect to personal behaviours about which people may well be reluctant to talk freely, is that changes in *reports* may reflect alterations in people's willingness to admit to things rather than changes in how they actually *behave*. Clearly this is a real possibility with respect to sexuality. However, that cannot be a sufficient explanation as the self-reports of greater pre-marital sexual activity have been accompanied by marked rises in the proportion of adolescents becoming pregnant—in spite of contraceptives having become both more effective and more readily available. The possible meanings of these changes over time are best considered by taking each aspect of sexuality and marriage in turn.

Sexual attitudes and behaviour

There is a lack of really satisfactory comparative data which might be used to assess changes in sexual attitudes and behaviour over time. Nevertheless, there can be no doubt that in the U.K. and the U.S.A. teenagers have both become more accepting in their attitudes to pre-marital sexual behaviour and also have started to engage in sexual activity at a younger age. Thus, in the U.S.A. the findings from studies of national samples suggest that whereas in 1915 three-quarters of women were virgins at the time of marriage, this was so for only about half in 1965 and a quarter in 1970 (Reiss, 1976). There have been accompanying intergenerational changes in attitudes to pre-marital chastity (Bell, 1971). Yankelovich (1974), in American surveys of 16- to 25-year-olds between 1967 and 1973 found an increasing proportion of young people who said they would welcome more acceptance of sexual freedom and a decreasing proportion who thought that casual pre-marital sexual relationships were wrong. These shifting attitudes followed the same patterns in both college and non-college youth, but the trends occurred earlier and went further in college students. Thus, between 1969 and 1973 the proportion regarding casual pre-marital sex as morally wrong fell from 34 per cent to 22 per cent among college youth but from 58 per cent to 34 per cent among those who were not at college. Among those not at college, housewives remained the most traditional of all groups in their values, including attitudes to sexuality. A study of girls at a large urban U.S. university showed that in 1958 10 per cent accepted pre-marital intercourse when dating (or 15 per cent when going steady) whereas in 1968 the figures had risen to 23 per cent and 28 per cent respectively (Bell, 1971). Interestingly, the rise was much less marked with respect to sexual activity when engaged—31 per cent to 39 per cent. It seems that the change has been more in connection with the type of relationship needed for sex to be permissible, than for sexual activity as such. Nevertheless, it should not be thought that there has been a massive rise in casual sexual relationships. Young people, and especially girls, continue to stress the importance of love and a degree of commitment in pre-marital sex, even though they no longer regard engagement or marriage as pre-requisites. Interestingly, however, a majority of adolescents still expect sexual fidelity after marriage, even though they do not expect it before then (Sorensen, 1973). The same studies also indicate that sexually experienced girls generally have a low number of sexual partners, although this is much less true of boys. Moreover, the available evidence indicates that the main shift in sexual attitudes applies to girls—there has been much less alteration in the views and activity of boys—although there has been some change of a comparable kind (Bell, 1971; Reiss, 1976).

The greater acceptance of pre-marital sex has been accompanied by changing views on personal freedom, by an emphasis on sharing and openness, by a greater tolerance of atypical sexual behaviour and by an increasing prevalence of 'women's liberation' ideas. Although perhaps most obvious in terms of changing attitudes to sexuality, these attitudes seem to be part of a broader set of views and ideals characteristic of what some have called 'the peace and love generation' (Starr, 1974). Yankelovich (1974) found that the proportion of college youth regarding consenting homosexual relationships as morally wrong fell from 42 per cent to 25 per cent between 1969 and 1973, and from 72 per cent to 47 per cent among a similar aged group not at college. In 1973, 64 per cent of college women and 47 per cent of non-college women rejected the view that women's place was in the home; similarly only 41 per cent of college women thought that having children without formal marriage was wrong, whereas 62 per cent of non-college women expressed that view.

On the other hand, Yankelovich (1974) found that most unmarried college students still look forward to marriage (61 per cent) and are interested in having children (76 per cent). The proportion regarding marriage as obsolete rose from 24 per cent in 1968 to 30 per cent in 1973, but this attitude remained a minority one. Only a few young people (12 per cent non-college and 13 per cent college) said that they would find conventional life intolerable. Quite a lot (21 per cent of non-college and 28 per cent college) expressed an interest in living in a commune for a short while but a mere 1 in 50 said that they wished for communal living in the long-term. Between 1969 and 1973, the proportion of college and non-college youth emphasizing the importance of religion fell (39 per cent to 28 per cent and 65 per cent to 42 per cent respectively) but the vast majority of young people continued to stress the traditional values of love and friendship.

Sorensen (1973) found an even lower proportion of adolescents rejecting marriage. Eighty-five per cent of 13- to 19-year-old boys and 92 per cent of girls wanted to get married and have children (this proportion did not vary with either age or sexual experience). A committed relationship was generally seen as crucial for the bringing up of children but there was some cynicism regarding the effects on that relationship of a legal bond.

We may conclude from these U.S. findings that there has been a substantial move (first in college groups and later in all sections of the population) towards greater sexual freedom among young people. There has been little alteration in the emphasis on love and commitment in personal relationships, but although marriage has remained the goal for most young people far fewer accept it as a *sine qua non* for sexual relationships. Moreover, there is a substantial minority of young people who reject marriage as the preferred form of long-standing relationship.

The U.K. figures tell much the same story. For example, in his 1964 survey, Schofield (1965 and 1973) found that by the age of 16 years 14 per cent of boys and 5 per cent of girls were sexually experienced. Ten years later, Farrell and Kellaher (1978) found that 26 per cent of 16 year-old boys and 12 per cent of girls said that they had their first sexual experience before the age of 16 years. Other surveys confirm that teenagers are now tending to start sexual activity at an earlier age (Cossey, 1978). The increasing proportion of pre-marital sexual activity is also reflected in the figures for the whole of the late teenage period. Whereas only 16 per cent of Schofield's sample of 15- to 19-year-olds said that they had had sexual experience at least once, in Farrell and Kellaher's sample of 16- to 19-year-olds in the mid 70s half

93

reported that they were sexually experienced. The comparison is not a direct one in view of the inclusion of 15-year-olds in the earlier study but, even when this is taken into account, it is obvious that over the mid-60s to mid-70s decade there was a substantial increase in the proportion of teenagers engaging in sexual activity. Schofield's (1973) follow-up at age 24 to 26 years showed that 80 per cent of the men and 61 per cent of the women had had premarital sex—the proportions being slightly higher among the better educated than those who left school at the first opportunity. However, there were few social class differences and Farrell and Kellaher (1978) found that working-class teenagers were more likely than the middle-class to express approval of premarital sex. There was no social class difference in the proportion of girls who were sexually experienced but sexual experience was more common in working-class boys. On the other hand, as in the U.S. studies, young people from a middle-class background were more likely to express approval of abortion.

Clearly, premarital sex has now become the normal pattern. On the other hand, for many young people the sexual experience had only been with the person they subsequently married. Altogether, 40 per cent of Schofield's total sample (and over half of those who were married) had either no sexual experience prior to marriage or had only had experience with their spouse-to-be (Schofield, 1973).

Sexually transmitted diseases

Although greatly influenced by the effectiveness of medical treatments and by people's willingness to seek treatment, the frequency of sexually transmitted diseases provides a rough and ready guide to the extent of promiscuity. The available statistics (Central Statistical Office, 1978) on cases dealt with for the first time at any centre show that there was a considerable increase in Britain between 1966 and 1971—from 127,000 cases to 219,000 cases. This rise included teenagers to the same relative extent as adults (young people under 20 years accounted for some 15 to 20 per cent of cases). Among teenagers, girls showed a greater increase in gonorrhea than did boys (Court, 1976). Since 1971, the total number of new cases per year has gone up further to

Trends in Marriage Rates for 16-19 Year Olds

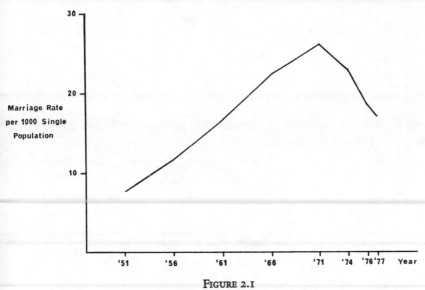

FIGURE 2.1

(Data from Court, 1976 and Office of Population Censuses and Surveys, 1979)

285,000 (in 1977); but in the population as a whole this increase in the 1970s has been largely confined to non-specific infections and to other conditions not requiring treatment, rather than syphilis or gonorrhea. However, gonorrhea in adolescents continued to rise up to 1973 (Court, 1976). The evidence is consistent with some increase in promiscuity.

Marriage
From the 1930s up to about 1971 there was a regular trend in the U.K. towards both earlier marriage and also towards a higher proportion of the population who were married, but during the last 6 years both trends have reversed (Central Statistical Office, 1978; Leete, 1979). Thus, the marriage rate per 1000 single people for 16- to 19-year-old males rose from 7·8 in 1951 to 27·2 in 1970 but by 1974 it had again fallen to 22·9 (Court, 1976). By 1977 it had fallen further still to 17·2 (Office of Population Censuses and

Trends in Divorce for Teenage Brides

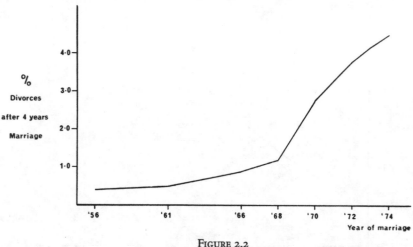

FIGURE 2.2
(Data from Leete, 1979)

Surveys, 1979—see fig. 2.1). The rates for teenage girls are higher throughout but the historical trend has been closely similar in both sexes. The overall rate of married women per 1000 total female population at age 35 to 39 years similarly rose from 739 in 1916–20, to 826 in 1950, and 895 in 1970, but fell slightly to 889 by 1974. This decline in marriage rates has affected all age groups, but has been most marked in teenagers. In 1977 only 13 per cent of 19-year-old girls were married, compared with 19 per cent in 1970 and 17 per cent in 1972 (Leete, 1979). This fall in first marriage rates has been most marked in Scandinavia where there has been a substantial rise in couples cohabiting, but it has also occurred in the U.S.A. and in other European countries (Leete, 1979). Exact figures are lacking but it seems highly probable that cohabitation outside marriage has also risen in both the U.K. and the U.S.A. Certainly this is suggested by the rising proportion of illegitimate children registered by *both* parents (see below).

For many years teenage marriages have been consistently associated with a much higher rate of divorce (Leete, 1979). Thus, among women aged under 20 years and first married in 1956,

96

19 per cent had been divorced after 20 years of marriage compared with 10 per cent for those married between 20 and 24 years and 5 per cent for those marrying between 25 and 29 years. The divorce rate among young people marrying in their teens has shown the same marked increase evident in the population as a whole (see fig. 2.2). Thus after just four years of marriage, among teenagers married in 1956, 4 per 1000 had divorced but for those married in 1974, 45 per 1000 had done so. It seems that teenage marriage now, as in years past, carries a very high risk of break-down. Whether this risk will apply equally to marriages taking place after a period of prior cohabitation remains to be seen.

Contraception

Accurate figures on contraception are not available for earlier generations of young people but it is evident that over recent years there has been a substantial increase in the use of effective contraceptive methods. Thus, between 1970 and 1975 there was a decrease from 14 per cent to 5 per cent in those relying on with-drawal and an increase from 19 per cent to 30 per cent in the use of the pill among women under 41 years (Central Statistical Office, 1977). Similarly, in 1975, 17 per cent of those first married during 1956–60 were using no methods of birth control, but this was so for only 8 per cent of those married during 1971–5. Among married couples two-thirds were using effective methods of contraception in 1967–8 but by 1973 this proportion had risen to four-fifths (Cartwright, 1976).

Even so, it is clear from Farrell and Kellaher's (1978) survey of 16- to 19-year-olds that many sexually experienced teenagers were not regularly using reliable techniques. Although only 8 per cent said they had never used any method of birth control, nearly half had not employed any form of contraception during their first sexual experience, and a quarter had relied on less reliable methods (withdrawal, the safe period, or chemicals). Furthermore, half of the sexually experienced did not always use birth control, although three-quarters usually utilized the sheath or pill. The young people most likely to be using birth control consistently were older middle-class girls; those least likely to be controlling their fertility (either through their own precautions or

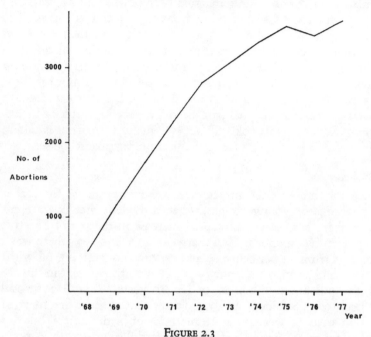

Trends in Abortions for Girls
under 16 years

FIGURE 2.3

(Data from Court, 1976 and Office of Population Censuses and Surveys, 1979)

those of their sexual partners) were young working-class boys not involved in stable relationships.

Abortion

There has been a huge increase in recent years in the number of abortions. In the U.S.A. the rise has been from 23,000 in 1969 to 892,000 in 1974 (Reiss, 1976). Even between 1972 and 1975 the abortion rate per 1000 women aged 15 to 19 years rose from 21 to 32, and the proportion of pregnancies being terminated almost doubled from 31 per cent to 56 per cent (Dryfoos, 1978). Similar increases have occurred in most European countries (Deschamps and Valantin, 1978) with abortions most frequent among young adolescents. Thus, in Sweden, 92 per cent of pregnancies in 14-

to 15-year-olds end in an abortion, but only 37 per cent in 18- to 19-year-olds. In the U.K., there was a three-fold increase between 1961 and 1967 in the number of therapeutic abortions carried out in National Health Service Hospitals (Central Statistical Office, 1972), but the main increase followed the 1968 Abortion Act. From April to December 1968 there were 25,000 abortions, in the next year the number rose to 58,000, in 1970 it rose again to 92,000 and in 1971 it reached 133,000. However, since 1972 the overall number of abortions in England and Wales (for women resident in the country) has remained fairly steady (Office of Population Censuses and Surveys, 1979). About half the abortions are for pregnancies in unmarried women, and for this group the number of abortions now substantially exceeds the number of live births (Thompson, 1976).

It should be noted that although the abortion rates has been steady overall during the last six years in the U.K., the pattern for young teenagers has been different (see fig. 2.3). The number of abortions in girls under 16 years has continued to rise steadily each year—from 2·30 per thousand in 1971 to 3·34 per thousand in 1974 and to 3·62 per thousand in 1977 (Office of Population Censuses and Surveys, 1979). To a lesser extent, it has also continued to rise in unmarried girls in the 16- to 19-year age group—from 17·4 per thousand in 1971 to 22·9 per thousand in 1974, and to 23·4 per thousand in 1977.

Birth: legitimate and illegitimate

As is well known, there have been various peaks and troughs in the birth rate; with a fall in the period between the two world wars, a very sharp rise after the Second World War and then a progressive and very marked fall after that. Thus, in the U.S.A. the birth rate fell from 23·7 per 1000 total population in 1960 to 14·7 in 1976 (U.S. Bureau of the Census, 1977). In the U.K., the fall was from 17·8 in 1966 to 11·6 in 1977. These figures are influenced, however, by the age distribution of the total population and a more valid picture may be obtained by considering age-specific birth rates. These confirm the trends. In 1964 the live birth rate per 1000 women aged 15 to 44 years was 93·0, higher than it had been for fifty years. After that it fell, at first gradually and then more sharply so that by 1978 it was down to only 60·6 (Office of Population Censuses and Surveys, 1979). However, this fall in births has *not* applied to young teenagers. To the contrary, the number of births to girls aged less than 16 years increased from 0·2 per thousand in 1951 to 1·7 per thousand in 1973, with a small decline to 1·4 per thousand in 1976 (Pearce and Farid, 1977). Among older teenagers there has been a fall in birth rate but it did not occur until rather later—from 1972 onwards (Office of Population Censuses and Surveys, 1979).

The pattern for illegitimacy is also different for teenagers. In the U.K. population as a whole, the illegitimacy rate per 1000 live births stood at about 7 per cent in 1850; then during the next 50 years there was a steady fall so that the rate was only 4 per cent at the turn of the century (Pearce and Farid, 1977). There were very sharp peaks at the time of both world wars but otherwise there was not a great deal of change until the late 1950s, when there was a steep rise up to 9 per cent in 1976. However, this overall trend conceals very sharp differences according to both age and marital status. Since 1966 there has been a steady fall in pre-marital conceptions, so that the number of births conceived pre-maritally dropped by a third from 1966 to 1975 (Thompson, 1976). Among women aged 25 years and over the number of illegitimate births registered by the mother only dropped steadily from 6·2 per thousand in 1961 to 1·9 per thousand in 1971, and to 0·3 per thousand in 1976 (Central Statistical Office, 1978). It would appear that more widespread effective contraception has led to fewer unplanned pregnancies.

But in teenagers the trend has been different (see fig. 2.4). The age-specific illegitimate fertility rates continued to rise after 1968, although there has been some decline more recently (Pearce and Farid, 1977). Thus, the illegitimacy fertility rate per 1000 for 15-year-olds rose from 0·7 for those born in 1940 to 2·8 for those born in 1950, and to 3·5 for those born in 1960. The comparable figures for 16-year-olds are 2·2, 7·3 and 7·8. For women up to the age of 20 years, 15·9 per cent of all births were illegitimate in 1960, but 28·6 per cent in 1975. Much the same has happened in the U.S.A. (see Bronfenbrenner, 1976) where the ratio of illegitimate births per 1000 live babies born has risen steadily from about

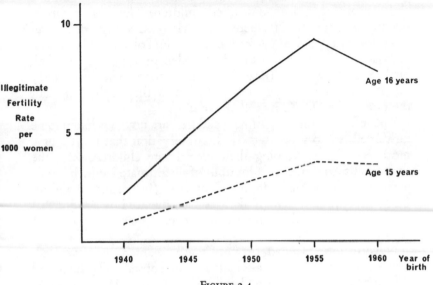

Trends in Illegitimate Births for Girls aged
15 and 16 years

FIGURE 2.4
(Data from Pearce and Farid, 1977)

40 in 1950 to over 120 in 1974. This trend has been most marked in young women so that over 80 per cent of all illegitimate children are being born to women under 25 years of age. Between 1966 and 1975 the out of wedlock birth rate for 15- to 17-year-olds rose from 13·1 per thousand to 19·5 per thousand (Dryfoos, 1978).

In part, this rise in illegitimacy rates among the young seems to be a function of less efficient use of contraceptive methods among teenagers. Thus, whereas the number of illegitimate births registered by the mother only has been falling among older women (see above), it has been rising among teenagers until very recently in the U.K. However, this does not seem to be the whole story as there has been an even greater rise in the number of illegitimate births registered by *both* parents. Among women under 25 years, the number rose from 3·4 per thousand in 1961 to 13·9 per thousand in 1971 (Central Statistical Office, 1978). It seems that in part the explanation lies in the increasing tendency for cohabitation and child bearing outside marriage. In so far as this is the case, it should not be assumed that the illegitimate children are necessarily unwanted children. This is particularly striking in Scandinavia where there has been a large decline in marriage rates and a marked increase in cohabitation outside marriage, with the result that in Sweden in 1975 a third of all births were illegitimate (Pearce and Farid, 1977). The illegitimacy rate in mainland Europe tends to be below that in the U.K. but the rate in the U.S.A. is well above it.

The inference that illegitimate children are now less likely to be unwanted is also supported by the observation that more single mothers are now keeping their illegitimate children, with the result that the number of adoptions of illegitimate babies by non-parents has fallen markedly in recent years (Leete, 1978 a and b). Of course, too, this trend is likely to be influenced by the decreasing social pressures for unmarried mothers to marry the father or get the child adopted.

Nevertheless, planned or unplanned, wanted or unwanted, teenage pregnancies are associated with substantially increased risks for both the mother and child (Court, 1976; Dryfoos, 1978; Deschamps and Valantin, 1978). They tend to receive late and insufficient antenatal care and have a higher rate of still births, premature births, and low birth-weight babies, with all the physical disadvantages these imply. Moreover, U.S. figures show that not only is the infant of a teenage mother at greater risk but also the teenage mother herself is more likely to die or suffer illness or injury (see Cossey, 1978). The death rate from complications of pregnancy, birth, or delivery is 60 per cent higher for girls who become pregnant before they are 15. Moreover, follow-ups of the children born to teenage mothers suggest that they show an increased rate of behavioural and cognitive problems (Shaffer et al, 1978). It remains uncertain how far these consequences stem from the age of the mothers, the children's illegitimacy, or the accompanying psychosocial disadvantage.

Conclusions

Clearly, there have been marked changes over recent years in the sexual attitudes and behaviour of teenagers. Sexual activity has begun earlier, premarital sexual relationships have become more frequent, and the number of teenage pregnancies has risen greatly. The trend towards increasing popularity of marriage has been halted and fewer teenagers now are marrying, although probably more are living together and having children outside marriage. The rate of illegitimate births to single teenage girls living alone has also remained quite high in spite of a greater utilization of birth control and a marked increase in the number of abortions. To some extent, these changes represent a change in attitudes and in life style but to an important degree they also represent a lack of family planning among young people, and especially among young working-class boys.

EDUCATIONAL STANDARDS

In recent years there has been a great deal of public discussion of the question of whether educational standards are falling. At first sight this appears to be a quite straightforward question which should be susceptible to investigations giving rise to clear and unequivocal answers. In fact, this is not so. The matter is both conceptually complex and methodologically difficult.

Purposes of education

Clearly we have to begin by asking what are the purposes of education, what are the educational aims and objectives? Answers to this question tend to range from learning reading, writing, and arithmetic to facilitating optimal personality development. Obviously, the answers must involve value judgements but there are ways of taking the matter of aims and objectives somewhat further. The issues may perhaps be clarified by taking two examples.

First, let us consider the meaning of educational standards in medicine. Naturally, the first requirement is for safe doctors. This demands a sound knowledge of a lot of factual material. However, also we need to have *effective* doctors. This, too, demands a great deal of factual knowledge but in addition there must be the facility to apply the knowledge to an almost infinite variety of human problems and conditions. So far so good; in principle we can test both by means of a combination of tests examining factual knowledge and tests assessing its application to patients. This is just what medical examinations aim to do and hence, in theory, it should be possible to determine whether medical graduates are as well trained or have as high standards today as they did a generation ago.

But, and it is a very large 'but', there is an essential dimension still to add and that is the fact that the body of knowledge needed to practise medicine is constantly changing. Indeed, even the pattern of diseases is altering. A physician retiring today at the age of 65 years who qualified some 40 years ago will have received his undergraduate training before the advent of antibiotics, before the availability of tranquillizers or anti-depressant medication, before an understanding of the physiology of neonatal care, before open heart surgery, before oral contraceptives, before kidney machines, and before immunization against poliomyelitis, tuberculosis, and a variety of other diseases. At a conservative estimate half of the knowledge he is applying at the time he retires will have had to have been acquired after the end of his formal medical training. Moreover, much of what he learned will have proved irrelevant and some of it will have been shown to be wrong.

The lesson is clear. One of the main educational objectives must be learning *how to learn*; how to acquire new knowledge and how to evaluate new claims and new discoveries. This involves learning skills but also it requires an attitude of mind. These may be much more difficult to assess but nevertheless they constitute essential elements in education. It would be no use at all seeing if medical students today got better or worse marks on the final exams that today's retiring physician took some 40 years ago. Not only would the questions be inappropriate and the answers be different but the exam would not assess learning to learn and the ability to evaluate, acquire and apply new knowledge—without which the doctor will be at best incompetent and at worst dangerous in the years to come.

Of course, it may well be thought that these issues are a long way removed from the question of educational standards in school. Most children are not going to go on to be doctors of medicine.

The issue with them may be thought to be more appropriately considered in terms of their ability to read and write or to do simple arithmetical calculations applicable to everyday life. Of course, the issues are different in degree but they are not different in kind. All of us as we grow older live in a rapidly changing world with changing demands, and education must fit us to deal with these altering conditions—whether they be in the operating theatre or on the factory floor.

Certainly we have got to acquire the same basic skills in the '3Rs' as those gained by our forefathers but we, as our grandparents before us, must be able to apply these skills. The issue is not whether we can read, spell, and do sums in an exam but rather whether we can *use* these abilities to read for pleasure, to follow newspapers, to acquire new knowledge, to deal with shopping and with the completion of income tax forms, and to fit us to cope with the demands of new technologies in the factory and in the home.

It was considerations such as these which have led to some of the changes in education. Teachers had become aware that for some children rote learning had led to a sterile and useless set of skills they could not apply outside the classroom. People might know their multiplication tables but they had no 'feel' or understanding of mathematics—a lack which put them at a severe disadvantage outside the school. It was in order to help children gain a real grasp of the subject rather than mere rote skills that styles of teaching were modified to provide a greater emphasis on discovery methods, on the understanding of meaning and of principles and on acquiring a learning set in which to find out about things is sufficiently rewarding in itself for learning to go on outside and after schooling. For example, these are some of the notions which underlie the so-called 'new science' courses.

Whether the new methods have succeeded in these aims, and whether a price has had to be paid for the shifts in emphasis remain important questions demanding answers. But, as a result of these alterations in teaching many of the older tests have become inappropriate and inapplicable. That is certainly the case with mathematics. How then do we know whether the new methods are any good—have they led to a raising or a lowering of educational standards? The question may be approached from several different directions.

Staying on at school

We may ask first what changes there have been in the proportion of children staying on at school. The figures for both the U.K. (D.E.S., 1969, 1977) and the U.S.A. (U.S. Bureau of the Census, 1977) show marked increases over the years. Thus, in the U.S.A., of people aged 25 years or greater in 1940, less than a quarter had completed four or more years of high school; but by 1970 the figure had risen to over half and by 1976 it had reached 64 per cent. The proportions with college education had shown comparable increases; from 4·6 per cent in 1940 to 11·0 per cent in 1970 and to 14·7 per cent in 1976. The statistics for the U.K. show much the same trend. For example, the proportion of children remaining at school after 16 years rose from 11·7 per cent in 1950 to 20·7 per cent in 1960 and to 32·1 per cent in 1970. Evidently there has been a steady increase in the proportion of children staying on at school for longer periods of education.

However, a closer look at the statistics shows a more complicated picture (see fig. 2.5). The proportion of children remaining at school after 16 years did indeed rise steadily up to 1973 (when the figure reached 37·2 per cent) but the following year it fell precipitously by a third to 26·8 per cent and it has remained at about this level ever since. The timing of this marked drop in the proportion of children staying on at school after 16 years makes it almost certain that it was a result of the raising of the school leaving age (ROSLA) to 16 years in 1972–3. The drop is all the more striking because before 1973 it represented staying on at school for *two* years after the school leaving age whereas after 1973 it represented staying on for only *one* year. Obviously the intention of making schooling compulsory for a further year was to *increase* the proportion of pupils remaining at school for a longer period of education. In practice, it seems to have had the reverse effect—a devastating *drop*. This is a striking example of the undesired negative effect of a piece of legislation which sought to increase something by making it compulsory, and it is surprising that it has received so little public attention up to now. The

106

Trends in Continuation of Education

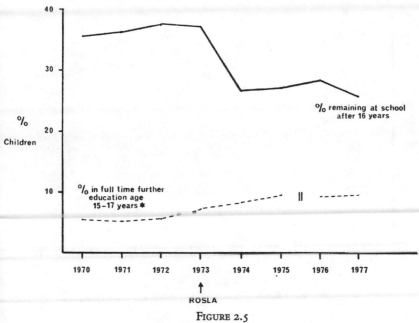

FIGURE 2.5
*Figures for 1976 and 1977 apply to 16–18 year olds.
(Data from Department of Education and Science, 1976, 1977 and 1979)

statistics (see fig. 2.5) indicate that some of the loss of pupils from the sixth forms may have been a result of their moving out of school into further education—but this accounts for only a minority of the losses (D.E.S., 1976, 1977, 1979). Rather the drop appears to have been a negative response to the experience of an extra year's compulsory schooling. Before 1973, the children staying on into the fifth year will usually have been well looked after and generally encouraged. Perhaps after the raising of the school leaving age this was less likely to happen because the change was introduced rather quickly without the time and resources needed to ensure that the extra year's schooling was properly planned to provide a useful learning experience for all pupils. Be that as it may, the effect seems to have been the opposite of what was intended.

Trends in School Absenteeism

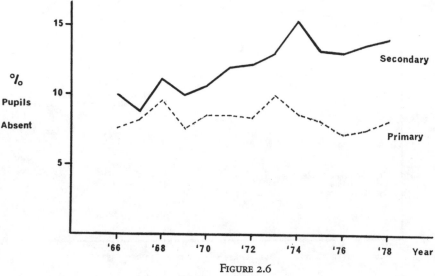

FIGURE 2.6
(Data from Inner London Education Authority, 1975 and 1979)

School attendance

National figures on patterns of school attendance over the years are not available but data are available for London over the course of the last century (Ivin, 1979). In 1873 the average percentage daily attendance was 65·8 per cent; by the turn of the century it had risen to 81·2 per cent, and from 1921 to 1938 in LCC elementary schools it held steady at about 87 per cent. The pattern for more recent years differs between primary and secondary schools (see fig. 2.6). Over the last 12 years the average non-attendance rates at primary schools have remained steady at about 8 or 9 per cent (ILEA, 1979). But the rates of non-attendance at secondary schools have increased from 9 or 10 per cent in 1966–7 to 14 per cent in 1978—the biggest jump being from 13 per cent to 15·4 per cent in the year after the school leaving age was raised from 15 to 16 years. In all years, non-attendance tends to be worst during the last year of compulsory schooling. In 1975, for example, the afternoon absence rate rose year by year from the low of 9·6 per cent for 12-year-olds to the high of 24·3 per cent for 15-year-olds—attendance in the sixth form was better with rates of 10 to 15 per cent absence (ILEA, 1975). The figures for girls were closely comparable.

In short, the figures suggest that attendance rates steadily improved up to about 1920, that they then held fairly steady for many years but that recently there has been a slight deterioration in secondary schools. Care is needed in the interpretation of the data both because they are heavily dependent on the accuracy and comparability of records from year to year and because absence rates are influenced by so many different factors. Most obviously, they will be affected by the prevalence of minor (and major) illnesses. Increasing rates may reflect improved health as much as greater commitment to schooling.

Literacy

Official statistics indicate a marked reduction in illiteracy since the beginning of this century. Thus, the U.S. figures (U.S. Bureau of the Census, 1977) show a progressive fall from 11 per cent in 1900 to 5 per cent in 1930 and to just over 1 per cent in 1970. However, these data derive from estimates rather than detailed measurement of populations. In the U.K., Start and Wells (1972) sought to provide a more precise estimate of trends in reading standards through the comparison of a series of national surveys of reading comprehension undertaken over the years since 1948 and up to 1971.

The findings are summarized in fig. 2.7. They show a steady rise in reading standards after the Second World War up to 1964, but then a levelling off or a slight fall. The statistics for illiteracy and semiliteracy (below 9-year level on 1938 norms) show much the same picture. For 11-year-olds the rates dropped from 25 per cent in 1948 to 13 per cent in 1964 but rose slightly to 15·5 per cent in 1970. For 15-year-olds the comparable drop was for 6 per cent to zero per cent with a rise in 1971 to 3 per cent. All the surveys omitted children at special schools and it is known that the proportion of pupils at schools for educationally subnormal children (who would undoubtedly include some of the worst

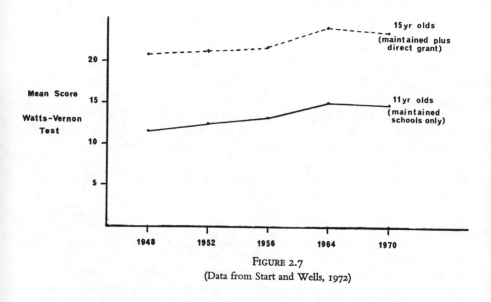

FIGURE 2.7
(Data from Start and Wells, 1972)

readers) rose considerably over the same period of time—from 3 per 1000 in 1955 to 6 per 1000 in 1970. Accordingly, it may well be that the increase in illiteracy during the 1960s and 1970s was actually greater than the national surveys suggested.

The figures are encouraging in terms of the overall picture of improvement over the last quarter of a century but give rise to concern with respect to the apparent recent slight fall in reading standards. But how valid are the comparisons? It is clear that there must be many caveats. Firstly, it is questionable how far the tests had the same meaning over the years. For example, there are several words such as 'mannequin parade', 'wheelwright', and 'haberdasher's' which have become outmoded. As a result, these (and other similar) items will have been less familiar and hence more difficult for pupils in recent years. It is evident that although the specifics of the tests have remained unchanged, their meaning and therefore their *effective* content has altered.

Secondly, the sampling was done on slightly different bases in the various testings. More especially, the 1970 survey was marred by a rather high school refusal rate—27 per cent. This may well have introduced a systematic bias but it is not known in which direction this will have operated.

Thirdly, all surveys are influenced by the proportion of children absent from school on the day of testing. This, too, introduces a bias as absentees tend to have lower educational attainments (Cox et al, 1977). If the absentee rate varied between surveys this could also have affected the results.

Fourthly, the findings will have been affected by the populations from which the samples were drawn. If these varied then the results may also vary as a consequence. Two movements may have led to biases. As the surveys excluded children at independent schools any change in the proportion of children being privately educated would be likely to affect the scores. Also, as the proportion of children from immigrant families (who had markedly lower reading scores on average) was greater in the more recent surveys this may have resulted in a lowering of reading levels. Start and Wells (1972) examined this point and showed that the effect on the mean was likely to have been fairly small (although it may have had a greater effect on the proportion of children with very poor reading).

It is impossible to determine the net effect of these various considerations, as some could tend to inflate and some to depress test scores. There must be real uncertainties as to the true state of affairs but on balance it seems likely that reading standards increased up to the mid '60s, but since then they have levelled off and may have actually fallen.

National examination results

Over the last 25 years there has been a very large rise in the proportion of school leavers in the U.K. with passes in the national examinations taken at the time of school leaving. This was so both with the GCE and CSE examinations taken at 16 years and the advanced levels taken at 18 years. Thus, the proportion of school leavers with at least five higher grade GCE 'O' level or CSE passes rose from 11·7 per cent in 1955–6 to 18 per cent in 1965–6

Trends in British Examination Results

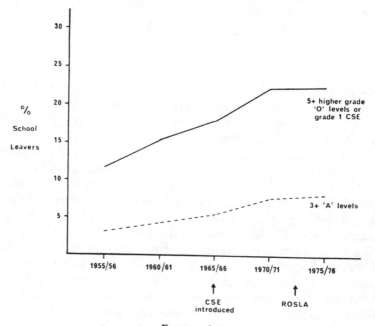

FIGURE 2.8
(Data from Department of Education and Science, 1964 and 1978)

and to 22·4 per cent in 1975–6. Similarly, the proportion of school leavers with at least three advanced level passes rose in the same years from 3 per cent to 5·6 per cent and 8·3 per cent. Some caution is required in the interpretation of these figures because of the introduction in 1965 of the new CSE examination with its somewhat different approach and its broader range of subjects. Nevertheless, this change does not appear sufficient to account for the steady rise in well qualified school leavers as the same rise was seen with 'A' level results which were unaffected by CSE (D.E.S., 1964, 1978a).

On the other hand, the overall picture is influenced by the type of subjects taken. Thus, although the proportion of girls with higher grade 'O' level passes in a combination of English, mathematics, science, and a modern language has continued to rise steadily, this has not been so for boys. The proportion rose to a peak of 10·6 per cent in 1966–7 but by 1976–7 it had fallen to 8·9 per cent; the comparable figures for girls being 8·5 per cent in 1966–7 and 9·8 per cent in 1976–7 (Central Statistical Office, 1978). This recent drop in the academic performance of boys is mainly attributable to the falling proportion of good passes in modern languages but it is also influenced by the lack of much improvement in the mathematics results. Thus the proportion of boys with higher grade 'O' level passes in both English and mathematics rose from 14 per cent in 1961–2 to 21·2 per cent in 1966–7 but in 1976–7 it had only marginally increased to 22·1 per cent. As with literacy, the general impression is one of considerable overall improvement since the Second World War but a levelling off over the last ten years or so.

There is always a tendency to interpret national figures of this kind in terms of circumstances in this country or in terms of particular political actions (e.g. the phasing out of selective education and the spread of comprehensive schooling). However, before making links of this kind it is essential to check whether comparable historical trends have occurred in other countries where these political actions have not taken place. The data from the U.S.A. are relevant in this connection (see Bronfenbrenner, 1976). New York has reported an increase over the years in the proportion of children failing to perform at minimum levels in reading and arithmetic. The findings from the educational testing service with respect to Scholastic Aptitude Test are even more alarming. This is a test taken by almost all high school juniors and seniors who plan to go to college. The figures show a steady and substantial decrease over the last decade in both the verbal scores and the mathematics scores. Other findings have shown a similar fall in science scores and in reading skills.

Before discussing the implications of these patterns, it is necessary to consider how far the examination results may have been influenced by either the marking of examination papers having become stricter or more lenient over the years; or by different populations of children taking the tests. The latter point is an obviously relevant one in that in both the U.S.A. and the U.K.

the proportions of children taking college entrance examinations and the proportion going on to further education has risen greatly over the last 30 years (Central Statistical Office, 1978; U.S. Bureau of the Census, 1977). This means that it is very likely that there have been major changes in the social composition and intellectual abilities of the students taking the examinations. It is probable that the candidates today include many more socially disadvantaged and/or intellectually less able pupils than was the case a generation ago. It is encouraging that a much larger segment of the population has been found capable of achieving academic success. However, the shift in the composition of the examination-taking group is likely to have had effects on the average scores obtained. This is especially likely if students with a weak chance of college entrance are now more likely to take extrance examinations in the hope that they might 'make it'. Bronfenbrenner (1976) reports that the educational testing experts dismiss this possibility as an explanation for the fall in examination scores but there does not seem to have been a rigorous investigation of the effects of changing populations on examination performance.

However, there has been a systematic attempt in the U.K. (Wilmott, 1977) to determine whether there have been any changes in examination marking standards. The approach followed in this study was to use reference tests against which examination marks could be compared—in this case an IQ test and an English test. The research strategy was based on knowledge that IQ correlates with school achievement; the correlations vary from subject to subject but are in the region of $0·3$ to $0·6$, i.e. accounting for some 10 per cent to 40 per cent of the variance. The argument is that if you know the calibrations of IQ and attainment over time you can use those to assess the standards of marking. The procedure is most easily explained by taking a specific example from the actual results obtained by Wilmott.

In brief, fig. 2.9, which deals with the findings for both boys and girls over all CSE subjects, shows a tendency for IQ scores to be getting lower but for examination grades to be remaining constant. The assumption is that the marking has become more lenient. But, there are many problems inherent in this interpretation. First, there is the matter of the population base. The

Trends in "IQ" Scores and Exam Grades for
CSE Candidates

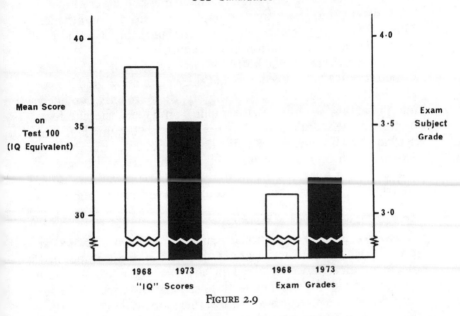

FIGURE 2.9

possibility that this may have altered is immediately raised by the substantial drop in mean IQ between 1968 and 1973. Almost certainly, this is a consequence of the very great rise in the number of children taking GCE and CSE examinations at 16 years. The implication is that examinations have become much more available to the less able candidates and hence that the general level of ability of the examination candidates will have fallen accordingly. The study could have dealt with this issue by determining the examination grades separately for each IQ band, but unfortunately this was not done. There are also various other minor problems in sampling—in particular that the sampling was by school and not by individual. This is important because a significant (and rising) proportion of children leave school and go on to colleges of further education to take their school based examinations. The investigation is also bedevilled by the fact that

115

the correlations between IQ and examination scores vary greatly across subjects, being very high for mathematics but very low for art and only moderate for geography or history, for instance. Wilmott (1977) was aware of this issue and probably it was not an important cause of distortion in the results.

A much bigger problem lies in the interpretation of the findings. If the mean IQ has gone down and the examination grades have remained constant (or even risen slightly) there are only two likely interpretations, assuming that sampling errors and the like have been adequately dealt with. Either teaching has become better or marking has become more lenient. Unfortunately, the findings provide no means of deciding between these two alternatives. This is a major limitation of the study as the first would be a cause for rejoicing whereas the latter would be a source of concern.

Conclusions on educational standards

The whole issue of educational standards has been discussed at some length because it illustrates the serious and complicated methodological issues involved in any evaluation of historical changes. Unlike the situation with psychiatric disorder where we lack comparable measures over time, there are available quantitative scores of educational performance which aim to be directly comparable from year to year. In spite of that, it has proved difficult, if not impossible, to arrive at any very firm conclusions as to how far things are getting better or getting worse.

On the positive side, there can be no doubt that educational attainments today in the population as a whole are very considerably better than they were a generation ago and vastly improved over the level two or three generations ago. These gains seem to have arisen largely as a result of the opening up of educational opportunities to a much greater proportion of the population. On the negative side, although the evidence is inconclusive, it appears likely that over the last decade or so there has been more of a plateau with few marked gains and probably some losses. It is not just that in some respects educational achievements have failed to rise in the '70s in the way that they had been doing in the '50s and '60s. The substantial reduction over the last 4 years in the percentage of pupils staying on at school after 16 years seems to indicate that some pupils have become rather disenchanted with what schools have to offer. The increasing non-attendance rates in secondary (but not primary) schools seem to tell the same story. Of course, it should not be expected that educational standards should go on rising indefinitely. Presumably a point will be reached when no further improvement is possible. However, it is quite clear that that is not the explanation for the apparent levelling off in recent years. The major disparities between secondary schools in rates of examination success even for children of comparable intellectual abilities (see Rutter et al, 1979) indicates that some schools do very much better for their pupils than do others. There is still plenty of room left for improvement!

The figures on educational levels have been presented in terms of overall proportions or averages for the population as a whole—as that is how official statistics tend to be recorded. However, any serious concern over standards requires a much more searching enquiry than that. An increased proportion of pupils with examination passes may be entirely due to the opening up of educational opportunities to a broader segment of the population (a most worthwhile goal in itself), and nothing to do with a tendency for a pupil of a given ability level to achieve more today than he would have done a generation ago. Indeed, it is quite possible to have *both* falling standards (in the latter sense) and better examination results (in the former sense). The main remaining query concerns the question of whether pupils of high abilities are doing better or worse today than in earlier years. Unfortunately, the available data do not allow any confident answer to that question.

DELINQUENCY AND VANDALISM

Delinquency

There are many reasons why crime statistics should be treated with considerable caution when considering the question of whether juvenile delinquency is increasing or decreasing in frequency (Rutter and Madge, 1976). First, from time to time there are alterations in the law as to what is regarded as an offence. These may at a stroke of the pen cause crime rates to go up or down simply by changing the definition of what is a crime. Secondly, the extent and pattern of police activity will influence both who and how many are convicted. Changing notions of the 'seriousness' of particular behaviours and of how to deal with them will influence the ways in which the police will act. West (1967) gives examples of this effect with respect to police practices in relation to male importuning and to female prostitution. Thirdly, people committing offences are not all treated equally. Various studies (see Rutter and Madge, 1976) have shown that in some areas low social status offenders may be dealt with more harshly if their crimes were committed in a middle-class rather than a working-class area, that middle-class offenders may be more often dealt with informally without a court appearance, and that black people and those of low social status may be treated more severely. Fourthly, for many crimes the offender is never found. Thus, the clear-up rate for indictable offences in England and Wales (i.e. the rate of offences in which an offender is identified) has stood at about the 40–45 per cent mark over the last decade. Clearly if the rate goes up or down to any extent it will affect the crime statistics. Fifthly, the crime rate will be influenced by changes in the opportunities for crime which are available (see Mayhew et al, 1976). For example, the more people who own motor vehicles the greater the likelihood of motoring offences. Similarly, the growth of large self-service stores may well have increased the opportunities for shoplifting. Or again, the major drop over the last eight years in illegal abortions (Home Office, 1978a) is almost certainly largely due to the greater availability of legal terminations of pregnancy. Sixthly, self-report studies show that the number of people who have committed delinquent acts far exceeds the number of people in the courts. Seventhly, the official statistics concern the number of people convicted each year, and not the number of *separate* individuals convicted. As a result, any changes in rates of recidivism will affect the crime statistics.

For these and other reasons, crime statistics provide a rather uncertain guide as to either changing levels of delinquency or a changing incidence of delinquent individuals. On the other hand, the difficulties should not be exaggerated. In the first place, self-reported delinquency (and especially severe and repeated delinquency) shows a substantial, although imperfect, level of agreement with administrative figures. In the second place, statistical adjustments can be made to deal with some of the factors, such as changes in the proportion of first offenders (see e.g. Little, 1965; McClintock and Avison, 1968). In the third place, some assessment of the likely bias introduced by changes in the law and in police practices can be made by examining similarities and contrasts in the historical trends shown for different offences.

Offences are divided into the indictable (on the whole the more serious ones) and non-indictable. The vast majority of indictable offences involve some form of stealing but crimes of violence and sexual offences are also included. Since about 1900 there has been a progressive and marked increase in indictable crimes, but a more variable pattern of change in non-indictable offences (McClintock and Avison, 1968). Five main changes are discernible. From 1900 until the beginning of the First World War the crime rate remained fairly stable; during the next 15 years it rose about 5 per cent per annum; it then fluctuated but remained roughly stable until 1954; then during the next decade crime increased at the record rate of about 10 per cent per annum. Since 1965 the crime rate has continued to increase but at a more variable and, in general, somewhat slower rate (Home Office, 1978a). Over this century as a whole, the increase in recidivism has been greater than that for first offences. McClintock and Avison (1968) estimated that, after allowing for population changes, convictions have trebled whereas crime has increased ninefold. Since the Second World War, crimes involving violence against the person have shown a particularly marked increase resulting in a threefold rise in the proportion of offences falling into that category. However, the increase in the number of offences of violence against the person goes back to the mid 1930s. From then until the mid '50s the percentage increase was about 6 per cent per annum; from the mid '50s to the present it has increased at a rate of about 11 per cent per annum (Home Office, 1978a). Also during recent years female crime has tended to increase at a faster rate than male crime.

Any changes over time in rates of juvenile delinquency need to

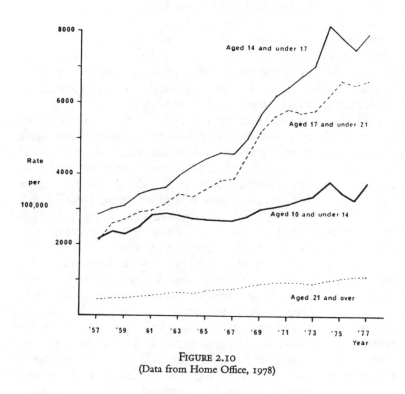

Indictable Offences per 100,000 Population
(Convictions and Cautions)

FIGURE 2.10
(Data from Home Office, 1978)

be viewed against the backcloth of historical trends in crime as a whole. In fact, it is clear that all these trends are more sharply evident in juveniles than they are in adults. Thus, as shown in fig. 2.10 the increase in crime rate among 14- to 17-year-old boys (and also 17- to 21-year-olds) during the last two decades has been rather greater than that in adult men. Part of the increase is due to a much greater use of cautioning by the Police for indictable offences. Between 1957 and 1968 less than a quarter of all male juveniles were cautioned; there was a marked increase between 1967 and 1971 from 24 per cent to 44 per cent; but the rate has remained fairly stable since then. Much the same happened with girls; between 1967 and 1972 the proportion of cautions rose from 35 per cent to 70 per cent (Home Office, 1978a). It is likely that some of these young people receiving cautions would have gone to court in earlier years but also it is likely that some would not have been charged. However, even if all cautions fell into the latter category this still could not account for anything like the whole of the increase in crime as the annual rate of juveniles found guilty in court (i.e. excluding cautions) has more than doubled over the last 20 years.

During the last decade there has been a slight decrease in the proportion of adolescent first offenders (from 67 per cent to 64 per cent in the 14- to 17-year age group) but this, too, does not explain the trend. We may conclude that the last 20 years has seen a very considerable increase in crime among adolescent boys in the U.K. U.S. statistics (Bronfenbrenner, 1976) show parallel changes over time. Juvenile delinquency rates rose sharply during the late '60s with particularly marked rises in violent crimes and in crimes associated with drug use.

One piece of apparently contrary evidence needs to be considered before leaving the topic of male delinquency. Robins et al (1975) in a study of crime in two generations reported a similar rate of juvenile delinquency in the fathers as in the sons (31 per cent in both), and in the mothers as in the daughters (14–16 per cent). West and Farrington (1977) do not present their data in the same form but their figures show that by age 15 years the delinquency rate in the sons (13·1 per cent) was little different from that in their fathers (11·5 per cent). Both sets of figures seem out of keeping with the marked increase in delinquency over time shown by the criminal statistics. However, there are several reasons why these two-generation studies might be expected to show a different picture. Firstly, both concern high-risk populations and it may be that the main rise in crime has affected what in previous generations have been low-risk groups. Second, not only are the samples special in various respects and hence not representative of the general population, but more particularly the two generations are special in *different* respects. One generation was chosen because it met various risk criteria but the other generation was chosen because it consisted of the fathers (or sons) of the first sample. As a result the two generations are likely to differ from the general population in different ways. Thirdly, in the Robins study the sons are atypical in a further respect in that they are predominantly first born. Fourthly, as both studies mainly concern just one boy per family the figures will be an underestimate of the total population prevalence (because delinquency is commoner in boys for large families and instead of counting *all* the boys in each large family only one was included). We may conclude that two-generation family studies do not provide a good test of historical trends and we are on safe ground relying on the crime statistics which show a marked increase in delinquency among adolescent boys during the last 20 years.

It is sometimes suggested that the rise in delinquency means no more than that young people have less respect for authority than adolescents did in the past, but that this is accompanied by an increasing concern for people. However, this seems an inadequate explanation in that one of the most spectacular rises have been in crimes involving violence against the person. Probably it is unwise to seek a single explanation to cover all delinquencies, as many different influences are operating.

The increase in crime rate for 14- to 17-year-old girls since 1957 has been even greater than that for boys—more than a six-fold increase compared with the three fold increase for boys. Care must be taken in comparing proportions of this kind (Smart, 1979), since when the initial level is very low (as it was with girls) quite small changes in absolute terms can lead to very large percentage increases. However, that is not the explanation here as the rise in female delinquency has led to a major alteration in the male–female ratio for delinquency in 14- to 17-year-olds (see fig. 2.11). In 1957 the ratio was 10·79 to 1, but by 1977 it had fallen to 4·97 to 1—more than a halving of the female crime preponderance. Again this disproportionate increase in female delinquency is also evident in U.S. figures (see Steffensmeier, 1978). The possible reasons for the shift in crime sex ratio have been much discussed recently without any adequate resolution of the issue (see e.g. Adler, 1977; Jensen and Eve, 1976; Giordano, 1978; Heidensohn, 1968; Steffensmeier, 1978; Smart, 1979). It has been argued that the increasing female criminality is a

Delinquency and vandalism

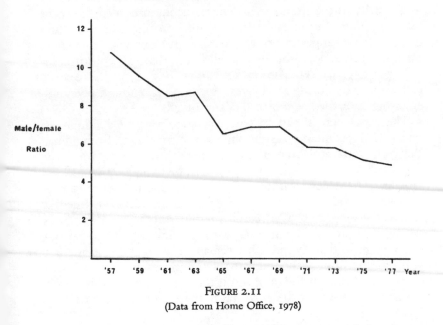

Sex Ratio for Indictable Offence Rates in
14 to 17 Year Olds

FIGURE 2.11
(Data from Home Office, 1978)

consequence of women's increasing emancipation or the effects of the women's liberation movement (Adler, 1977). However, it is difficult on that basis to account for the increasing percentage of women offenders in the 1935–46 decade, but not the 1946–55 decade (Smart, 1979). Others have suggested that to a considerable extent the increase is due to the ever-increasing self-service stores facilitating shop lifting, which has always been a traditional female crime (Steffensmeier, 1978), but that does not explain the fact that violent offences by women have risen to an even greater extent than the various forms of theft (Home Office, 1978a). In the U.K. a further possible factor is the effect of the increasing proportion of adolescents from West Indian families during the 1960s and '70s. This is relevant because disruptive and antisocial behaviour is relatively commoner in black girls than white girls (see Rutter and Madge, 1976). However, the proportion of West Indian

123

youngsters in most parts of the country remains too low for it to be plausible that they could have had much effect on the statistics —especially as the rise in female delinquency preceded the main influx of West Indian families. It is not possible entirely to rule out possible changes in police practices and responses to female offenders but it does not seem at all likely that this constitutes a sufficient explanation. The rise in delinquency among adolescent girls, especially during recent years seems a real enough phenomenon but its cause has still to be determined.

The last change in pattern with respect to juvenile delinquency which requires mention is the shift in the peak age of offending. Between 1962 and 1971 the peak age of offending for boys remained at 14 years, but in 1972 it changed to 15 years and has remained there since (Home Office, 1978a; Home Office, 1979). In contrast, the peak age of offending for girls has remained at 14 years throughout. The reason for this shift in peak for boys remains uncertain. It coincides with the raising of the school leaving age so that the peak has remained throughout in the last year of compulsory schooling. It is tempting to attribute a causal connection between the two, but if they are linked in this way it remains obscure why the peak has not also shifted for girls.

Children in the care of the local authorities

Children are received into the care of local authorities for a wide variety of reasons ranging from abandonment by parents to delinquent acts by the child. The characteristics and circumstances of children in care vary greatly but they all reflect in one form or another family problems experienced by the child or presented by his behaviour. Accordingly, admissions into care may be taken as one, very indirect, reflection of the rate of problems in childhood and adolescence. The statistics (Central Statistical Office, 1972, 1974, 1978) show that during the 1950s and 1960s there was a steady rise in the absolute number of children admitted into care— largely as a result of 'fit person orders' and 'other reasons', both of which probably largely arise as a result of behaviour by the child or adolescent which gives cause for concern. The rise has continued during the 1970s with respect to children at or above compulsory school age—from 74,000 in 1971 to 89,000 in 1977.

Due to changes in legislation, the categories of reasons for admission into care have altered somewhat, but still the main increase seems to have been a result of admission because of concern about the child's or adolescent's behaviour.

Considerable caution is needed in the interpretation of these figures because they rely so heavily on decisions by the courts on how 'maladjusted' or 'delinquent' behaviour will be dealt with. The increase of admissions into 'care' could reflect no more than a growing tendency to use 'care proceedings' rather than some other form of action. In fact, the figures show that this has not happened (Home Office, 1978a). To the contrary, there has been a reducing tendency for the courts to use care orders as judged by the *proportion* of persons aged under 17 years dealt with in this way. But the number of offenders has risen (see above) so that the absolute number of care orders reflects this. The published figures on admissions into care concern total numbers of children rather than proportions of the population at risk. The latter would be lower simply because of the rising number of children and adolescents during the late '60s and '70s. For these and other reasons the figures on children in care provide no firm guide to the overall level of adolescent problems.

Vandalism

Over recent years there has been much concern over vandalism (not only in western countries but also in eastern Europe) and there has been a general impression that the problem is increasing (see, for example, Home Office Standing Committee on Crime Prevention, 1975; Stone and Taylor, 1977; Central Policy Review Staff, 1978). At first sight this seems to be demonstrated by the fact that of all offences recorded as known to the police, criminal damage has shown by far the greatest increase in recent years—from 17,000 offences in 1969 to 124,000 in 1977. However, these statistics refer only to cases where the damage exceeded a cost of £20. It is obvious that the severe inflation in recent years would be enough in itself to account for much of the rise. Also, it is relevant that there is an exceptionally low rate of reporting to the police (see Clarke, 1978), particularly of the most common but less expensive types of vandalism (such as breaking of windows on housing estates, or damage to street lights, or slashing of seats on buses). Accordingly, changes over time in the number of cases of criminal damage may well reflect alterations in public sensitivity and awareness of the problem, and hence their tendency to report cases. In addition, it is evident that the available statistics are very patchy and inadequate and quite unsuitable for the accurate assessment of historical trends with respect to vandalism as a whole. In addition, it must be said that technically there is no such offence as 'vandalism'. It is generally taken to mean wilful damage to public or private property and amenities but of course this covers a most disparate set of activities ranging through smashing up abandoned cars or old prams on rubbish dumps, the breaking of windows in unoccupied houses, football excursion train hooliganism, the desecration of school lavatories, political graffiti, and damage as a byproduct of theft. Rather than attempt any overall measurement of vandalism, a better appraisal may be obtained by focusing on certain specific areas of damage.

Thus, the Post Office keeps records of vandalism to public telephone booths. Figure 2.12 gives the figures for the 1970-8 period in terms of the number of cases of damage per number of kiosks. Several things are evident from the graphs. Firstly, it is clear that the tendency for vandalism to increase was not only halted but was reversed during the early 1970s. This is likely to have been a result of the extensive strengthening programme with respect to the equipment; so that the coinbox cover and cash compartment are now made of heavy gauge steel, the handset is made of shatterproof plastic and the dial is not only made of steel but is recessed to allow little opportunity for leverage. Secondly, in the country as a whole, although vandalism has slightly increased in recent years, there is no indication of any marked change. Thirdly, however, it is evident that not only do the levels of vandalism vary greatly between different parts of the country but so also do the historical trends. In 1970 the vandalism rate in the south-west was below half the national average; apart from an increase in 1977-8 it has progressively fallen over the last six years and the rate is now less than a quarter of the national average. In sharp contrast, the London rates have always been high and although, as in the rest of the country, vandalism decreased in the

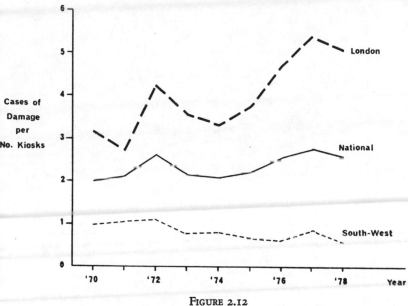

FIGURE 2.12

(Data from Post Office Telecommunications, 1979)

mid-'70s, the rate has risen again during the last four years to reach a level twice the national average. We may conclude not only that preventive measures have probably had an effect in reducing vandalism but also that this effect has been far from uniform throughout the country. In the metropolis things have got worse to some extent whereas in rural areas this has not been the case.

The British Transport Police annual reports provide information on damage to railway stock and property. Summary offences (which are mainly ticket frauds and Railway bye-law prosecutions for trespass, minor forms of stone throwing, and the like) as a whole have remained at a pretty constant level over the last 18 years but the number of juveniles who were prosecuted halved between 1960 and 1969. During the last 10 years there have been both increases and decreases but the overall level is slightly below

127

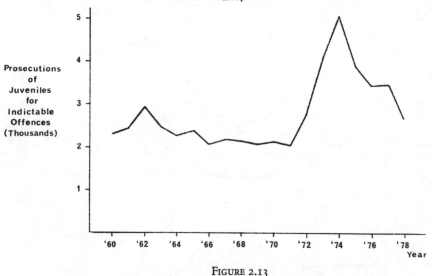

Trends in Juvenile Crime on British Railways
and London Transport

FIGURE 2.13
(Data from British Transport Police annual reports 1960–78)
*The indictable offences mainly included offences under the Criminal Damage Act;
Offences Against the Person Act (putting objects on lines, dropping missiles on trains,
removing sleepers, etc.); Malicious Damage (intending to obstruct railway engines, etc.);
Public Order Act (threatening words and behaviour and other forms of what might be
considered 'hooliganism')

that of a decade ago. The number of indictable offences per year
among juveniles, on the other hand, rose slightly in the early
'60s, then fell again to remain fairly steady until a very sharp rise
in the early '70s, followed by a further fall back to the level of
the early '60s (see fig. 2.13). The indictable offences include quite
a mixed bag of offences under various Acts but many deal with
behaviours which clearly involve wilful damage of a kind which
might properly be regarded as vandalism. Again, it seems that
various actions are likely to have been effective in reducing the
problem. For example, the extensive use of police escorts on
'football special' trains and the planning of routes to keep apart
rival groups of supporters has been followed by a marked improvement in the behaviour of football supporters on trains and

railway stations. Evidently preventive policies can be made to be effective.

Damage to school property is another area where it should be possible to obtain data on historical trends. However, apart from arson (where apparently the number of major fires showed an increase from 12 in 1965 to 90 in 1976—Stone and Taylor, 1977), no very satisfactory figures are available. It is clear that schools and authorities vary greatly in what they consider reporting, there is no common standard for measurement, and most statistics are kept in the form of costs of repair. A recent Home Office project in Manchester (Gladstone, in preparation) illustrates how inflation may cause those figures to distort historical trends. Between 1969 and 1977 the cost of repairing damage identified as vandalism in schools more than quadrupled from about £42,000 to £179,000. However, over that same period building costs also rose considerably and when costs were adjusted for inflation it became apparent that there had been little change over the 8 years. On the other hand, as both these data and others (Stone and Taylor, 1977) show, any single figure for trends is bound to be misleading in view of the huge variations between schools in rates of vandalism (see also Rutter et al, 1979). Some schools show a picture of steady improvement over the years whereas in others there is evidence of a steadily worsening problem.

Conclusions

Crime statistics clearly show that rates of delinquency have increased considerably throughout this century and especially since the Second World War. It is difficult to determine just how far the official figures have been influenced by alterations in the public reporting of crimes or by changes in police practice. However, it seems most unlikely that these account for the historical trends. Almost certainly, there has been a real increase in acts of delinquent behaviour. Of course, this is and should be a matter of real concern but it does not necessarily follow that this means that there has been a similar increase in the number of adolescents who are prone to behave in delinquent ways, although this may have taken place.

Two points require particular emphasis in this connection.

Firstly, several studies utilizing self-report data have shown that a *majority* of boys engage in delinquent activities from time to time, although most of them do not get caught (see, e.g. Belson, 1975 and 1978; Clarke, 1978, West and Farrington, 1973 and 1977). Of course, most of these activities concern fairly minor delinquencies such as 'buying cheap' (i.e. receiving stolen property), damaging property, or stealing from slot machines, but the findings do indicate that sharp qualitative distinctions can not be drawn between delinquents and non-delinquents (in spite of the fact that overall there are very marked differences between the two groups in life style). Secondly, the vandalism data indicate that whether or not delinquent acts take place depends not only on the existence of particular kinds of 'delinquency-prone' individuals but also on the extent of crime opportunities (see chapter 3). Given poorly supervised badly maintained public property many young people may engage in vandalism, whereas far fewer will do so with well supervised, well maintained private homes. Similarly, whether or not adolescents steal may depend not only on their family background and personality characteristics but also on the opportunities they see before them, and on concepts of what is regarded as 'fair game' because it doesn't belong to any particular individual or because it is thought of as a perk of the job. Preventive policies will need to be concerned with these factors as well as with those which serve to increase individual predispositions to behave in unacceptable ways.

PSYCHIATRIC DISORDER

Any adequate appraisal of historical trends in the incidence or prevalence of psychiatric disorder would require comparable epidemiological studies of the general population at a series of successive time periods. Unfortunately such data are not available and it is necessary to have recourse to official statistics on hospital attendance and admissions and to the data from studies of specific disease categories. All have major deficiences as indices of changes over time in overall rates of disorder but taken together they may provide some guide as to whether patterns are altering.

Psychiatric hospital care

Psychiatric hospital data are probably the least use of all, because they are likely to be influenced much more by the facilities made available than by the psychiatric needs of the population. However, for what they are worth, the figures show that adolescents aged 15 to 19 years accounted for about 10 per cent of all resident patients in mental illness hospitals and units in 1971 (Court, 1976). The proportion rose from 6·3 per cent in 1954 to 9·3 per cent in 1963, and to 9·8 per cent in 1971. The absolute numbers fell between 1963 and 1971 but rather less than that for adults and the age and sex specific rates for admission continued to rise up to 1971. The comparable proportions for children under 15 years rose from 1·2 per cent in 1954 to 2·7 per cent in 1963 and to 5·1 per cent in 1971—a very large rise in both relative and absolute terms. Since 1971 the figures have fallen slightly. Outpatient attendances for children show much the same pattern of a big rise during the 1960s but much less change during the 1970s. It seems likely that these figures do little more than reflect the great increase in psychiatric facilities for children and adolescents during the late 1960s (Court, 1976). Nevertheless, in the opinion of psychiatrists running child and adolescent units, there were still many unmet needs—particularly with respect to older adolescents where the pressure on beds was thought to be increasing. Whether this means that psychiatric disorder among adolescents is becoming more frequent, or whether the pressure reflects an increasing awareness or decreasing tolerance of adolescent problems, or rather whether the demands for admission are a result of a growing public appreciation of what psychiatric adolescent units have to offer (an appreciation only likely to become apparent after the relatively recent establishment of such units) can only be left to speculation.

Suicide

Suicide is extremely rare in pre-pubescent children both in the U.K. (Shaffer, 1974) and the U.S.A. (Bakwin, 1957), but its frequency rises sharply during the teenage period so that it comes to rank as one of the half dozen most common causes of death among older adolescents, although its frequency is still well below that in adult life.

Over the years there have been a variety of peaks and troughs in rates of suicide, with decreases during both World Wars and an increase at the time of the economic depression in the 1930s. However, during the last few decades there has been a gradual but steady decline in the suicide rate so that the standardized mortality ratio for male suicide has fallen from 117 in 1961 to 86 in 1976 and for female suicide from 115 to 80 over the same period (Central Statistical Office, 1978). But the pattern for 15- to 19-year-olds has been different. In spite of a fall in other age groups, suicide in young people continued to increase in frequency up to the early '70s (Adelstein and Mardon, 1975). The suicide rate in adolescent girls has continued to rise right up to the present time so that it has doubled over the last 20 years (Office of Population Censuses and Surveys, 1978). The rate for adolescent boys has also very greatly increased since the early '50s, although there has been a slight reduction in recent years. The trend in the U.S.A. has been similar with a sharply rising suicide rate among both black and white teenagers (U.S. Bureau of the Census, 1977) so that as in the U.K. the rate for 15- to 19-year-olds has more than doubled over the last two decades.

There are many reasons why suicide rates might alter over time. In the U.K., safer domestic gas, improved hospital care of the poisoned, better treatment by general practitioners of their depressed patients, a change for the better in the psychiatric services both in hospitals and the community, and the rapid spread of the Samaritan movement have all been advanced as possible reasons for the falling rate of suicide in the population as a whole (Jennings et al, 1978). However, it is not at all obvious from these suggestions why suicide rates should be increasing among adolescents at a time when they are decreasing in adults. Access to drugs which could kill is a possible factor, but the very widespread prescription of tranquillizers, sedatives, and hypnotics applies at least as much to adults as to adolescents. Of course, too, socio-cultural factors are likely to be important as suggested by the immense variation in suicide rates between different countries (Bakwin, 1957). During the 1950s the suicide rate for adolescent girls in Japan, for example, was 18·7—a rate many times that in either England and Wales (1·1) or the U.S.A. (1·6). The Japanese rate for adolescent boys (26·1) was similarly increased over that for other countries. It should also be noted that this is not the first time that there has been a concern over the particularly high rates of adolescent suicide. During the latter half of the nineteenth century, the suicide rates for children and adolescents in Saxony were 10 times those of the U.S.A. in the mid 1950s; in Moscow during the years 1908–9 more than two-fifths of all suicides were in children or adolescents compared with the few per cent only in modern U.K. or the U.S.A ; and in France, too, suicide rates for young people were particularly high at the turn of the century (Bakwin, 1957).

It is evident that we have a poor understanding of these major variations in suicide rate over time and over place. Certainly, although suicide in adolescents is usually associated with some kind of emotional or behavioural disorder in conjunction with psycho-social stresses (Shaffer, 1974) we cannot assume that the trends in suicide rates reflect trends in rates of psychiatric disorder. Nevertheless, some explanation is needed for the marked increase in suicide rates among adolescents at a time when suicides in the population as a whole are becoming progressively less frequent.

Attempted suicide

Although suicide rates increase sharply during adolescence (see chapter 1) the rates for young people are still far below those for the old. Attempted suicide, or parasuicide (as perhaps it is better called) on the other hand, is very much an adolescent phenomenon. Like completed suicide, attempted suicide rates, especially in girls, have risen very greatly during the late '60s and early '70s. Figure 2.14 shows the data from Edinburgh for age-sex specific admission rates for attempted suicide among 15- to 19-year-olds. Although these data refer to a particular city there is every reason to suppose that the pattern shown is similar to that elsewhere (Kreitman, 1977). It is clear that since 1962–3 admissions for parasuicide (meaning deliberate non-accidental self-injury or self-poisoning not resulting in death—irrespective of whether actual death was intended or planned) have risen tenfold for adolescent boys and

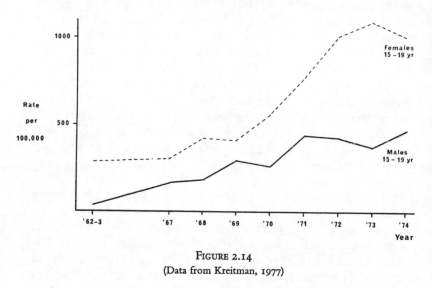

Admission Rates for Attempted Suicide
in Edinburgh 1962 - 1974

FIGURE 2.14
(Data from Kreitman, 1977)

five-fold for adolescent girls. However, whereas the male rates mainly accelerated during the 1962–8 period, the female rates have risen much more sharply during the period since 1969. In both cases the increase was considerably greater than that for other age groups, although there had been some general rise.

The increase in admissions for parasuicide could reflect either more people poisoning or injuring themselves or the same number of people doing so more often. In fact, to some extent both seem to have occurred but the main increase, especially for girls, is certainly due to a greater number of persons attempting suicide for the first time. The age-sex specific rates for first-ever admissions for suicide are shown in fig. 2.15. The rate for girls has gone up steadily since 1969 (with a slight fall in 1974) so that over a five-year period it has almost doubled; the increase for boys has been less regular but that rate, too, has tended to go up.

The reasons for the rising parasuicide rate in young people remain rather obscure (Kreitman, 1977). It cannot be accounted

134

First-Ever Attempted Suicide Rates
in Edinburgh 1968-1974

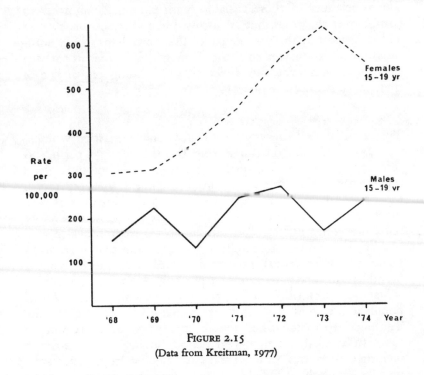

FIGURE 2.15
(Data from Kreitman, 1977)

for in terms of any change in drug abuse, in that the proportion of parasuicide patients with drug abuse did not increase over the period studied. The rise for girls could be associated in part with increasing alcohol use in that the proportion of parasuicides following consumption of alcohol among women aged 15 to 24 years doubled between 1968 and 1974 (Holding et al, 1977). Also, it might be suggested that the increase in parasuicide is largely a consequence of more liberal prescribing by doctors. However, it seems improbable that this is the explanation in that there has been no change since 1962 in the proportion of poisonings by prescribed rather than non-prescribed drugs. Parasuicide is associated with a variety of social problems including criminality, unemployment, marital difficulties, and childhood separations. The associations of these variables with parasuicide showed no change over the years, but as discussed elsewhere in this chapter and in chapter 4, the prevalence of these problems in the community generally has been rising. It may well be that in part the increasing parasuicide rate reflects the increasing prevalence of these social stressors.

Anorexia nervosa

Typically, anorexia nervosa occurs in young unmarried women, the disorder having begun during the late teenage period. A recent survey of adolescent girls at independent schools in England suggested that the disorder occurred in about 1 in every 100 of those aged 16 years or more (Crisp et al, 1976). However, it was much less frequent among girls at comprehensive state schools, reflecting either earlier observations of a greater prevalence in middle-class groups or the effect of a boarding school environment. Nylander (1971) produced comparable figures from a Scandinavian survey—a rate of 1 per 150 adolescent girls.

Data on historical trends are not available from general population studies but they are provided by clinic studies. Theander (1970) identified female inpatients in a region of southern Sweden over a 30-year period, finding a marked rise in incidence over this time—11, 25, and 58 cases in successive decades. Similarly, Kendell et al (1973) showed through the use of case registers in Scotland, London and the U.S.A., that the number of cases of anorexia nervosa reported each year rose over periods of 4 to 10 years in all three areas. Duddle (1973), reporting on psychiatric referrals to a university student health centre, also noted a sharp rise over the 1966–71 period in the number of anorexia nervosa cases—from none out of 104 psychiatric referrals in 1966 to 13 out of 118 in 1971. There is uncertainty as to how far the rise in incidence in all three series is due to better identification rather than to a true increase in frequency of the disorder. However, the consistency of the finding of a rising frequency, together with the extent of the rise, suggest that probably the disorder is becoming more frequent.

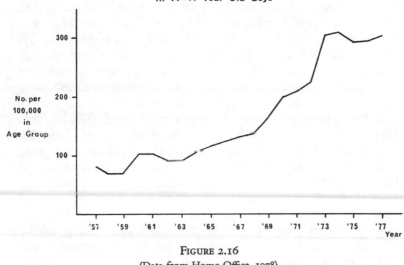

Psychiatric disorder

Trends in Drunkenness Offences
in 14-17 Year Old Boys

FIGURE 2.16
(Data from Home Office, 1978)

Alcoholism

There are many problems in the accurate assessment of the prevalence of problem drinking and of alcoholism (Edwards et al,
1973 and 1978). Estimates tend to be based on the known physical
and mental complications of alcoholism; thus calculations are
based on deaths from cirrhosis of the liver or on hospital admissions for alcoholic psychosis. Alternatively, the extent to which
alcoholics come into contact with services may be used as a guide,
so that reference is made to the number of arrests for drunkenness
or driving while under the influence of alcohol. There are objections to each of the measures, and surveys of the general population show rather higher rates of problem drinking than expected
for the various medical and administrative indices. Nevertheless,
all the various indices agree in the picture they give of changes
over time (Donnan and Haskey, 1977). From the early years of
this century until the mid 1940s or '50s there was a steady fall in
the U.K. in alcoholic problems. There was then an upturn after
the Second World War, but the rates in 1975 were still well

137

below those in 1911. Thus, the death rate per million for cirrhosis in males was 115 in 1911 but 38 in 1975, and over the same period of time offences of drunkenness fell by half. But during the decade between 1965 and 1975 alcoholism seemed to increase markedly. In the population as a whole there was a 90 per cent increase in convictions for drunkenness in males and a 400 per cent increase for females. The increase has been particularly marked in young people (Home Office, 1978a), as illustrated in fig. 2.16.

Other indices of alcoholism show similar trends (Donnan and Haskey, 1977). Thus, deaths due to alcoholic cirrhosis have increased sharply since the 1950s in young people aged 15 to 24 years as well as in other age groups; and admissions to mental illness hospitals as a result of alcoholism or alcoholic psychosis have risen substantially over the last two decades. The general pattern clearly points to a substantial rise in the problem of alcoholism—especially in women and especially in young people. The same trend has been apparent in the U.S.A. Between 1960 and 1973 there was a 135 per cent increase in the number of adolescents arrested for offences attributed to alcohol (Kelley, 1974). However, while the historical trend in the two countries over recent years has been similar the absolute rate of alcolism in the U.S.A. is almost certainly very much higher.

Drug use and abuse

Although no directly comparable figures are available for much earlier time periods, there is no doubt that drug use among adolescents in both the U.K. and the U.S.A. has become very much more widespread than it was in previous generations. This is most striking with respect to marihuana. Up to 1945 there was little evidence of its use in the U.K., between 1945 and 1960 there was a slow increase, and from 1960 to 1965 a very much more rapid rise in the usage of the drug—especially among young people (Edwards, 1974; Bewley, 1975). By the late '60s and '70s, surveys of college and university students in the U.K. showed that some 10 to 40 per cent had used marihuana; in the U.S.A. the rates found were rather higher, being generally in the 20 to 60 per cent range (Blumberg, 1977). The use of marihuana among high school students in the U.S.A. has been almost as high, but it is likely that the usage in U.K. school children has been much less—a reflection in part perhaps of the fact that school children in the U.K. tend to be younger than in the U.S.A. because fewer 16- to 18-year-olds stay on at school. However, most usage has been occasional rather than regular (Kandel et al, 1976; Kosviner et al, 1974) so that only about some 6 per cent of students in the U.K. and 8 per cent in the U.S.A. have been found to be regular or heavy users of cannabis. It has been suggested that marihuana use in young people may be levelling off now, but good data on this point are lacking (National Commission on Marihuana and Drug Abuse, 1973). Opinions differ on the dangers and damage from cannabis (see Edwards, 1974, for a thoughtful review of the evidence). Certainly, it is far less harmful than the opiates, but there are sufficient pointers to probably psychological ill-effects from heavy usage for there to be a real concern about the consequences of a high proportion of adolescents taking marihuana.

In the U.S.A., the use of hallucinogenic drugs originated in the early 1960s among middle-class white youngsters (Braucht et al, 1973). Its use spread to lower socio-economic and ethnic minority groups but it remained more widespread among college students. Surveys around the 1970 period indicated that some 4- to 12 per cent of college students had tried hallucinogens at some time (Blumberg, 1977). Exactly comparable figures are not available for the U.K. but it is clear that far fewer adolescents have tried hallucinogens (Bewley, 1975).

During the period of the Second World War, there was evidence of an increase in the misuse of stimulant drugs and of barbiturates—often in combination (Bewley, 1975). Accurate figures for drug use in the general population are not available but among boys on remand from the courts, 7 per cent were found to have taken stimulants (Cockett and Marks, 1969). In the U.S.A., the level of usage among students rose from 5 to 20 per cent—being greater at college level than at high school (Blumberg, 1977; National Commission on Marihuana and Drug Abuse, 1973). It seems uncertain whether stimulant usage is still increasing or whether it is now becoming less prevalent.

Both the level and pattern of opiate usage differ markedly between the U.K. and the U.S.A. Narcotic addiction is thought to

Use of Opiates and Hallucinogens by
High School Students

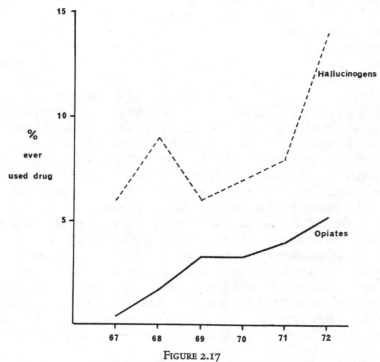

FIGURE 2.17
(Data from US National Commission on Marihuana and Drug Abuse, 1973)

be some 18 to 36 times as common in the U.S.A. as in Britain. In the U.S.A., surveys of students suggest that at least 1- or 2 per cent have tried opiate-type drugs (Blumberg, 1977; National Commission on Marihuana and Drug Abuse, 1973) and in some studies the rates have been substantially higher—for example 7 per cent of black students in the Kendell et al (1976) study had used heroin. Most experimented only briefly in their late teens and did not continue its usage or progress to a state of dependency. Nevertheless, the problem of opiate dependency in the U.S.A. is a considerable one—especially in the city ghettoes but also in

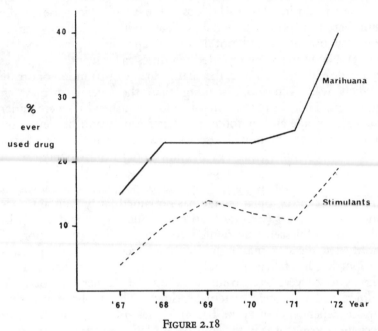

Use of Marihuana and Stimulants by
High School Students

FIGURE 2.18
(Data from US National Commission on Marihuana and Drug Abuse, 1973)

the suburbs. Accurate figures on historical trends in opiate usage
are difficult to obtain but it seems that it may have been increasing
at least up to the early 70s, as judged by drug arrests and deaths
from heroin use (Bronfenbrenner, 1976; Conger, 1973).

The suggestion that drug abuse has been increasing among
young people in the U.S.A. over the last decade is also supported
by the findings from the surveys undertaken by the U.S. National
Commission on Marihuana and Drug Abuse (1973). Figure 2.17
indicates the trend for use of hallucinogens and opiates by high
school students over the years 1967 to 1972. Both drugs, but
especially opiates, showed considerable rises. Figure 2.18 shows
the same for marihuana and stimulants—again there has been an
increasingly widespread usage.

141

In the U.K., before 1950, opiate addiction among adolescents was extremely rare (dependence being largely confined to middle-aged adults from the medical and paramedical professions). However, during the early '60s there was an increase in the number of people dependent on opiates, with a spread to younger men whose usage did not have therapeutic origins (Bewley, 1975). New cases were reported ten times as frequently in 1968 as a decade earlier. However, the change in age distribution of opiate addicts was even more striking than the overall increase in numbers. Thus, in 1959 no heroin addicts in the U.K. were under 20 years of age and in 1960 only 1 per cent were; however, by 1968 the proportion had risen to 32 per cent (James, 1971). Several community surveys documented the rapid increase in heroin usage during this period (see e.g. de Alarcón, 1969). However, at least as judged by the prescriptions to addicts at treatment centres, opiate usage has remained fairly constant over the last few years (Central Statistical Office, 1977 and 1978). In all years, adolescents accounted for only a tiny proportion of notified addicts (a maximum of 8 per cent in 1971) and this proportion has fallen markedly during the '70s, so that in 1977 the 15 to 19 year age group made up only 1 per cent of male addicts and 2 per cent of female addicts. The implication is that opiate dependence may be becoming less of a problem among teenagers than it was in the late 1960s. Nevertheless, this inference must be extremely tentative in view of reliance on official notifications which fail to include many cases of opiate usage and which provide a rather uncertain guide to the true level of the problem.

Conclusion on psychiatric disorder

Altogether, the evidence does suggest that psychiatric problems among adolescents may be increasing. Rates of suicide and of para-suicide in teenagers have risen considerably in recent years and there are indications, too, that anorexia nervosa may be becoming more common. Almost certainly, alcoholism has greatly increased in frequency among young people and the use of drugs has become very much more prevalent. It is likely, too, that drug dependency has also become more frequent among adolescents although there are suggestions that drug problems are no longer continuing to increase.

What is much less certain is whether these historical trends all have the same explanation. It is also unknown whether the total prevalence of psychiatric disorder has risen, or rather whether it is just that the patterns have altered to some extent. For example, many of the trends could be a consequence of the greater availability of drugs and the greater acceptance of their use. However, it is doubtful whether this is a sufficient explanation and the tentative conclusion is that there may have been some general increase in psychiatric problems among adolescents, although whether this increase has been large or small is quite unknown.

CONCLUSIONS

It is clear that the general pattern of adolescent development and disorder has not altered to any substantial extent in recent years. The characteristics and concerns of adolescents today are closely similar to those of a generation ago and even to those of several generations ago. In particular, the evidence suggests that there has *not* been a widening of the supposed 'generation gap' and the increase in sexuality during adolescence has always been a feature of this age period. Young people, today, are probably as idealistic as they have ever been and they continue to be concerned with personal relationships and with personal values.

On the other hand, there have been changes. Although most young people look forward to getting married and to having children, there is no longer a belief that engagement or marriage are pre-requisites for the development of sexual relationships. Contraceptive methods are being used more widely by all age groups and there is a much readier recourse to abortion as a means of dealing with unwanted pregnancies. Nevertheless, in spite of these trends, births to teenage girls continued to increase until quite recently; moreover, more unmarried mothers have been keeping their babies rather than having them adopted. Also, in common with patterns in older age-groups, the proportion of marriages ending in divorce has risen sharply.

In spite of a widespread belief that educational standards have

143

been falling, this belief seems to be largely unjustified. As measured by rates of literacy, by national examination results, by staying on at school, or by the proportions going on to further education, it is evident that standards have improved very greatly over those of two or three generations ago. On the other hand, there is some cause for concern in terms of the suggestions that there may be a flattening or even some fall-off during the last decade. The recent reduction in the percentage of pupils staying on at school after age 16 years is particularly worrying in terms of the implication that continuing education is ceasing to prove attractive and worthwhile for some young people.

The picture with respect to delinquency and vandalism is also a mixture, with reasons for both concern and optimism. The ever-increasing rise in delinquency rates is certainly worrying, but probably it reflects increased crime opportunities as much as an increase in the proportion of individuals prone to behave in delinquent ways. The suggestions that the steps taken to reduce crime opportunities may be having an effect in some areas are encouraging, and certainly they provide pointers to avenues of action worth further exploration.

How far the same applies to the historical trends with respect to psychiatric disorder among adolescents is not known. There are strong indications that certain sorts of disorder are increasing in frequency and to some extent these increases may be a byproduct of the greater availability and use of drugs. However, this does not seem to be the whole story and it is necessary also to search for possible changes in society which may be serving to put young people at psychiatric risk. These are discussed in chapter 4, but first it is necessary to prepare the scene by considering the range of possible influences on adolescent behaviour.

3

Influences on
adolescent behaviour

INTRODUCTION

The title of this chapter refers to influences rather than to causes because it deals with some of the more general factors which impinge on adolescent behaviour, rather than those items which are specific in the aetiology of particular syndromes or disease states. Obviously, the latter are crucial to the understanding of the causation and course of each condition; moreover, the clinical care of individual patients depends on such knowledge. However, my purpose here is not to provide a textbook account of individual syndromes but rather to survey the range of different influences which may serve as predisposing or precipitating factors for the variety of psychosocial problems presenting in adolescence, and to consider the effects of different forms of preventive and therapeutic interventions. Hopefully, this may both provide pointers to the alterations in society generally which require attention as possible explanations for the changes taking place in adolescent behaviour, and also serve as a guide to the factors to be taken into account in planning preventive and therapeutic services.

Concepts of causes

In medicine there is a well-established tradition of searching for *the* 'causes' of different diseases, the assumption being that in most cases there is one main cause. The approach has paid off richly as the identification of specific causes has led to the development of specific remedies. Colin Dollery's (1978) Rock Carling monograph provides some good examples of such successes. In psychiatry, too, it is likely that specificities of this kind may be discovered for some of the main disease states, although few examples have been found up to now. However, it is important to recognize that this is not the only causal question which can be posed (see Rutter and Madge, 1976).

The first point to appreciate is that the notion of a basic or fundamental cause often requires a rather arbitrary decision on what to regard as the beginning. This may be illustrated by considering the syndrome of so-called 'deprivation dwarfism' (see Rutter, 1972c; McCarthy, 1974). This is a condition found in young children who usually come from grossly disturbed families and who are of extremely short stature. The dwarfism is not associated with any physical disease or illness and at first it was thought that lack of love or emotional privation of some kind impaired growth even when the intake of food remained adequate. This now seems not to be the case, at least in most instances. The answer is more humdrum—the children have not received enough to eat. To that extent the dwarfism is 'caused' by starvation. However, that leaves open the question of why the children had not been adequately fed. The answer often lies in parental neglect or the child's depression following chronic stress. Therefore it could be said that parental neglect or lack of love is the real cause. But that only puts the question back one stage further. Why did the parents neglect the child? The answer may lie in current social disadvantages (e.g. loss of job or homelessness) or in adverse childhood experiences which failed to provide the proper basis for parenting. Are these then the causes? Or do we need also to ask why *this* child was deprived rather than his brother? Perhaps the answer to that question lies in his temperamental make-up, or the circumstance that his birth had been unwanted, or the fact that his parents had not had him for the first two months after birth because he had been in intensive care. Of course, in a sense all of these variables are causes and appropriate action requires an understanding of the process as a whole.

The second point is that with psychosocial disorders multi-factorial causation is the rule, although the relative importance of different factors varies with different sorts of disadvantage. Of course, to some extent that is true with medical conditions generally and an example serves to emphasize how the most effective point of intervention varies according to both the state of knowledge and the environmental circumstances. Tuberculosis is due to infection by the tubercle bacillus and specific means of prevention and treatment are now available. However, it is also known that genetic factors play a major role in determining individual differences in a person's resistance to infection by the bacillus (see Carter, 1977). But, in addition environmental influences also play a part in predisposition. The fact that tuberculosis is still so common in parts of Asia and that it was rife in concentration camps during the Second World War emphasises the role of malnutrition. Improved standards of nutrition, and of public hygiene generally, might well do much to reduce susceptibility to tuberculosis if more specific remedies were not available, and even when they are available a combined approach may be most effective of all.

The third point is that causation tends to be thought of in terms of the 'who' question; that is the reason why one person has a disorder or problem rather than another. That is a most important causal question but it is not the only one and in some circumstances it may not even be the most important. For example, we may need to ask the 'how many' question. The implications of the distinction are evident in the example of unemployment. The answer to the 'who' question, that is why this man is unemployed rather than that one, comes down to personal factors in large part. Those who are old, who lack work skills, who have chronic physical incapacities, or who show marked personality disorders, are the ones most likely to be left without jobs. On the other hand, these factors have got little or nothing to do with the 'how many' question, that is the question for example as to why the unemployment rate has risen five-fold over recent years. Here, the answer is more likely to lie in the national (or international) economic situation, in political decisions, and in regional job opportunities. Whether the same applies in the mental health or social fields is uncertain. But, for instance, it may well be that the reasons why the delinquency rate has increased so much since the Second World War are different from the reasons why George becomes delinquent but Peter does not.

The last point is that in planning services it is not enough to know the reasons why disorders *arise*, we must also understand why they *continue*, and why they do or do not lead to functional *impairment.* For example, many boys commit delinquent acts but only a proportion come to the notice of the police, and of those that do, only about half continue in delinquency. Some $2\frac{1}{2}$ per cent of the population are intellectually retarded in so far as they have a measured IQ below 70, but only some of these require special schooling because of educational difficulties or failure. Many boys have a propensity to behave in disruptive or disturbing ways but whether this actually results in vandalism, or truancy, or scuffles in class, depends on the school environment they experience.

These few examples do not exhaust the different ways of looking at causation but perhaps they suffice to make the point that the concept of causation involves a variety of different processes and a range of points at which intervention may be effective. In the discussion that follows, the factors which may influence adolescent behaviour are considered without detailed examination of their *modus operandi* in the various possible networks of causal chains and processes, as this would take us too far into a consideration of individual syndromes. However, attention is briefly paid to a few aspects of this issue in the concluding chapter on services.

FAMILY INFLUENCES

The very extensive literature on different types of family influences on the behaviour and development of children and adolescents has been extensively reviewed by Martin (1975), by Rutter (1972c, 1977b and c, 1979e; Rutter and Madge, 1976) and by Hinde (1979), so that only a very brief appraisal of the main issues will be given here.

Hinde (1979) has clearly outlined some of the crucial features of family dynamics which have to be borne in mind when considering possible causal effects. Firstly, the child has a relationship with each family member so that father–child and sib–sib interactions must receive attention as well as those of the mother and child. Secondly, relationships always involve mutual influences. Just as parents influence their children so children influence their parents. Thirdly, relationships affect each other, so that mother–child relationships are affected by the relationship between the two parents, and how one parent behaves with the children is influenced by whether or not the other parent is also present. Fourthly, the family structure changes with time. Fifthly, family structure is influenced from outside as well as from within. Social conditions and family life circumstances (as with satisfactions or disappointments at work) will affect family interactions. Sixthly, to a considerable extent relationships and structures are self-regulatory. For this reason an influence that appears to be important in the short-term may be unimportant in the long run.

Family discord, disharmony and disruption

Numerous studies have shown the importance of severe parental discord and disharmony as a precursor of adolescent problems of various kinds, but especially of conduct disorders and delinquency, of teenage pregnancies, of unmarried motherhood, of subsequent marital breakdown, and of difficulties in infant care. Much of the earlier literature was concerned with 'broken homes' rather than discord, but it is clear that disturbed relationships rather than separation is the most important variable (Rutter, 1971b). This is shown by the repeated observation that whereas parental divorce is strongly associated with these outcomes, parental death is not. Moreover, conduct disorders are associated with family discord and disharmony even when the parental marriage is intact and there have been no breaks or separations. Furthermore, Power and his colleagues (1974) found that among boys who had already made a court appearance for delinquency, those from intact homes with severe and persistent family problems were more likely to become recidivist than those from broken homes (or those from intact homes without serious problems). Lambert, Essen and Head (1977), in their longitudinal study of children removed from their homes into the care of the local authority found that most of the behavioural disturbance was manifest *before* the removal. We may conclude that family discord and disharmony are indeed the damaging factors, although separations may add to the stresses.

However, four further points require emphasis. First, although discord and disharmony appear to be the most important features, it should not be assumed either that parental divorce is without

149

adverse effects or that divorce brings disharmony to an end. Neither seems to be the case (Hetherington et al, 1978). The divorce action often serves to increase tensions and conflict between the parents as matters of both finance and access to the children are being sorted out. Moreover, it has been found that divorce is often associated with a *worsening* of behaviour during the year after the break-up even though in the long run it is followed by a substantial improvement (see chapter 4 for a fuller discussion of this issue).

Secondly, the effects are not irreversible. Rutter (1971b) found that the disorders were less frequent in children who later came to live in harmonious homes (either because parental conflict had been resolved or because the parents had separated and remarried) and Hetherington et al (1978) showed that two years after divorce children's emotional and behavioural disturbance had much improved.

Thirdly, however, the associations are much stronger with persistent disorders than they are with transient difficulties. This is so with respect to both psychiatric problems (Rutter et al, 1976) and delinquency (West and Farrington, 1973, 1977).

Fourthly, although early family discord is associated with later behavioural disturbance in adolescence this does not usually seem to represent any kind of delayed or 'sleeper' effect. Rather, the evidence indicates that early family difficulties are associated with the early development of troublesome behaviour which in turn leads on to adolescent problems. West and Farrington (1973), for example, found that a child's separation from his parents for reasons other than hospital admission or parental death was associated with an increased risk of delinquency (32·2 per cent vs 17·1 per cent for children without such separations). However, this association ceased to be significant once the prior association with troublesome behaviour at age 10 years had been taken into account.

Family communication patterns
There have been considerable methodological difficulties in the measurement of family communication and patterns of dominance and the research findings in this area are rather contradictory and

inconclusive. Nevertheless, the balance of findings indicates that discussions in families with a disturbed child or adolescent tend to give rise to more tension and disagreement than they do in normal families (Rutter, 1977c). There does not seem to be anything very distinctive about the sequence or patterns of communication but families with a disturbed child often show more negative feelings when talking together and may give more conflicting messages. But, perhaps the most striking characteristic of many families with a disturbed adolescent is their inefficient communication, both in the sense that discussion tends to be associated with fruitless disputes, and in the sense that it often fails to give rise to an agreed solution. Very few studies have made distinctions between diagnostic groups and it is not known whether communication difficulties are associated with particular types of psychiatric disorder. Strong claims have been made that communication deviance is specifically associated with schizophrenia arising in adolescence or early adult life but it seems doubtful whether this is so (Rutter, 1978).

Parental criminality and psychiatric disorder

A variety of early studies reviewed by Rutter (1966) suggested a link between mental disorders in parents and psychiatric problems in their children. This observation has since been confirmed by many systematic investigations of both clinic and general population samples using several different research strategies (see Rutter, 1977c, also Rolf and Garmezy, 1974; Weintraub et al, 1975 and 1978; El-Guebaly and Offord, 1977; Welner et al, 1977; Gamer et al, 1977; Cooper et al, 1977). Many studies have made comparisons according to the diagnosis of the parent's mental condition but although chronic disorders and conditions associated with abnormalities of personality seem to carry a greater risk for the children, on the whole diagnosis has not appeared a crucial variable. The disorders in the children have also not followed any particular pattern and there has been a lack of evidence indicating any close connection between the parental diagnosis and the type of the child's disorder.

Doubtless, several different mechanisms—including genetic factors—are involved in these links between parental illness and child disorder. However, it has been evident that parental mental disorder is often associated with marital discord and disharmony, with conflict over child rearing, with irritability or hostility to the children, and by impaired family communication. The presence of family discord has been shown to be associated with the development of problems in the children of parents with mental conditions, and it seems that the children are at risk in large part because of the accompanying family disturbances and marital problems. A further feature is that the children seem more likely to develop emotional or behavioural difficulties if the parental symptoms directly impinge on the children or affect child-rearing.

When a parent is ill, the children are more likely to be placed in the care of the local authority or removed from home in some other way and this, too, has been found to be associated with the development of psychiatric problems. Quinton and Rutter (1979), in a study linking childhood experiences with functioning in early adult life, found that in large part parental deviance or disorder was followed by problems in adolescence and adulthood just because the parental abnormalities led to a string of adverse experiences and stressful happenings.

The implication is that the risk to the children is not an inevitable consequence of the parental illness but rather is a result of the involvement of the children in abnormal parental behaviour and of the association between parental illness on the one hand and family discord, maladaptive communication, and impaired parent-child interaction, on the other (Rutter, 1977c). The age of the child does not seem to be a crucial factor in these effects but there has been a tendency for younger children to be most affected. Once again, the association with psychiatric disorders in adolescence is mainly with those persisting from an earlier age rather than with those arising *de novo* (Rutter et al, 1976).

Parental criminality has been most studied in relation to delinquency in the offspring. It is well established that criminality in either parent much increases the risk of delinquency in the children (West and Farrington, 1973; Rutter and Madge, 1976). Thus, Robins et al (1975), in a sample of black Americans, found that 45 per cent of the sons of a criminal father were delinquent compared with only 9 per cent of those whose fathers had no criminal record; the comparable figures for girls were 24 per cent and 0 per cent. Similarly, Farrington et al (1975) in a sample of working-class white London families found that where the father had had at least two adult convictions 39·5 per cent of the sons were recidivist delinquents compared with 8·4 per cent of boys whose father had never been convicted. However, it is not just a question of intergenerational associations with respect to crime as criminality in fathers is also strongly associated with psychiatric disorder in the children—at least at age 10 years (Rutter et al, 1975c). The association, then, is well demonstrated but the mechanisms it reflects remain unclear. It does not seem to be a function of criminal parents inculcating their children in crime, nor does it seem that the parents directly encourage delinquency by an attitude of tolerance towards lawbreaking. In part, it appears that families with criminal parents have other adversities and provide a less satisfactory pattern of upbringing and in part it may be that the criminal parents provide a model of delinquent behaviour. Genetic factors, too, may be involved. As with other family influences the associations are most marked with *persistent* disorders in the adolescent offspring.

Discipline and supervision

Discipline and supervision have been studied through a wide variety of measures, many of which have proved to be unsatisfactory. There have also often been problems in the interpretations of findings because the data have been retrospective (so making it difficult to disentangle cause from effect), because the measures have been attitudinal or inferential (so that it has been uncertain what the parents actually did), and because the results applied to variations within the normal range (making extrapolations to extreme groups rather dubious). Nevertheless, in spite of these limitations there is a reasonable degree of consistency of findings in terms of the parental patterns associated with delinquency and aggressive behaviour—far less is known on the antecedents of emotional disturbance (Rutter, 1977c).

The particular methods of discipline employed appear to be rather unimportant on the whole; properly applied a wide range of techniques seem to be reasonably effective. On the other hand, the consistency and efficiency of the discipline and the affectional context within which discipline takes place are relevant. Markedly inconsistent or haphazard discipline is associated with an increased likelihood of conduct disorders and delinquency. This is probably because it provides no clear guidance to the child as to what behaviour is expected of him, and because inconsistency tends to be associated with parental tension and conflict. It has also often been found that delinquents tend to be poorly supervised by their parents who neither know where they go nor attempt to regulate their activities. The timing and quality of parental responses to the children's behaviour are also influential. The parents of youngsters showing problem behaviour appear to differ from other parents in being less good at recognizing when and how to intervene, in giving less encouragement and praise for good behaviour, in responding erratically and inconsistently to bad behaviour, and in giving an undue amount of attention when the child is misbehaving. A vicious circle of maladaptive interaction all too readily develops in which parental reprimands and nagging provoke and perpetuate the very behaviours they aim to prevent. Thus, Patterson (1977) in a detailed study of sequences of family interactions in the home showed that disapproval tended to increase the likelihood that the child would show hostile behaviour, and physical punishment increased the likelihood of social aggression. Many studies have noted that extreme parental criticism, brutality or harsh discipline, rejection, and hostility are associated with high rates of aggression, delinquency, and disorders of conduct in the children. These negative behaviours are often associated with family tensions, conflict, and discord, and the ill effects probably stem from both the disturbed family relationships and also from the fact that discipline is less likely to be adhered to by the children when the parents are neither loved nor respected.

In practice, many of these features of unsatisfactory discipline and poor parent-adolescent relationships frequently go together (see e.g. McCord and McCord, 1959; West and Farrington, 1973) making it hard to disentangle just which are the crucial elements putting the young people most at risk. However, haphazard discipline combined with poor supervision (so that there is a lack of clear goals or aims), and harsh discipline in the context of an unloving relationship seems particularly liable to be damaging.

Institutional rearing

Several studies have indicated the hazards associated with being reared in an institution with multiple changing caretakers (see Rutter, 1979e). In the school environment institutional children tend to be attention-seeking, restless, disobedient, and unpopular, and at home they both seek affection more than other children and also fail to develop close attachments to their parent-surrogates. These abnormalities in social behaviour seem to stem from the children's relative lack of selective bonding in infancy. Interestingly, however, it is evident that an institutional upbringing need not impair intellectual development.

Family size

It is well established that, on average, individuals from large families (that is those with at least four or five children) tend to have a lower level of verbal intelligence and of reading attainment, and also that they are at a greater risk of becoming delinquent or developing conduct disorders. The mechanisms are ill-understood but are almost certainly multiple. Firstly, large family size is quite strongly associated with overcrowding and socio-economic disadvantage. Secondly, there is probably less intensive interaction and less communication between the parents and the children in large families if only because parental time has to be distributed more widely. Thirdly, parental discipline and supervision may be more difficult when there are a lot of children to look after. Fourthly, some of the children may have been unwanted. Fifthly, in some cases the lack of family limitations may reflect general parental qualities of inadequate foresight and planning. At the moment, data are lacking to give appropriate weights to these various alternative explanations but it seems clear that, whatever the reason, children in very large families have an increased risk of psychosocial and educational problems.

Poverty and low social status

There is a huge body of research on the effects of being brought up by parents of low social status or in a family with a low income or in an overcrowded home (see Rutter and Madge, 1976). That such an upbringing is associated with substantial disadvantages is not in doubt. It is also well demonstrated that low socio-economic status and overcrowding are good indicators of risk for educational retardation and to a lesser extent of delinquency. What remains less certain are the processes involved in these associations. Some suggested explanations are discussed in Rutter and Madge (1976).

STRESS EVENTS

Surprisingly little is known about the impact of stress events in adolescence and undoubtedly this is a topic requiring much further study. In adults there is good evidence that acute life stresses are associated with the onset of depression (Brown and Harris, 1978). The timing of the stresses, the much higher rate of stresses among depressed people than among well-matched control populations, the fact that the stresses studied were not brought about by the individual himself, and the confirmation within general population samples of the findings from studies of hospital patients all indicate that the stresses are of considerable causal importance. A variety of events may serve as stresses but those most strongly associated with depression seem to involve the experience of a threatened or actual loss (such as separation from the family or life threatening illness in a loved one) or an actual or perceived life failure (such as examination failure or a rebuff from a close friend). It would seem plausible that such stresses might also play a part in the aetiology of the depressive disorders arising during adolescence but data are lacking on how far this is in fact the case. There is some indication that bereavement is a significant precipitant of psychiatric disorder in adolescence (Rutter, 1966); it is reported that acute stresses (especially disciplinary crises, disputes with a friend, or a threat of family break-up) often precede suicides and attempted suicides in adolescence (Stanley and Barter, 1970; Shaffer, 1974; Haim, 1974);

and Heisel et al (1973) found stresses associated with psychiatric disorders and certain physical conditions in children. On the other hand, Gersten et al (1977) in a study of New York 11- to 23-year-olds found that stressful life change events were not related to their measures of psychological disturbance. However, little weight can be attached to this negative finding in view of the relative crudity of their measures, and especially their failure to examine timing with respect to onset in the detailed way which Brown and Harris' (1978) studies suggest is necessary. The pointers are there but systematic investigations are required to provide sound empirical evidence on the nature and extent of the risk.

Early life events have also been identified as precursors of disorders in later childhood and early adolescence. For example, Douglas (1973) found that of children in the National Survey who had experienced at least four disturbing events (such as admission to hospital, birth of a sib, or moves of home) in the first four years, 7·6 per cent were enuretic at 11 years and 3·1 per cent at 15 years, as compared with 4·6 per cent and 1·4 per cent respectively of those who had experienced no events of this kind. Similarly, enuresis at 15 years was three times as common in children admitted to hospital at least twice, as in those not admitted to hospital or admitted only once. Recurrent or prolonged hospital admissions in the first five years were also found to be significantly associated with delinquency, with troublesome behaviour, and with an unstable job pattern in adolescence (Douglas, 1975). Quinton and Rutter (1976) confirmed that repeated hospital· admissions were associated with later behavioural disturbance and with psychiatric disorder (at age 10 years) but also showed that this association was most likely to occur in children who experienced chronic family adversities or psychosocial disadvantage. More recently, Douglas and Mann (1979) have shown that long or repeated hospital admissions in the first five years are also significantly associated with psychiatric problems in the 15- to 26-year age period (of those with such admissions 14·4 per cent had problems compared with 9·3 per cent in the rest of the population).

It seems then that *early* stress events as well as concurrent life stresses are associated with problems and difficulties in adolescence.

157

While the indications are that these stresses play a part in the causal processes, the ways in which they increase vulnerability remain ill-understood. The fact that an event at age four years is linked with disorder at age 14 years does not necessarily mean that single stresses can still have an effect 10 years later. Indeed, the fact that the association is most marked when there is a background of chronic deprivation suggests that the event frequently constitutes just one element in a longer chain or pattern of stresses rather than something which operates in isolation. In this connection it is relevant that it is *multiple* hospital admissions which put the child at risk—single admissions do not have that effect. Many questions remain unanswered. Do stresses in the first five years predispose to disorders in adolescence without there being any emotional disturbance in the intervening years; or is it that early stresses lead to early disorder which then continues on into adolescence? Similarly, do early stresses predispose to disorders in adolescence even when there are no concurrent psychosocial stresses or disadvantage in the teenage period; or is it that early stresses are associated with adolescent problems simply because early stresses so often lead on to later stresses and it is these later stresses which constitute the immediate cause or precipitant? Or yet again, as Brown and Harris (1978) suggest, do early stresses create a *vulnerability* which on its own does not cause disorder but which may enhance the damage done by later stresses? Data which might decide between these alternatives are lacking.

BIOLOGICAL FACTORS

Biological factors of many different kinds play an important part in shaping the course of development generally and in determining people's predisposition to disorders of various types. Thus, there is evidence that polygenic influences are important in the timing of puberty, in the origins of temperamental differences, and in the course of intellectual development (Shields, 1979); as well as in the genesis of psychiatric disorder, learning difficulties, and some forms of criminality (Shields, 1977). Sometimes these findings tend to be dismissed on the grounds that they have no practical implications in that very few of the effects are strong enough to even contemplate eugenic policies, and that there is nothing that can be done to alter a person's genetic make-up after he is born. Both objections are valid but they do not mean that knowledge on genetic influences is without practical implications. In the first place, it appears that constitutional variables to some extent shape environmental responses (see Rutter, 1977a; Dunn, 1979). Thus, malnourished infants have been found to receive less maternal attention than those who were better nourished; children with language impairment tend to elicit different forms of parental communication than those elicited by youngsters with well developed language skills; and temperamentally difficult youngsters often become scapegoated when family tensions increase. It is necessary to appreciate that to some extent how children are dealt with by adults and by their peers will be a function of the children's own characteristics. Secondly, genetic factors may give rise to both ordinal and disordinal interaction effects with the environment (Shields, 1979). An ordinal interaction implies that environmental factors affect individuals of different constitutions to a different *degree*, but in the same way. Thus, there is evidence that boys are more sensitive than girls to certain kinds of environmental stress. Also, an hereditary predisposition to criminality seems to have its effect through its rendering individuals more susceptible to environmental stresses. A disordinal interaction implies that environmental factors affect individuals of different constitutions in *opposite* ways. Reactions to sedative drugs in people of differing personality traits provide an example of this effect. Knowledge of these biological effects is necessary if we are to be in a position to develop optimally effective preventive and therapeutic services.

Autosomal chromosome anomalies are known to cause several syndromes associated with mental retardation, of which Down's syndrome is much the commonest. However, it is clear that anomalies of the sex chromosomes can also influence cognitive and emotional development. An extra Y chromosome (XYY), for example, is known to be associated with a predisposition to impulsive and delinquent behaviour (see Shields, 1979). However, many XYY individuals appear behaviourally normal and the mechanisms involved in this predisposition remain obscure.

Physical features also have developmental implications (Rutter, 1977a; Rapoport, 1979). An unpleasant facial or physical appearance increases the likelihood of social rejection; delinquents tend to be less physically attractive than other people; and there is some slight suggestion that the surgical treatment of minor deformities and disfigurements may sometimes lead to improvements in morale and in behaviour. Chronic physical handicaps in childhood and adolescence are also associated with a somewhat increased risk of psychiatric and educational problems (Rutter, Tizard and Whitmore, 1970; Haggerty et al, 1975). The same applies to blindness and deafness (Freeman, 1977). The processes by which these emotional and behavioural susceptibilities arise are not fully understood but it is clear that the adverse psychosocial sequelae apply to only a minority of physically or sensorially handicapped individuals, and that the mode of response or adaptation to the handicap is important.

Brain damage is especially likely to predispose to psychiatric disorder and educational retardation (Rutter, 1977e). Several epidemiological studies have shown that psychiatric disorder occurs more frequently in young people with brain damage than in those of comparable IQ and physically crippling but no brain injury. A recent prospective study of children and adolescents who suffered severe head injuries has confirmed that this is a *causal* association by showing that the psychiatric problems *increase* in frequency after the injury in a way that does not happen with accidents not involving brain damage (Rutter and Chadwick, 1979).

Several different mechanisms appear to operate in this predisposition to psychiatric disorder resulting from brain damage (Rutter, 1977e). First, there is the behavioural disruption due to abnormal brain activity as reflected in gross generalized epileptic disturbance on the EEG. Secondly, there are the crucial cognitive effects due to both general intellectual impairment and also specific reading retardation. These may be influential because educational failure often leads to social opprobrium and stigma at school—an effect through society's response to poor scholastic attainment as well as from the direct problems stemming from cognitive deficits. Thirdly, there are the probable effects of brain damage on temperament and personality. Fourthly, there are the adverse secondary effects of treatment—from the side-effects of drugs, from recurrent admission to hospital, and from the restriction of physical activities. Fifthly, there are the family responses to the brain damaged child. All these considerations carry important implications for the planning of treatment (Rutter, 1977e). However, from the point of view of prevention it is also important to recognize the role of perinatal factors in the causation of cerebral palsy (Alberman, 1979). Improved social conditions and improved obstetric care should make it possible to prevent some cases of cerebral palsy; prevention of accidents should also reduce the number of cases with a post-natal causation.

In the last few years, attention has come to be focussed on the possible role of environmental lead (from industrial and traffic pollution, from lead water pipes, and from the ingestion of lead in food or through pica in young children) as a cause of sub-clinical brain damage associated with cognitive deficits and behavioural disturbance (see Rutter, 1979g). Sweeping claims have been made about the supposed importance of lead intoxication as a factor in the high rate of delinquency and learning problems found among children and adolescents in socially disadvantaged inner city areas. The research findings are somewhat contradictory and open to more than one interpretation. Nevertheless, the balance of evidence suggests that a high body lead burden may lead to slight intellectual impairment (a deficit of one to five points on average) and less certainly to behavioural problems, even when there is no encephalopathy or other symptoms indicative of lead poisoning. Uncertainty remains on just how high the lead levels must be for this to occur. Clearly it is important to be alert to the need to reduce sources of lead pollutions in the environment; however, the findings so far suggest that lead intoxication plays no more than a most minor role in the genesis of adolescent disorders.

Lastly, it is clear that mental retardation very substantially increases the risk of psychiatric disorder (Rutter, 1971a; Corbett, 1977b). On the whole the types of disorders in mildly retarded children are fairly similar to those in children of normal intelligence but the distribution of disorders in severely retarded children is considerably different. However, it is not just mental retardation which predisposes to emotional and behavioural problems; even within the normal range of intelligence youngsters of somewhat below average intelligence or scholastic attainments are more at risk. Thus, West and Farrington (1973) found that the average IQ of delinquent boys was 95·1 compared with 100·9 for non-delinquents. This difference was almost entirely due to the recidivists; the IQ scores of one-time delinquents did not differ from those of the general population. The vulnerability associated with educational retardation and with a lower IQ applies also to psychiatric disorder in adolescence, but only to that which persists from earlier childhood, not to disorders arising for the first time during the teenage period (see chapter 1).

FILMS AND TELEVISION

On average, children spend two to three hours per day watching television. Many of the programmes contain scenes portraying violence of various sorts and much concern has been expressed over the possible adverse effects of young people viewing so much aggression and violence, particularly when such behaviour is glorified or at least portrayed as justified (Surgeon-General, 1972). Numerous studies have shown correlations between violent behaviour and watching violence on television but there have been many difficulties in sorting out how far these associations reflect causal influences. Three main research strategies have been employed. Firstly, statistical control techniques have been applied to cross-sectional data. For example, Belson (1978) used this approach in his study of 1565 London boys aged 12 to 17 years. He showed that high *exposure* to television violence was significantly correlated with frequent *use* of violence, even after controlling for the various background factors associated with violent behaviour. On this basis, and because the reverse did not hold (i.e. after controlling for background factors associated with TV viewing), he concluded that the TV violence had predisposed to violent behaviour. The effect seemed to be most marked when the TV violence occurred in the context of close personal relations and when it was presented as justified. It was suggested that the main mechanism was the reduction or breaking down of inhibitions against being violent.

Secondly, naturalistic longitudinal studies have examined correlations over time. Thus, Lefkowitz et al (1977) showed that boys' preference for violent television correlated 0·21 with his concurrent aggressiveness and 0·31 with his aggressiveness 10 years later. Because the reverse did *not* apply, i.e. aggression in third grade did *not* correlate significantly with television viewing 10 years later, it was concluded that the TV viewing had predisposed to aggression rather than the other way round. Interestingly, however, this pattern did not apply with girls.

Thirdly, experiments have been undertaken both in the laboratory and in more natural settings. For example, Berkowitz et al (1978) studied delinquent boys living in cottages within minimum security institutions. Boys in cottages where highly aggressive films were shown on five consecutive nights were compared with boys in cottages where non-violent commercial films were shown. The results showed that a diet of aggressive films stimulated the boys to increased aggression during the movie week and to a lesser extent in the following period as well. Some of the influence was clearly imitative in nature.

The results of other studies are closely similar and as the findings of each of the different research strategies point in the same direction, it may be concluded that the prolonged viewing of violent television programmes has some effect in predisposing adolescent boys to behave in violent ways.

A recent report (Barraclough et al, 1977) suggests that other forms of publicity may also have unintended effects. A statistical association was found between the newspaper reporting of suicide inquests and suicides in men under 45 in the following week. This, taken in conjunction with the observation that suicides increase briefly after the publicity given to suicides of famous people and with other evidence of 'suicide contagion', suggests that newspaper reporting as well as television and films may cause imitations of undesired behaviour.

SCHOOLING

The American reports by James Coleman (Coleman et al, 1966) and by Christopher Jencks (Jencks et al, 1972) and their colleagues led to the general belief among academics that schooling had only a marginal impact on children's behaviour and academic performance. It came to be accepted that schooling made so little difference that for most practical purposes its effects could be ignored. It is now clear that this view was mistaken and that, to the contrary, schooling constitutes a most important influence on adolescent behaviour.

This shift of opinion has been brought about by the increasing weight of evidence that there are large differences between secondary schools in almost all aspects of children's performance— in their attendance, behaviour, scholastic attainment, and even delinquency rates (see Rutter, Maughan, Mortimore, Ouston and Smith, 1979). Thus, Power et al (1967) found huge differences in delinquency rates between twenty secondary schools serving one inner London borough, even after excluding academically selective schools. Gath et al (1977) showed much the same for an outer London borough, finding that secondary schools differed widely in their delinquency rates (as reflected in probation) and rates of referral to child psychiatric clinics. In a quite different geographical area, Reynolds (Reynolds and Murgatroyd, 1977; Reynolds et al, 1976) found major variations between secondary schools in rates of academic attainment, attendance, delinquency, and also unemployment, four months after school leaving. In the U.S.A., too, it has been found that schools varied greatly in their rates of vandalism and that these variations were systematically associated with characteristics of the schools themselves (Goldman, 1961; Pablant and Baxter, 1975).

These and other similar results led to a reappraisal of the negative conclusions from earlier studies (see Rutter, et al, 1979). Three main issues stood out as relevant. Firstly, the finding that schools had little effect largely referred to their impact on measures of children's verbal ability, whereas the positive findings applied to *taught* subjects and to behaviour. Secondly, the original surveys were concerned almost entirely with one or other aspect of resources whereas the new evidence suggested that what mattered were the school's qualities as a social organization, in terms of attitudes, values, and mores. Thirdly, Jencks' analyses were mainly designed to determine whether improvements in the quality of schooling would reduce inequalities in attainment by making children more alike. The recent research confirms that raising the quality of education does not (and could not) achieve homogenization, but on the other hand the strong implication is that it may have a decisive impact in raising overall standards of behaviour and attainment.

However, the demonstration that schools *vary* in rates of vandalism or examination success is not tantamount to showing that the variations in adolescents' behaviour and achievement are due to school influences. Several further steps are required before causal inferences are justifiable. The first issue is whether the differences reflect something intrinsic about the schools themselves or, rather, something about their intakes of pupils. Perhaps the variations between schools mean no more than that some schools *admit* far higher proportions of children of low ability or with disturbed behaviour. The evidence from our recent study of twelve inner London secondary schools showed that this was *not* a sufficient explanation (Rutter et al, 1979).

In order to examine this issue, some 1500 children in one inner London borough were systematically assessed at age 10 years just prior to their transfer to secondary school, were reassessed in the same way four years later at age 14, and then reassessed once more at the time of school leaving with regard to their success in national examinations. Measures of behaviour, of delinquency rates, and of school attendance were also obtained. Figure 3.1 shows the findings on national examination results, the vertical giving the average weighted examination score per child and the horizontal the findings in turn for each of the twelve study schools which took the bulk of the children. It is evident that examination success was strongly correlated with the child's level of intellectual abilities as assessed prior to entering secondary school. However, it is also clear that the variations between secondary schools were so marked that the average score for band three children (the lowest 25 per cent ability group) in the most successful school was

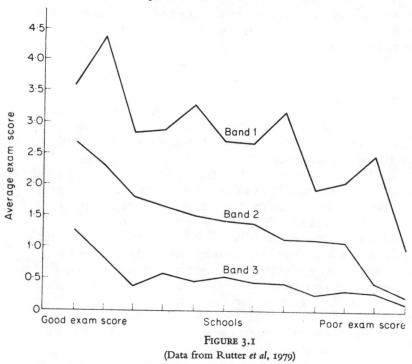

FIGURE 3.1

(Data from Rutter *et al*, 1979)

as good as that for band one children (top 25 per cent ability group) in the least successful school. Similar differences between schools were found with respect to all the other outcome measures of pupil behaviour, of attendance, of drop-out rates, and of delinquency. Statistical analyses showed that the marked school variations in each different type of pupil outcome could not be accounted for in terms of any of the available measures of individual intake characteristics. The school variations must have been due to 'something else'.

The second step was to determine how far this 'something else' concerned features of the schools as social institutions or organizations. A systematic study was made of each of the twelve secondary schools with detailed assessments of a wide range of aspects of school life, organization, or functioning. Over 200 teachers were

166

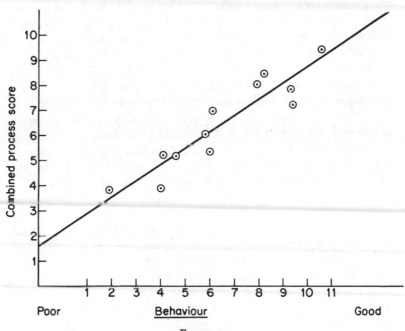

FIGURE 3.2
(Data from Rutter *et al*, 1979)

interviewed, questionnaires were obtained from over 2700 pupils, moment by moment observations were made throughout over 500 lessons, and measures were obtained on the state and decor of the buildings, and on staff-pupil interactions in school corridors and playgrounds. The various school features were put together into a 'combined school process score'. This dealt with items as varied as academic emphasis, styles of classroom management, patterns of rewards and punishments, and pupils' opportunities for responsibility and participation. Figure 3.2 shows that there was a very substantial correlation between this overall school process score and children's behaviour as observed in the school and as reported by themselves. The pupil behaviour measure included items such as late arrival at lessons, chatting and calling out in class, overtly disruptive behaviour, damage to school property, and absconding during the school day. Each point on the graph represents the scores for one school on both measures—the school characteristic on the vertical and pupil outcome on the horizontal. The regression line indicates a positive association. The differences between schools *were* systematically and strongly associated with characteristics of the schools themselves. Firm conclusions about causation can only come from controlled experimental studies in which school practices are altered to determine if this results in changes in the children's behaviour or progress. Such investigations have yet to be undertaken but in the meanwhile there is the strong implication that school processes do influence pupil outcomes and that schooling does have important effects on adolescents' behaviour and scholastic attainment.

However, if this conclusion is to be of much practical benefit it is necessary to go on and ask *which* were the features of schools which seemed to make the difference and which led to better behaviour and attainments. The evidence showed that physical aspects, such as the size of the school, or the age of the buildings, were not particularly important; no one system of academic or pastoral organization had over-riding advantages; and both the overall pupil-teacher ratio and the average size of school class made little difference to outcome. It was also evident that the total amount of punishment was not the crucial feature.

Rather, the aspects of school life which seemed to matter all reflected the school's qualities as a social organization and as an environment for learning. Eight sets of variables require mention. First, it appeared important that schools should have a reasonable balance of intellectually able and less able children, although it mattered less how these were distributed in social or ethnic terms. The exact mechanisms underlying this association are not fully clear but it appeared that they operated through effects on the peer-group. Probably when a preponderance of pupils in a school are likely to be unable to meet the expectations of scholastic success, peer group cultures with an anti-academic and anti-authority emphasis may form.

Secondly, it was found that the ample use of rewards, praise and appreciation, tended to be associated with better pupil outcomes. This probably reflected both the importance of effective feedback to young people on what is and what is not acceptable

168

behaviour and achievement; and also the value of encouragements and a focus on success in setting the emotional tone of the school and hence in influencing pupil morale.

Thirdly, quite apart from rewards for specific pieces of work or behaviour, a pleasant and comfortable school environment was associated with better outcomes. This meant good working conditions, responsiveness to pupil needs, and also good care and decoration of the buildings. U.S. research, similarly, has shown that vandalism tends to be less in schools which take trouble to look after the buildings well and to maintain attractive decor and pleasant grounds (Pablant and Baxter, 1975).

Fourthly, ample opportunities for children to take responsibility and to participate in the running of their school lives appeared conducive to good attainments, attendance, and behaviour.

Fifthly, the evidence indicated that children made better progress both behaviourally and academically in schools which placed an appropriate emphasis on academic matters. Successful schools tended to make good use of homework, to set clear goals, and to have an atmosphere of confidence that pupils could and would succeed in the tasks they were set. Several studies have also shown modest, but positive, associations between the time spent actively involved in particular subject work and attainment in those subjects (Bennett, 1978).

The sixth school feature concerned the models of behaviour provided by teachers. Outcomes were better in schools where the teachers were good time-keepers and were willing to see pupils about problems at any time. Pupil behaviour was worse, on the other hand, in schools where teachers tended to react to provocation and disruptiveness by slapping the pupils or pushing them about.

The seventh set of variables concerned group management in the classroom. The individual school class constitutes a social group and, as with any other social group, skills are involved in its management. The findings suggest the importance of preparing lessons in advance, of keeping the attention of the whole group, of unobtrusive discipline, of a focus on good behaviour rather than disruptive acts, but with swift action to deal with disruption when this is necessary. Lastly, the evidence indicated that pupil outcomes tended to be better when both the curriculum and approaches to discipline were agreed and supported by the staff acting together. A combination of firm leadership together with a decision-making process in which all teachers felt that their views were represented and seriously considered seemed most effective.

It remains somewhat uncertain just how this rather hetero-geneous mixture of variables comes together to create a school environment which fosters good behaviour and academic success. However, the implications are that they determine the nature of the values and norms of behaviour set by the school; they influence the extent to which these values and norms apply to the school as a whole in a manner which creates cohesion and unity; and they affect the degree to which pupils accept the norms established by the school.

PHYSICAL ENVIRONMENT

Most of the research on schools has focused on features which may be expected to operate through their effect on young people's propensity or motivation to behave in certain ways. However, there is also some indication that there is a different mechanism which plays a part—namely the extent to which the environment provides, or does not provide, opportunities for certain sorts of behaviour. For example, Pablant and Baxter (1975) found that vandalism was less frequent in schools where the property was clearly visible to nearby residents and where the surrounding area was well illuminated. Conversely, high vandalism schools tended to face railroad tracks, motorways, or vacant land. The implication is that neighbourhood vigilance reduced vandalism. This issue has been more extensively studied in connection with housing estates and transport.

The American architect Oscar Newman (1973 and 1975) has greatly influenced thinking on this topic through his concept of 'defensible space', meaning personal territory with a clearly identifiable status and a layout which enables people to know their neighbours and easily spot strangers. On the basis of the distribu-tion of vandalism and of the types and locations of crime on New

York housing estates, he hypothesized that physical design features might either predispose to or protect against crime. He argued that large apartment blocks, particularly those which were high rise, were crime-prone because large areas were neither private and therefore supervised by residents, nor truly public and therefore constantly used and overseen by passers-by. The semi-public areas increased the likelihood of vandalism both because they were not felt to belong to any particular group of residents (and hence not looked after or protected by them) and because surveillance tended to be difficult by the nature of their design. The crucial physical variables appeared to be the size of the housing project, the number of housing units sharing an entrance to the dwelling and the building height. Although not as strong predictors of crime as the characteristics of the residents on the estates, the physical design features nevertheless seemed to influence the extent of crime.

More recently, Sheena Wilson (see Clarke, 1978) has tested some of Newman's ideas in a study of 285 blocks of dwellings in London. She found, as did Newman, that most damage occurred in those semi-public areas such as lifts and stairways which were out of sight of dwellings. Child density (i.e. the number of children per dwelling) had the strongest association with the level of vandalism but physical design features were also of some importance. Vandalism was particularly high in large blocks with extensive semi-public space which could not be supervised easily by residents and in blocks with impersonal entrances which could be used as a through way to other locations. Damage was also more common in blocks with little or no landscaping of the grounds. The presence of flower beds, trees, and grass was associated with lower rates of vandalism and it may be that the provision of a pleasant environment makes it less likely that people will want to damage it; quite apart from a well supervised environment making it less likely that opportunities for vandalism will arise. Of course, not all of the vandalism will have been undertaken by adolescents or children but it is clear that it is particularly common in this age group (Clarke, 1978).

Similar issues have been investigated in relation to other circumstances and situations. For example, Mayhew et al (1976) showed that cars with steering wheel locks were much less likely to be stolen than cars without this device. In the U.K. it seems that the greater security of new cars simply increased the risk of theft for old cars. Car stealing was not reduced; rather it had been displaced from one sort of car to another. On the other hand, in Germany, where anti-theft devices were required to be fitted to *both* old and new cars the incidence of theft was substantially reduced. Making the stealing of cars more difficult made car theft less common. The really determined thief would still find a way of overcoming the protective devices but it appears that much stealing is opportunistic. If the easy opportunity is not there, some potential thieves may not steal. Similarly, when the design of telephone booths was altered to make vandalism and theft less easy, this seemed to reduce damage in country areas and small towns, although it did not do so to the same extent in large cities (see chapter 2).

Another legislative measure which had an effect on theft was the requirement introduced in 1973 that riders of motor cycles should wear protective head gear. While the measure was designed to improve road safety it was followed by a marked reduction in the theft of motor cycles. Presumably some opportunist thieves were deterred from stealing motor cycles by the likelihood of their being stopped if seen riding without a crash helmet. A study of damage on buses by the same research group (Mayhew et al, 1976) showed that areas of low supervision (the upper deck and back seats) were most likely to be vandalized. Moreover, damage was greatest on one-man operated buses without a conductor. Supervision seems to have a pronounced effect in reducing vandalism.

It is not known how far physical prevention truly reduces crime and how far it simply displaces it from one area to another or from one type of activity to another. However, it seems likely that the two are not truly independent. Any protective action that still leaves open a wide range of similar crime opportunities is unlikely to do more than serve as a means of displacement. On the other hand, when it is possible for protective actions to be sufficiently widespread in their effects so that there are few readily available alternatives left open a real overall reduction in crime may take place. Recidivist delinquency may well be linked with rather persistent styles of behaviour but much crime, even in recidivists, is likely to be situational (see Mayhew et al, 1976). Thus, Clarke and Martin (1971) showed that absconding from approved schools (for delinquents) was more frequent during the dark evenings of November than the light nights of June; the same applies to property offences. Similarly, many years ago, Hartshorne and May (1928) showed that the frequency with which children cheated was influenced by situational factors such as the teacher in charge of the tests and the amount of supervision provided. Only a few children are completely honest all the time —most will behave dishonestly given the right circumstances.

Moreover, it should not be thought that situational influences apply only to crime. De Alarcón (1972) argued that the ready availability of drugs was a crucial factor in the epidemic of heroin and methedrine abuse in one English town. Similarly, the severe reduction in the toxicity of domestic gas which has taken place since 1963 in the U.K. has resulted in a dramatic reduction in suicides from this cause—from 2461 in 1962 to 50 in 1974 (Adelstein and Mardon, 1975). This decrease was only partly offset by a rise in poisonings from other substances and it is likely that the reduced toxicity of domestic gas has resulted in a real saving of life.

AREA INFLUENCES

From the pioneering studies of Burt (1925) and of Shaw and McKay (1942) onwards, it has been repeatedly shown that delinquency rates vary markedly according to geographical area— being highest in poor, overcrowded areas of low social status in industrial cities, and lowest in more affluent spacious rural areas (see Rutter et al, 1975a; Rutter and Madge, 1976). However, high delinquency areas may exist in new housing estates as well as in city slums. Moreover, delinquency rates have been shown to vary between boroughs, between wards in a borough, between enumeration districts within a ward, and even between streets in a small neighbourhood, so that the high risk areas may be very small as well as quite large. The explanation for these findings

173

remains rather uncertain and there is disagreement on how far the area differences reflect variations in family difficulties and disturbance and how far broader ecological influences. But any explanation put forward must account for the observation that delinquency areas seem to remain rather stable over time (Wallis and Maliphant, 1967; Castle and Gittus, 1957) and that on the whole the areas with high rates of juvenile delinquency also have high rates of adult crime, social problems, alcoholism, and psychiatric disorder (see Rutter and Madge, 1976).

Suicide rates also vary by area, tending to be commoner in those characterized by social disorganization and social isolation, but not by overcrowding and unemployment (Sainsbury, 1955). Parasuicide rates, too, show marked geographical variations, being most frequent in areas of poor housing and poverty (Kreitman, 1977). These tend to be the same areas with high rates of delinquency, illegitimate births, divorce, and mental hospital admission. The main ecological associations seem to concern a wide range of social problems and social disturbance rather than just specific diseases or behaviours.

Unfortunately, there are many problems in the interpretation of these findings (see Rutter et al, 1975a). Firstly, most investigations have relied on delinquency statistics or hospital attendance figures so that it is uncertain how far the variations reflect differences in social control procedures rather than real differences in prevalence. Secondly, the findings often leave it unclear how far area influences have led to disorder and how far disorders have led people to live in a socially dilapidated area. Thirdly, it has rarely been possible to determine the extent to which the particular features of an area impinge on adolescents with problems rather than on other groups. Thus, because delinquency is common in an area of poor housing it does not mean that delinquents themselves have poor houses. It may be that it is mainly young adults or old people rather than the teenagers living in the area who experience housing disadvantage.

The Inner London–Isle of Wight comparative study was planned to take account of these methodological problems so far as possible. Closely comparable research techniques were applied by the same research team to the two areas, with a principal focus on 10-year-olds and their families. Psychiatric disorder and behavioural disturbance was twice as common in inner London as on the Isle of Wight; and a series of methodological checks confirmed that this was a valid finding of a true difference in prevalence (Rutter et al, 1975a). Moreover, the difference was *not* due to any drift of disturbed children into London, as the difference applied equally to those born and bred in the two areas. A similar two-fold difference was found for severe reading difficulties (Berger et al, 1975).

The correlates of these various problems in the two areas were investigated in order to explore possible reasons for the differences in prevalence. Four sets of variables (family discord, parental deviance, social disadvantage, and certain school characteristics) were found to be associated with emotional and behavioural disturbances in the children in both areas. In almost all cases these same adverse factors were much more common in London than on the Isle of Wight and it appeared that the high rates of psychiatric disorder and specific reading retardation in London 10-year-olds were due in large part to the fact that a relatively high proportion of London families experienced marital discord and disruption, that many of the parents showed mental disorder and antisocial behaviour, that the families often lived in poor social circumstances, and that schools were more often characterized by a high rate of turnover in staff and pupils.

This inference was confirmed by re-comparing the two areas after controlling for the presence of family adversities (Rutter and Quinton, 1977). It was found that there was no longer any significant difference between London and the Isle of Wight in rate of child psychiatric disorder. The higher rate in London was entirely explicable in terms of the greater frequency of family disadvantage. Of course, that only pushes the question back one stage further to ask why London families were more likely to be disadvantaged and what it was about life in a metropolis which predisposed to adult mental disorder, crime and family discord. No satisfactory answers to these important questions are yet available (Quinton, 1979). It does not seem to be a matter of lack of family supports nor does it seem to be a function of poor housing or overcrowding. Furthermore, high rates of disorder are

175

Influences on adolescent behaviour

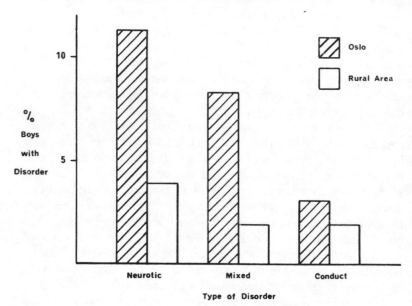

Figure 3.3
(Data from Lavik, 1977)

not a necessary consequence of urban living as there are cities and individual towns with relatively low rates of problems. The crucial adverse features of life in some inner city areas have yet to be identified.

These data refer to 10-year-olds and hence to pre-adolescent children. However, the same differences have been found with teenagers. Thus, Lavik (1977) found that psychiatric disorder was twice as common in Oslo adolescents as in adolescents living in a rural area in Norway. The difference applied to both sexes and to both neurotic and conduct disorders but the least disparity between the areas concerned neurotic disorders (see fig. 3.3). As in the London–Isle of Wight study, family disruption was associated with a higher risk of psychiatric disorder and was more frequent in the city area.

176

Area influences

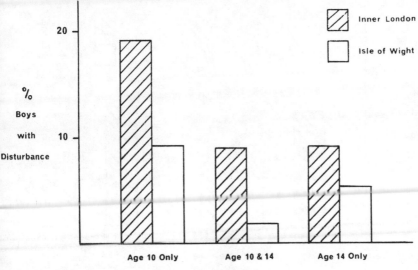

Behavioural Disturbance Among Boys in London and the Isle of Wight

FIGURE 3.4

Because rather comparable area differences are evident with respect to both pre-adolescent and adolescent disorders, it is particularly important to determine how far the differences in adolescence refer to disorders persisting from earlier childhood and how far to those arising *de novo* during the teenage period. The observation that the area differences seem to reflect differences in serious family adversities might imply that the former is the case. The London–Isle of Wight comparison shows that this is indeed so.

Interview data were not available for 14-year-olds in the same way that they were for 10-year-olds. However, teacher questionnaire ratings were available at *both* ages for a cohort of 1968 children followed over a four-year period on the Isle of Wight and for 2010 children followed for the same duration in inner London (at follow-up some had moved from the area but these children have been included in the analysis). By combining the

177

Influences on adolescent behaviour

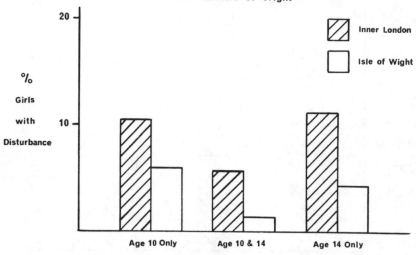

FIGURE 3.5

data for the two ages it is possible to determine the proportions of children in each area showing emotional or behavioural disburbance at age 10 years *only*, at age 14 years *only* and at *both* age 10 and 14. The findings for boys are shown in fig. 3.4. The biggest difference between London and the Isle of Wight concerned disorders present at 14 years which had persisted from age 10 years (9·0 per cent vs 1·9 per cent) and the least difference those arising *de novo* in adolescence (9·1 per cent vs 5·3 per cent). Persistent disorders also showed the largest area difference in girls with a four-fold increase in London over the Isle of Wight (5·8 per cent vs 1·4 per cent—see fig. 3.5). As expected from other findings, in both areas the persistent conditions were mainly conduct disorders but, relatively speaking, persistent emotional disorders were increased in London to about the same extent (in boys 2·4 per cent in London vs 0·5 per cent on the Isle of Wight). It is clear that the excess of disorders among adolescents living in inner London stems from disturbances which have been present

178

Ecological and social group influences

from a much earlier age rather than from any new influences arising during adolescence itself.

ECOLOGICAL AND SOCIAL GROUP INFLUENCES

The discussion of area differences naturally leads on to a consideration of ecological effects and the influence of social groups. Bronfenbrenner (1979) has been foremost among social scientists in arguing that human development must be viewed from an ecological perspective, and his recent book provides a powerful documentation of the evidence in support of this argument. His thesis is both that the behaviour of individuals is powerfully influenced by the social environment in which they find themselves and also that development involves a person's evolving conception of the ecological environment and his relation to it, as well as his growing capacity to discover, sustain and alter its properties. However, in the present context, the issue which requires emphasis is that an individual's behaviour at any particular moment is affected not only by his own developmental history but also it is powerfully shaped by the social group and the social environment in which he is interacting at that time.

This is well demonstrated in the classical 'Robber's Cave' experiment by Sherif and his colleagues (1961). Eleven-year-old boys who had not previously met one another were brought together for an experimental summer camp. Within a matter of days strong social groups had formed and the conflict inherent in competitive games and social activities soon led to strong intergroup hostilities. Bringing the groups together for social events did nothing to reduce the friction; rather the contacts served as yet further opportunities for conflict. On the other hand, joint activities towards a superordinate goal removed the tensions and brought both harmony and cooperation. The implication is that social forces develop a momentum of their own which is not wholly dependent on the particular personalities involved; but also that the nature of the social situation serves to determine whether the interactions are cohesive or disruptive in character.

The influence of role expectations on social behaviour was shown by the simulated prison study by Zimbardo and his

179

colleagues (Haney, Banks and Zimbardo, 1973). Middle-class college students were randomly allocated the roles of guard or prisoner and kept in a functional simulation of a prison environment in which they were expected to act in accord with their assigned roles. Within days violence and rebellion broke out, the guards harassed and intimidated the prisoners and in some instances behaved brutally towards them. The prisoners, on the other hand, showed signs of disintegration and some developed emotional disturbance and had to be released. Only in a few cases were these behaviours attributable to pre-existing personality traits. Rather, it seemed that the stressful social situation, in conjunction with prevailing social stereotypes, became the prime determinants of behaviour within that situation. 'Evil acts are not necessarily the deeds of evil man, but may be attributable to the operation of powerful social forces.'

Both investigations involved contrived situations but they concerned life-like circumstances and the studies lasted weeks rather than the usual hour or so in the laboratory. Moreover, naturalistic observations in schools, hostels, factories, and other institutions, point to similar conclusions (see Kelvin, 1969; Rutter et al, 1979; Bronfenbrenner, 1979). It seems clear that social groups and social expectations, as well as personal predispositions, serve to shape human behaviour. Few of the reports refer specifically to adolescents but it is clear that the general principles apply to all age groups, including teenagers.

POSITIVE OR AMELIORATING INFLUENCES

So far in this chapter the discussion has mainly focused on negative influences, disadvantaging circumstances and stress factors. This bias accurately reflects the clinical and research literature which has had a most regrettable tendency to focus exclusively on the ills of mankind and on all that can and does go wrong. However, it is important to point out that all the evidence shows that even in the most damaging environments many children come through relatively unscathed. It is not that they have been unaffected by their experiences; they may well have been left with susceptibilities and inner insecurities of various kinds. But there is still the world of difference between those individuals who become ordinary reasonably well adjusted people in spite of chronic stress and disadvantage and those who become delinquent, mentally ill, or educationally retarded. So far not much is known on the reasons why some young people appear relatively invulnerable but there are pointers to the importance of *positive* influences on development and of ameliorating or compensating factors (see Rutter, 1979f). It may well be that an increased understanding of why some children are *not* damaged by deprivation would provide a much needed potential for effective prevention of psychosocial disorders in adolescence. Here it is possible only to indicate what seem to be the slender leads pointing to the avenues worth further exploration.

Firstly, the interactions between stresses appear crucial. Surprisingly, it appears that the presence of one chronic stress provides *no* increase in the risk of psychiatric disorder. On the other hand, when two or more stresses occur together the risk goes up four-fold and more. In other words, stresses potentiate each other so that the combination of chronic stresses provides very much more than a summation of the separate stresses considered singly. The implication is that it may be of considerable value to eliminate some stresses even if other stresses remain. Secondly, at least with some aspects of development, environmental traumata are most damaging to those individuals who are genetically vulnerable. That means that the presence of a genetic predisposition makes it more important, not less so, to do everything possible to improve environmental circumstances. Thirdly, there are marked individual differences with respect to both sex and temperament in how children respond to deprivation or disadvantage. While we have only a very limited understanding of *how* these individual differences exert their influences, it seems that one effect is their shaping of other people's responses to the children. Accordingly their impact is potentially modifiable.

Fourthly, as discussed above, it is clear that schools can do much to foster good behaviour and attainments. While they cannot be expected to compensate for lacks at home or for deficiencies in society as a whole, they can constitute a force for the good in a disadvantaging environment. Fifthly, there are suggestions that high self-esteem and a sense of achievement may constitute a protective factor. If children can be helped to develop a concept of personal worth through their successes and their acquisition of competence and through a focus on that which they do well rather than on the areas of failure, this may well help them cope better with the difficulties they face. Sixthly, the scope of opportunities open to young people is likely to play a part in their ability to weather later difficulties. One of the striking features of the later careers of youngsters from unhappy, deprived, and disadvantaged homes is that they tend to marry young, to have babies early, and to live with someone from a similarly deprived background. Good evidence is lacking but the indications are that those who make the best ultimate adjustment in spite of an unpromising start tend to manage to avoid a teenage pregnancy, continue longer in education, and marry someone from a more favoured background. Obviously many factors are operative here and these include individual differences in motivation and temperament. But also a postponement of marriage and child-bearing allows the widening of horizons implicit in further education or vocational training, increases the likelihood of making a marriage when the personality is more mature and stable, and broadens the choice of marriage partners and life opportunities.

Seventhly, within the family there is evidence of the protective effect of both strict parental supervision and also of the maintenance of one good relationship throughout periods of discord and disharmony. It appears that such a relationship can exercise a quite substantial protective effect although it remains rather uncertain whether relationships outside the immediate family are as effective as those within the home. Lastly, although little studied up to now, there are pointers to the importance of learned coping skills. Children are not passive recipients of stress; rather they are active participants in the environment and how they respond to and cope with the hazards they face will make a difference to the effects of those stresses.

The fragmentary evidence which underlies these suggestions has been summarized by Rutter (1979f). It is obvious that we are nowhere near the stage when any kind of overall conclusions can be drawn but what is clear is that the phenomenon of resilience under stress is a real one and that a better understanding of what factors are protective in these circumstances and how they operate would have important implications for the planning of services.

INTERVENTIONS

The literature on preventive, therapeutic, and legal interventions to deal with problems experienced or exhibited by adolescents is large. As several good reviews of most of the relevant empirical studies have been published fairly recently, only a very brief summary of the main findings will be given here.

Judicial responses to delinquency

In spite of a substantial body of research, there is very little indication that any of the various judicial responses to delinquency have any significant effect in reducing the likelihood of further offending. Indeed, the evidence from West and Farrington's (1973) longitudinal study of working-class boys in London strongly suggests that a court appearance *increases* the likelihood of continuing delinquent acts (Farrington, 1977). Youths with similar self-reported delinquency scores at age 14 years were compared with respect to their scores at age 18 according to whether or not they had received a guilty finding in court. The average scores of the boys with a guilty finding increased from 59·5 to 69·3 over the four years, whereas the average score of those not appearing in court fell from 59·4 to 51·3. This contrast could not be accounted for in terms of differences in family background between the two groups. The strong implication is that a court appearance increases the likelihood that delinquency will intensify, but the mechanism by which this occurs remains uncertain. One effect of the court appearance seems to be an increased hostility to the police and it may be that this in turn leads to more delinquent behaviour. It also appears that the public labelling as a delinquent makes a boy more willing to admit delinquent acts— perhaps because he has come to see himself as a delinquent now that he has been formally identified as such, with the result that delinquency becomes more acceptable as a form of behaviour.

Whatever the explanation it seems that court appearances may sometimes have a counter-productive effect.

It is against that background that the studies of different forms of judicial response to delinquency must be considered. Both with juveniles and with adults different types of sentences all seem to have much the same results (Brody, 1976; Clarke and Cornish, 1978). Most research has been concerned with varieties of residential treatment (see Cornish and Clarke, 1975; Clarke and Cornish, 1978) and the findings here have been fairly consistently negative in showing no overall advantage of any particular type of regime (authoritarian or permissive; therapeutic community vs paternalistic control; etc.) as measured in terms of further offending during the years after release from the institution. On the other hand, it is clear that it would be wrong to conclude either that residential care is without effect or that it does not matter what sort of approach is used in the institution.

In the first place, there is good evidence that institutional environments *do* have an impact on the boys' behaviour while they remain in the institution, even though there may be less effect on subsequent rates of reconviction. For example, Sinclair (1971) showed that rates of absconding and offending by boys in probation hostels varied greatly between hostels. Failure rates were lowest in hostels where the warden related closely to the boys in his charge, was strict about the boys keeping to the rules, and was in agreement with his wife about the way the hostel should be run. The wardens who were harsh or lax or emotionally distant or in disagreement with their wives over discipline tended to have high drop-out rates from their hostels. However, it should be noted that the failure rates were characteristic of wardens, not of hostels. The differences between successive wardens in the same hostel were as wide as those between wardens in different hostels. Clarke and Martin (1971) have shown similarly marked differences between approved schools in rates of absconding and Tutt (1976) has shown the same with respect to community homes with education on the premises. Absconding correlates with later reconvictions and it appears that 'acting out' problems by absconding is not generally therapeutic but merely provides the boys with fresh opportunities to commit delinquent acts and to further establish delinquent patterns of response (Sinclair and Clarke, 1973). Dunlop (1975) found that approved schools which placed an emphasis on responsible behaviour and on trade training tended to have particularly low reconviction rates. We may conclude that the characteristics of residential institutions do matter, but the crucial features do not coincide with theoretically derived styles of regime.

Secondly, there is some tentative evidence that different types of offender respond differently to contrasting therapeutic regimes (Gibbens, 1977). For example, in one large scale project 'amenable' institutionalized delinquents characterized as bright, verbal, anxious, aware of their problems, and showing insight, responded better to individual counselling than to the standard authoritarian regime but the 'non-amenables' actually did worse with this form of treatment. Other studies suggest that the immature youths who lack neurotic features may respond better to a more directive, paternalistic, disciplined approach; and that insight-oriented counselling may be harmful. The evidence is far too fragmentary for any firm conclusions but there is a suggestion that the negative findings from so many studies may be due in part to the same treatment regime making some types of delinquent boys better and other types worse. Certainly, this possibility warrants further exploration.

Thirdly, it is relevant that outcome studies of institutionalized delinquents are assessing their behaviour in an environment which is quite different from that they experienced during their residential care (Clarke and Cornish, 1978). This would not matter if the 'treatment' was being applied to some personal disorder which was independent of environmental circumstances but clearly that is not the case. Although obviously there are consistencies in the ways individuals behave, nevertheless there are also differences according to situation. Thus, in a long-term follow-up of Borstal boys Gibbens and Prince (1965) found that aggressive independently-minded youths often resented supervision and improved when it stopped; conversely, passive inadequate boys responded well only to firm labour. The dilemma is that residential treatments usually have little chance of influencing the home environment so that frequently the youths are returning to the same adverse environment from which they entered the institution. Community interventions, on the other hand, although concerned with the home environment, often lack the power to bring about much change in it.

Behavioural treatments for delinquents

An alternative approach to delinquent behaviour has been to apply systematically behavioural principles (derived from social learning theory and operant conditioning) either in the person's own home or in some form of institution. The results so far are encouraging but the evaluations are not yet conclusive and many questions remain (Davidson and Seidman, 1974; Braukman and Fixsen, 1977; Yule, 1978). Patterson and his colleagues have developed systematic methods for training parents of aggressive children. Follow-up studies comparing treated families with those on a waiting list or given just general discussions showed a significantly greater reduction of deviant behaviours in the treated group (Patterson, 1974). The results are certainly impressive and there is no doubt that useful therapeutic techniques have been devised. However, the control groups were far from ideal and rather a lot of subjects were lost from the follow-up (see Kent, 1976 and Reid and Patterson, 1976, for a discussion of these and other methodological points); less success was achieved with stealing (Reid and Hendricks, 1973); and less intensive interventions based on the same approach have proved not so effective (Ferber et al, 1974). Moreover, the treatment methods require a high degree of parental cooperation which will not always be forthcoming.

Wolf, Phillips and Fixsen (1975) have applied behaviour modification methods within community-based, family style group homes for adolescent delinquents or pre-delinquents—the 'Achievement Place' programme. The boys are thought to lack appropriate social skills and the goal:

> is to establish through reinforcement, modelling and inter-
> action, the important behavioural competencies in social
> (including interpersonal relationship skills), academic, pre-
> vocational and self-care skills that the youths have not
> acquired.

The whole house is run on token economy lines, with a self-government system and comprehensive behavioural skills training. There is an emphasis on problem-solving techniques and on the encouragement of desirable behaviours rather than the suppression of deviant behaviours. The Achievement Place model demonstrates that behavioural techniques can be used flexibly and imaginatively within a group home for delinquents and that improvements in social skills and self-control can be achieved (see Davidson and Seidman, 1974). Boys treated in this way had a better outcome than those admitted to a traditional reformatory (Wolf et al, 1975), but so far there has not been a systematic evaluation with random allocation to treatments.

Behavioural methods of treatment for delinquents both within and without institutions appear promising but it is too early to know how much can be achieved by this approach. Moreover, as Yule (1978) has pointed out, these approaches share the problems of *generalization* and *maintenance* of change evident in studies of custodial and other judicial responses to delinquency. It is clear that adolescents' behaviour is more situation-specific than once believed and unless generalization of effects is deliberately planned for, it is unlikely to occur spontaneously. This will usually necessitate interventions in the home and the school with an emphasis on treatment in the natural environment. Also, greater understanding is needed of the mechanisms involved in the maintenance of change. It seems likely that there will have to be a focus on the development of self-control and of social coping skills rather than just the elimination of undesired behaviours.

Community interventions to deal with delinquency
There has been a shift over recent years from seeing community interventions in terms of personal counselling on an individual basis to approaches which involve groups in the community and community activities as a whole. This has come about in part because the evaluations of personal counselling as a means of either preventing or treating delinquency have been consistent in showing the *in*effectiveness of this therapeutic approach. One of the first systematic studies was that by Powers and Witmer (1951) of the Cambridge-Somerville Youth Study. The aim was

to provide boys from a high delinquency area with a close intimate friendship with a counsellor in order to prevent delinquency. Boys were randomly assigned to treatment and control groups and follow-up showed similar delinquency rates in both. For a variety of reasons there was a high turnover of counsellors and less frequent contact than intended but it is unlikely that the programme failed just for that reason as several subsequent attempts to prevent delinquency by similar means have also been largely unsuccessful (Tait and Hodges, 1972; Craig and Furst, 1965; Meyer et al, 1965).

More recently, there have been several attempts to use mental health programmes in schools to prevent problem behaviour and delinquency (e.g. Gildea et al, 1967; Kellam et al, 1976) but follow-ups have shown no gains compared with control groups. On the other hand, Rose and Marshall (1974) showed that school counselling and social work were effective in reducing delinquency in the experimental schools studied. Unlike the other programmes, the main emphasis was on providing focused help for individual children with current problems rather than a preventive service for all but whether this was a crucial difference leading to success is unknown.

In recent years the concept of 'intermediate treatment' has gained ground (DHSS, 1973). The term does not describe a well delineated treatment method but rather encompasses a variety of interventions with individuals and groups in the community. The approaches have so far been subject to little systematic evaluation and it is not known how much can be achieved in these ways.

The Kent Family Placement Project (Hazel, 1977 and 1978) has sought to develop time-limited family fostering as an alternative to residential placement for delinquent boys and out of control girls. Foster parents are provided with a salary (rather than the usual nominal fee) and there is extensive support through group meetings. No systematic comparison with a control group has been undertaken but the initial results seem encouraging.

There has been very little research into the value of improving leisure opportunities for adolescents (in the hope of countering delinquency by providing alternatives to hanging around street corners with a tough group or gang) and what little evidence there is is inconclusive (Clarke, 1978). Nevertheless, one study reported a decrease in offending in an area where a youth club was established, whereas rates continued to rise in comparable areas lacking this facility (Brown and Dodson, 1959). Also, epidemiological data for an English city showed a striking coincidence between areas lacking recreational facilities and youth clubs and areas with high rates of juvenile delinquency (Central Policy Review Staff, 1978). The same document also provides three examples of 'success stories' in which community-wide policies have been associated with reductions in delinquency rates. Other reports (see Clarke, 1978) have also suggested the value of a contractual approach in which financial support for youth activities is given in exchange for a reduction in vandalism.

The Wincroft Youth Project for detached youth in a slum area of Manchester (Smith, Farrant and Marchant, 1972) represents one of the most ambitious and far reaching attempts at community intervention as a means of reducing delinquency. This consisted of a social work programme with an emphasis on the extensive use of volunteers, on first contacting the delinquent boys on their own territory in a coffee bar setting, and on combining group work with individual casework as relationships developed. The 54 boys in the programme were chosen on the basis of their delinquency and/or their delinquency proneness as judged from scores on the Bristol Social Adjustment Guides. Controls were chosen from a comparable socially deprived area and were matched on the selection criteria; they were also comparable in family circumstances. Fewer project boys than controls were convicted during the follow-up period (37 per cent vs 55 per cent at the first follow-up and 50 per cent vs 62 per cent a year later). Self-report data confirmed that there was more delinquency and more serious delinquency in the controls; however, the groups did not differ with respect to their scores on the Jesness inventory, on employment or on relationships with parents. The outcome was best for those not already delinquent at the outset and with relatively low maladjustment scores. The benefits were therefore both quite modest and most evident with the least disturbed boys. Nevertheless, the results are encouraging in suggesting that community interventions may be of some value.

Treatment for psychiatric disorders in adolescents

There is a large literature on methods of treating psychiatric disorders in children and adolescents but few of the techniques have been really satisfactorily evaluated (see Robins, 1973; Kolvin, 1973). Perhaps the most extensive body of research concerns the use of drugs (see Shaffer, 1977; Barkley, 1977; Klein and Gittelman-Klein, 1978). It is well established that stimulants, such as methylphenidate, have a short-term beneficial effect on children who present with poor attention, overactivity, and disruptiveness in class. However, there is no evidence that the drugs have any impact on the long-term social, psychological, or academic adjustment of the children, and the value of stimulants in treating the more persistent disorders of adolescence remains quite uncertain. In view of the frequency of mood disturbances during adolescence it might be expected that anti-depressants would be particularly useful for this age group. This may be the case, as there are positive findings from the few well-controlled studies undertaken so far, but up to now their use has been so little investigated that no definitive conclusions are possible. The major tranquillizers have been shown to be of some value in the treatment of some of the more severe disorders of behaviour but it is with schizophrenic conditions that they are of most value.

Behavioural techniques have been equally widely studied although, as with drugs, the investigations have concerned younger children much more than they have adolescents (see Gelfand and Hartmann, 1968; Yule, 1977). Accordingly, it remains rather uncertain how far the modifications of teacher-child interaction in the classroom which appear so effective in younger children are also of benefit with teenagers. Nevertheless, there are reasonable indications that behavioural methods are of value at least with specific phobias, with school refusal, and with aggressive behaviour in the home. How far they are *superior* to other treatments is less certain and little is known on the long-term benefits with chronic disorders.

Social casework methods have been evaluated only to a limited extent (see Sussenwein, 1977). It has been clear that when goals and methods have lacked focus and direction there have been few if any benefits. On the other hand, there is evidence that social work can be effective when well undertaken. One of the few investigations to compare different varieties of casework was Reid and Shyne's (1969) systematic comparison of short-term focused methods and an open-ended approach with 120 families presenting difficulties in marital or parent–child relationships. The short-term group showed a better outcome in terms of various aspects of personal and family functioning; examination of the course of therapy suggested that the greater benefits of the brief approach lay in its better definition of goals and better treatment focus.

There have been several systematic controlled evaluations of group counselling or group psychotherapy with variable but mainly positive results, the benefits tending to be more marked at follow-up than immediately after treatment (Robins, 1973). Little progress has been made in the assessment of individual psychotherapy with adolescents and there is as yet no adequate basis from which to assess its efficacy. Conjoint family therapy has been increasingly used during the last decade for a wide variety of clinical problems. Satisfactory evaluative studies have been very few (see Lask, 1979; Wells and Dezen, 1978) but there are some indications of its efficacy—especially with short-term behaviourally-orientated approaches dealing with maladaptive interaction patterns in the families of delinquent teenagers (Alexander and Parsons, 1973). In view of the frequency with which adolescent disorders persisting from childhood are associated with parental discord and disharmony, the results of marital therapy are perhaps also relevant to the treatment of teenage difficulties. Again, much of the evaluative research has been rather unsatisfactory (Gurman, 1973) but Crowe's (1978) systematic and sound study does show the efficacy of well planned marital therapy and particularly of directive behaviourally-oriented marital approaches, with the benefits maintained over an eighteen-months follow-up.

Hersov and Bentovim (1977) have described the use of psychiatric inpatient units and day hospitals but there are no adequate data on their efficacy in the case of adolescents (Capes, 1973).

Because adolescent disorders may have their roots in early

childhood it is necessary also to consider whether there is any evidence that preventive counselling undertaken then can be of benefit. Little evidence is available but two studies (Cullen, 1976; Gutelius et al, 1977) suggest that the counselling of parents on child-rearing techniques as part of routine child health supervision may have benefits, at least in the short-term. Further investigations with random assignments to treatment are needed to evaluate these approaches more rigorously.

This very brief summary of evaluations of treatments for psychiatric disorders in adolescents indicates the rather patchy state of knowledge but also it is evident that some techniques of limited effectiveness are available. While they do not provide anything like satisfactory answers to the range of psychiatric disorders presenting in adolescence, they do provide something of immediate value and more importantly they give leads on avenues of therapeutic intervention which are worth exploring and developing.

CONCLUSIONS

The synoptic overview in this chapter of some of the main influences which affect adolescent behaviour has emphasised that these include ecological and situational forces on group behaviour as well as factors which determine individual predispositions and vulnerabilities. It was also evident from the research findings surveyed in the first chapter that, to a considerable extent, adolescent behaviour constitutes a continuation of patterns established in earlier childhood. Hence, in this chapter, it has been necessary to extend the discussion of influences to those which have their initial impact during the pre-adolescent years. Similarly in the next chapter the consideration of historical changes in society and in the family which carry implications for adolescents will include features which impinge on younger children as well as to those which have a direct effect on teenagers.

4

Changes in society
and the family

Possible changes in adolescent behaviours, attitudes, and problems need to be viewed against the backcloth of the many changes taking place in society generally, and more especially in family roles and circumstances. This is necessary to determine how far changes in adolescence are simply part of a broader pattern of historical change which is affecting all age groups similarly, and how far the changes in adolescence are different and specific to that age group. For that reason, this chapter unlike others is mainly concerned with younger children or with adults. Adolescence constitutes the link between, with teenagers carrying the strengths or scars established in childhood and looking forward to the adult world but not quite part of either. As we have seen there are a variety of special features characteristic of adolescence. However, there are also continuities with both earlier and later stages of development so that changes in society and in the family are likely to have implications for adolescence and for the identification of factors that need to be taken into account in planning services. The changes are most conveniently discussed under five headings: (a) changes in life expectancy; (b) changing patterns of family building; (c) changing expectations and circumstances of women; (d) changing patterns of married life; (e) other changes in society.

CHANGES IN LIFE EXPECTANCY

Mortality and morbidity
Throughout much of the world better living conditions and better medical care during the last hundred years have been associated with major improvements in life expectancy. Far fewer people are dying in childhood or in early adult life and far

Changes in society and the family

more are reaching old age. Thus, in England and Wales the total infant mortality in the first year of life has fallen from 117·1 per 1000 live births during 1906–10, to 29·7 in 1951, and to 13·8 in 1977 (Court, 1976; Office of Population Censuses and Surveys, 1979). The changes in other industrialized countries have followed a similar pattern but in many the improvements have been greater so that relatively speaking both the U.K. and the U.S.A. have fallen somewhat behind the rest of the developed nations. Countries such as France and Japan which had markedly worse infantile mortality rates in 1951 (over 50 in both cases) now have substantially better ones.

Death rates during middle childhood have also improved markedly. For example, for British children aged five-to-nine years it has fallen from 3·74 in 1901–05, to 0·31 in 1974, and for the 10 to 14 year age group from 2·19 to 0·28 over the same time period, and for the 15- to 19-year age group from 3·11 to 0·64. In each case the greatest improvements took place prior to 1955, and especially during the 1945–55 decade, but there have been some gains since then.

Similar changes have taken place in the death rates for young adults. For example, in the age group 20 to 24 years the death rate for women fell from 2·25 in 1938 to 0·42 in 1977. The life expectancy at birth for females has risen from 42 years in 1851 to 49 years in 1901, to 71·2 years in 1951, and to 74·9 years in 1971 (Finer, 1974). For those who live to age five years the increases are less striking but they are still substantial—from an expectation for girls of living to 55 years in 1851, to 62 years in 1901, to 73·5 years in 1951, and to 76·2 years in 1971. The changes in life expectancy from middle-age onwards have been very small (Central Statistical Office, 1978). It is not that the elderly are living much longer but rather that a much higher proportion of the population survives to become long-lived.

It is not only that mortality rates have fallen steadily throughout this century; also the health and development of children has improved. Over the last 70 years children aged five to seven years in average economic circumstances have gained in height by one to two centimetres each decade and at ages 10 to 14 years they have gained some two to three centimetres each decade (Court

1976). Comparisons between the Isle of Wight studies in the 1960s (Rutter, Tizard and Whitmore, 1970) and Burt's surveys in the 1920s (Burt, 1937) also document the major improvements in children's health. Conditions such as rickets and tuberculosis have been almost eliminated in the U.K. and general standards of nutrition have much improved.

In parallel with children's improving nutritional status in the western world there has been a definite trend towards accelerated maturation in height and weight in both boys and girls during the last 100 years (Tanner, 1970). The result has been that full growth is now achieved at a much earlier age than in past centuries (i.e. 18 or 19 years rather than 25 years or so). Similar trends have occurred with respect to sexual maturation so that it has been estimated that the menarche has been advanced by about four months per decade since 1850 in western Europe, although the trend may well now have halted. This tendency towards earlier puberty may have played some part in the trend towards earlier sexual activity among adolescents (see chapter 2). However, the observation that young people today are reaching physical maturation considerably earlier than in previous generations may also have rather different implications. The increasingly advanced maturation has happened to coincide with a progressive extension of education to later and later ages. The consequence of these two contrasting processes has been an increasing *potential* clash between the necessity for children to remain economically dependent on their parents and their ability and need to be psychologically independent. It is not known how far this has in fact occurred nor whether it has actually led to increasing family tensions in late adolescence but the possibility exists. There is a need to help young people gain emotional maturity and social independence while still in full-time education, and to help parents appreciate and adapt to the changing needs and growing responsibilities of their adolescent children as they reach adulthood while still at home studying.

Hospital admissions

It might be expected that the major improvements in health would have meant that fewer children are being admitted to hospital today than in days gone by. In fact this has not happened. Indeed, Douglas (1975) found that first born children of mothers aged 23 years or less in the 1964–73 generation were *twice* as likely to have been admitted to hospital in the first four years as those in the 1946–50 generation. Moreover, they were nearly *three* times as likely to have had multiple admissions. It was only in the proportion with long admissions (more than a week) that there had been a slight reduction over the last 20 years. This increase in recurrent admissions to hospital may well have led to some worsening of the risk of emotional and behavioural disturbance in later childhood and adolescence. As both Douglas (1975) and Quinton and Rutter (1976) found that repeated hospital admissions are associated with an increased risk of later disturbance or disorder, the evidence that hospital admissions are becoming more frequent is a cause for concern. This is especially so as many admissions are largely for social reasons (Wynne and Hull, 1977) and it is children from disadvantaged and discordant homes who are most at risk (Quinton and Rutter, 1976).

Attitudes to childhood

It is probable that the great reduction in infantile mortality and the increased likelihood of children surviving to reach adulthood will have had a major effect on people's attitudes to children. In the nineteenth century most parents produced children with the expectation that at least one of them would die. That is no longer the case today. We do not know what effect this has had on people's attitudes to children, but certainly the changes in infantile mortality have been accompanied by marked alterations in concepts of childhood. A hundred years ago there was very little realization that childhood was a separate state; children tended to be seen as just little adults who lacked stature and intelligence but who were without special needs otherwise (Ariès, 1962). There was no appreciation that events and happenings during the early years might have a special importance, and certainly no recognition that the ways parents talked, played, and did things with their children, might have a major influence on their development. This has all changed during the course of the last hundred years or so. In the mid-nineteenth century legislation was first introduced to judge the fitness of children to enter employment; the Education Acts of 1870 and 1880 first made schooling compulsory; school clinics and the school psychological service began to be established soon after the turn of the century; a few years after that paediatrics became recognized as a speciality with its own body of knowledge; child guidance clinics were first set up in the 1920s and 1930s; and the wave of legislation following the Beveridge Report of 1942 extended the special provision for children (see Court, 1976). Nevertheless, general recognition of the importance of psychological experiences in childhood took longer to come, and it was only following Bowlby's (1951) report to the World Health Organization that this became widely accepted. Whether or not there is any causal connection between them, it appears that as the physical hazards of childrearing have lessened so we have come to have a greater appreciation of children's psychosocial needs.

Perinatal hazards and later handicap

It is well known that serious adversities experienced during the period of foetal development and during the birth process itself may lead to brain damage and therefore to cerebral palsy and/or mental retardation (see Birch and Gussow, 1970; Rutter and Madge, 1976). Accordingly, it might be expected that the great reduction in infantile mortality could well be followed by comparable improvements in the incidence of cerebral palsy and mental retardation and hence by reduced proportions of seriously handicapped adolescents. As we shall see, there is some uncertainty as to whether this has in fact happened, but it is not self-evident whether the neonatal improvements should have made things better or worse with respect to resultant handicaps. In so far as improved obstetric and neonatal care leads to a reduction in the biological hazards during the age period it should have benefits. But, of course, it could be that for every child now normal who has been saved from cerebral palsy or mental handicap, there is another child who would have died but who now survives with brain damage. Moreover, better medical care and better social conditions during middle childhood may mean that seriously handicapped children who would have died of infections in an earlier era are now living on to reach adult life. This has meant, for example, that compared with earlier generations many more children with Down's syndrome are now surviving to adolescence (Carter, 1959).

It has proved quite difficult to assess the net effect of these various competing tendencies. Tizard (1964) compared the prevalence of severe mental retardation in Middlesex in 1960 with that found by E. O. Lewis (1929) in the 1920s for urban ones in England and Wales. The rates in the two surveys were closely comparable (3·71 per 1000 vs 3·45) but, if anything, the prevalence of retardation in the 7- to 14-year age group had fallen marginally. Other recent epidemiological studies have given figures closely similar to Tizard's (Kushlick and Blunden, 1974). In that more retarded children were living longer it was inferred that the incidence at birth of conditions associated with mental retardation had probably fallen. Scandinavian surveys suggest that the incidence of cerebral palsy has dropped markedly in recent years especially for diplegia (Hagberg et al, 1973 and 1975) and it has been thought that this has been a result of the improved obstetric and neonatal care which has led to the great fall in infantile mortality. Studies in the U.K. (Alberman, 1979) do not indicate any substantial drop in the rate of cerebral palsy but direct comparisons across time periods are limited by differing samples and methods. High quality intensive care for very small babies has meant that many infants who would have died in previous generations are now surviving. Follow-up studies show that these survivors have a gratifyingly low rate of serious mental and physical handicaps (Stewart, 1977) but too few children have been followed for long enough to assess the true level of lesser degrees of cognitive and psychiatric disability present in later childhood and adolescence. Altogether, we may conclude that the improvements in perinatal care are most unlikely to have increased the rates of disability in adolescence. There are some indications that they may have already somewhat reduced the incidence of handicap and certainly this should be achieved in the near future. On the other hand, the increasing survival of handicapped children may mean that there will be less change in the prevalence of handicapped adolescents.

Orphans

The reduced death rates in early adult life have meant that fewer children now are being orphaned by the death of their parents than was the case at the turn of the century (Finer, 1974). However, most of the changes in this respect took place some years ago and there has been little alteration in recent years in the number of children whose parents die when they are young. Obviously, the reduction in the number of children orphaned is a good thing but unfortunately it has not meant that fewer children are experiencing broken homes or that fewer are being brought up in a single parent household. The fall in parent deaths has been more than compensated for by the great increase in parental divorces. It is just that the pattern of marriage breakdown has altered. In the early part of this century death broke more marriages in the younger age groups than divorce; but this ratio has now reversed (Finer, 1974).

There is also another consequence which may not be wholly good. It has been suggested that as more and more people are growing up without experiencing the death of loved ones, so people are failing to acquire the coping mechanisms for dealing with bereavement (Gorer, 1977). The grief rituals of the past seem to be going but it is uncertain how far they have been replaced by anything better.

The extended family and support from kin

Because more people are reaching old age and are remaining physically fit for longer one might suppose that there ought to be more family supports available. More grandparents should be around to help with child care and to provide assistance at times of family crisis and stress. Of course, potentially this is so but in practice it has not generally worked out in this beneficial way. In part, this is because in the U.K. and the U.S.A., housing policies and patterns of employment have often separated the generations and so have removed the sources of kin support. Increased geographical mobility, too, has meant that young people often move so far away from their parents that when children are born the grandparents are too distant to offer much practical support.

A further factor, however, is the fact that more women are going out to work (see below), with the result that many grandmothers have their own job outside the home and are not available to help out with child care in the way they were in generations past.

There is another consequence of society including more old people. Better social conditions and better medical care have meant that more physically and mentally *handicapped* old people are living on unable to fend for themselves. Pneumonia is no longer carrying off the chronic sick in the way that it used to. The consequence is that increasingly families are facing greater burdens as a result of the need to look after ailing and aged grandparents and great grandparents, or they are having to leave the old people to fend for themselves, or go into an institution. The latter course may relieve the family burden but perhaps at the price of increasing the load on the family conscience or gradually eroding the values placed on human life and family ties. The figures show that the proportion of households with someone over retirement age living on their own more than doubled between 1961 and 1976 and the number of residents in old people's homes provided by local authorities increased by almost as much over the same time period (Central Statistical Office, 1978). These, and other, figures have led many people to become greatly concerned about the weakening of family ties.

However, it is far from certain that this is in fact happening (Quinton, 1979). In the first place, it is clear that most families with dependent children are still in close contact with the grandparents. Better public transport and the greater availability of telephones have made regular communication much easier even when the generations are living apart. Secondly, it is not self-evident that it is in everyone's interest for the generations to live altogether with the overcrowding and family tensions that this sometimes entails. Even when housing policies allow multi-generation homes it seems that people are choosing not to take up that opportunity. Many elderly people remain full of energy even though past the age of retirement and they strongly resist being expected to live with their children. Perhaps it may be preferable to maintain close ties and support without actually living under the same roof. Thirdly, the historical trends in family size (see below) have altered the situation in two important respects. When most families had four or five children there was a wider choice of offspring with whom the grandparents might live. Out of the four or five sons and daughters there was a reasonable chance that one would get on sufficiently well with their elderly parent and be in suitable accommodation to have them live with them. Now that families tend to have only one or two children the choice is reduced and the pressures are likely to feel greater and less acceptable. Conversely, however, it also means that the marked drop in the number of old people sharing their son's or daughter's home has not resulted in the same drop in the proportion of children being brought up with grandparents. Nevertheless, there has been a substantial reduction in the U.K. since 1961 in the number of young married couples living with their parents (Central Statistical Office, 1978).

CHANGING PATTERNS OF FAMILY BUILDING

Family size

The annual fertility rate for women aged 15 to 44 years was 114·9 per 1000 women in 1901; there was a brief temporary sharp rise just after the First World War but otherwise there was a steady fall until the mid-1930s, when it reached a low of 59; the fertility rate then rose slightly over the next 20 years to reach 71·6 in 1951; there was then a progressive rise to a peak of 93·0 in 1964; and since then a steady fall once more to a trough of 58·7 in 1977 and a minimal rise to 60·6 in 1978 (Central Statistical Office 1972 and 1978; Court, 1976; Office of Population Censuses and Surveys, 1979).[1] This marked fall in fertility rate over the last 15 years has been apparent in almost all major western European countries and has been even more marked in the U.S.A.

As a result of this recent fall in birth rate there has been a progressive reduction in the number of children per family so that the average number of births per woman now stands at less than two. This *ought* to have largely positive consequences. Poverty has been strongly associated with large family size and the need to support

[1] The precise figures for each year vary slightly between these different sources but they agree on the overall pattern of trends.

201

a large number of children (see Rutter and Madge, 1976). Thus, Abel Smith and Townsend (1965) showed that in 1953-4 the poverty rate in the U.K. was nearly *ten* times as great for families with four or more children as for families with just one child. Of families with a father in full-time work only 8 per cent of those with two or three children lived in overcrowded accommodation whereas one-third of those with at least four children did so. As the pattern has moved from a mode of three or four children to a mode of just two there *should* be an accompanying reduction in the proportion of children brought up in conditions of poverty and overcrowding. Moreover, there ought to be a similar reduction in those experiencing homelessness as this, too, is associated with large family size (see Rutter and Madge, 1976). In that these economic and housing disadvantages are associated with higher rates of problems of various sorts in childhood and adolescence, and as large family size is quite strongly associated with both reading difficulties and delinquency, it would seem that there ought to be a resulting decrease in adolescent disorders. In fact, this has not happened, as already discussed. We consider possible explanations later in this chapter.

Patterns of child bearing

Alongside this recent reduction in family size there has been an increasing tendency to delay child bearing for several years after marriage (Central Statistical Office, 1978; Court, 1976; Leete, 1979). In part this is a result of a very marked reduction in the number of births conceived premaritally—a fall of a third between 1966 and 1975 (Thompson, 1976). But this is far from the whole story as there has also been a lesser reduction in the number of postmaritally conceived first births in the early years of marriage. Thus, in spite of an increasing number of women marrying younger over the last dozen years there has been a substantial fall in rates of first births conceived in marriage for all age groups (Leete, 1979). It is clear that since the mid-'60s there has been a progressive tendency for couples to wait longer after marriage before having their first child. Thus, in 1961 for women marrying at ages 20 to 24 years for the first time, less than half were still childless after two years, whereas by 1975 the proportion had risen to three-quarters (Central Statistical Office, 1978). Whether this reflects a change in the choice of time for child bearing or rather whether it simply means that more effective means of contraception are available now is uncertain.

Again, this should have benefits in that potentially it ought to mean that children are more likely to be born to mature parents better able to cope with the task of bringing up children. In view of all that is known about the hazards experienced by children born to teenage mothers (see Shaffer et al, 1978) this ought to be a force for the good and perhaps it will be. But also it raises other issues which may not be wholly beneficial in their effects.

Because more families are being started several years after marriage, more women will have established careers for themselves outside the home. The other possible implications of a greater proportion of working mothers are considered below, but here the point to note is that there may be resulting changes in attitudes to children—of seeing children as an unwanted intrusion into working life rather than as one of the main goals of marriage. Obviously, this is far from a necessary consequence but clearly it is a possibility which could have adverse consequences for the upbringing of children. Certainly, commentators have expressed concern that children may be becoming less valued than in years gone by.

This is a real enough danger, but in fact the evidence suggests that so far this has not happened. Indeed, if anything, the reverse may be the case. For example, the proportion of illegitimate children being adopted has fallen rapidly during the last decade (Central Statistical Office, 1978), and many more single mothers are electing to keep their illegitimate children (Leete, 1978 a and b). This is not because fewer childless couples are wanting to adopt— to the contrary this has shown no sign of dropping. Rather it seems that the stigma of illegitimacy has lessened so that there may be less social pressure on unmarried mothers to marry the father or get the child adopted. However, whatever the reason, it appears that more women are wanting to bring up children even if this means doing so outside marriage.

Whether this is a desirable trend is another matter. At least in the past the outlook for illegitimate children has been much less

Changes in society and the family

good than that for adopted children or for children born to married couples (Crellin et al, 1971). In considerable part, the increased rates of educational and emotional/behavioural problems in illegitimate children seem to be due to the financial and social disadvantages of single parenthood (see Ferri, 1976; Rutter and Madge, 1976). These do not seem to have lessened greatly in recent years and there must be concern about the prospects for illegitimate children who remain with their single mothers. It may also be that single parents find it more difficult to supervise and discipline their children. The National Child Development Study findings (Fogelman, 1978) showed that school attendance was particularly poor among children in households without a father. Interestingly, this poor attendance largely accounted for the children's poor school attainments. Mathematics scores, for example, in children from fatherless households who attended well were average. Certainly, it will be important to take steps to reduce the disadvantages suffered by children in single parent households (Finer, 1974) but also there may be doubts about the desirability of this form of upbringing.

Contraception, abortion and sterilization

Of course, the changes in patterns of child bearing have been the result in large part of the greater use of contraceptive measures and of deliberate family planning. This should have benefits in terms of the birth of fewer unwanted children and hence of fewer rejected and neglected children. The disadvantage experienced by such children are shown by what happens to children born after abortion has been refused (Forssman and Thuse, 1966). A surprisingly high proportion of boys and girls develop satisfactorily in spite of this most unpromising start (Dytrych et al, 1975) but, as one might expect, their rate of problems is increased above that in the general population. Obviously, a reduction in the numbers of unwanted children would be a good thing (preferably by contraception as few people would want abortion to be anything other than a last resort).

Whether this has in fact happened is less certain. As discussed in the last chapter the illegitimacy ratio in both the U.K. and the U.S.A. has risen greatly in recent years (Bronfenbrenner, 1976;

Pearce and Farid, 1977). Of course it cannot be assumed that these children are necessarily unwanted as many of the single mothers keep their children; moreover, it is teenagers and women in their early 20s who are the main source of illegitimate births. On the other hand, studies of families with problems in parenting indicate that young people from severely unhappy stressful homes not infrequently become pregnant as a means of escape from an intolerable home situation (Quinton and Rutter, 1979)— not a good beginning. The fact that illegitimate births have remained particularly high in teenagers suggests that this process may still be operating. It should be added that the proportion of preschool children who are in the care of the local authority has not dropped in recent years indeed it has risen slightly from 3·2 per 1000 in 1961 to 3·8 per 1000 in 1977 (Central Statistical Office, 1978; Office of Population Censuses and Surveys, 1979).

Another possible index of the rates of unwanted and rejected children is the rate of severe physical child abuse. There is no doubt that in recent years people have become much more aware of this distressing phenomenon. Whether or not child abuse has actually become more common, however, seems in doubt (see Smith, 1978). The figures suggest, perhaps, an increase during the 1960s but a decrease in the last few years probably as a result of greater vigilance and earlier action. No dependable conclusion is possible, overall, on whether the proportions of unwanted and rejected children are increasing or decreasing.

The general acceptance of the desirability of family planning has also led to a far greater use of therapeutic abortion. This, too, is designed to reduce the number of unwanted children but there is also the possibility of undesired side-effects in terms of altered attitudes to child bearing and to children. A recent study in England (Kumar and Robson, 1978) showed that primiparous women who have had previous therapeutic abortion appear much more prone to depression during their first pregnancy which results in a live born child than women who have not had a termination (38 per cent vs 8 per cent). Of course that does not mean that abortions should be restricted (the need to reduce unwanted births is great) but it does indicate that having an abortion is not a psychologically neutral event. The implication is that a greater use of counselling at the time of abortion might be helpful in dealing with the guilt and anxieties thereby raised.

Sterilization too has become more widespread. Between the late '60s and early '70s sterilization rates were not only rising steadily but also they were increasingly impinging on quite young couples with comparatively few children soon after the initial decision to have no more (Bone, 1978). Thus, in 1961–5 only 4 per cent of sterilizations concerned couples with two children or less, but in 1971–5, 33 per cent did so. It is estimated now that about a quarter of couples with a wife now aged 30 to 34 years will have been sterilized by the time she has reached 35 years. This is a function of the increase in sterilization being greatest in young couples. It is also apparent that the pattern of sterilization is different in young couples. In those with the wife under 30 years of age, male sterilization outnumbers female sterilization by two-to-one, but in the population as a whole they are roughly equal in number. Whereas these findings apply to a post-adolescent age period it is likely that the pattern reflects some of the changing attitudes to child bearing and to family planning among young people today.

CHANGING ROLES AND EXPECTATIONS OF WOMEN

During the period since the Second World War there have been major changes in the roles and expectations of women and it is likely that these will have had implications for adolescents, both in terms of their own family experiences and in terms of their approach to adult life. The general emancipation of women has almost certainly led them to have greater expectations of marriage and of what they want from marriage. This should have beneficial results in so far as it leads to a richer and fuller family life. As women come to expect more of marriage so also are they likely to contribute more to marriage. But as expectations rise so also is it likely that dissatisfactions will increase if marriages fail to fulfil these expectations. It is relevant in this connection to note that in western societies marriage seems to have a protective effect on men with respect to both their physical and mental health—but it does *not* have the same beneficial effect on women (see Rutter, 1970c).

Another aspect of the emancipation of women is their increasing career needs and expectations. Because child bearing is now usually restricted to a small number of years and because people are living longer, more women are going to have a substantial period of their working life left after their children have grown up. It is reasonable that they have careers outside the home which will enable them to take advantage of the opportunities thereby created. Up to now there have been very substantial and wide-spread sex differentials in wages and salaries with women's earn-ings far below those of men in both the U.K. and the U.S.A. (see Rutter and Madge, 1976; Suter and Miller, 1973). Work oppor-tunities for women have been limited by the sex labelling of jobs and by overt sex discrimination in employment. Also many of the occupational disadvantages are linked with sexual discrimina-tion in educational provision and in attitudes transmitted during schooling. Woman's dissatisfaction with the lower wages generally paid to females and with the worse career expectations open to them is likely to increase and society will need to respond to the needs to remove these disadvantages.

Nevertheless, in the long run, discrimination as such may not prove to be the central issue (Fogarty et al, 1971). Rather there is a need to adapt work opportunities to women's pattern of life, with time off for child bearing and part-time work while children are dependent. Of course, these requirements apply to men as well. *Both* parents need to be involved in the care of their children and fathers, too, need to have flexible working hours to enable them to take time off work to accompany their children to the dentist or to hospital. Similarly it should be possible for either parent to stay home to be with a sick child.

One feature of women's increasing involvement in careers has been the rising proportion of girls continuing in further educa-tion. Thus, the proportion of females among full-time university undergraduates in the U.K. was 25·4 per cent in 1953–4; it rose to 28·3 in 1970–1 and still further to 35·8 in 1976–7 (Central Statistical Office 1972 and 1978). Part-time Open University students have always included a higher proportion of women but

Changes in society and the family

even so the proportion has risen from 34·9 per cent in 1973-4 to 41·5 per cent in 1976-7.

Working mothers

So far as children are concerned the most obvious effect of the changing roles of women has been the steady increase in the proportion of working mothers (General Household Survey Unit, 1978). The number of married women in the labour force in the U.K. has risen from 2·7 million in 1951 to 6·7 million in 1976 (Central Statistical Office, 1978). The main change has been the increasing tendency for women with dependent children to go out to work. Thus, even between 1971 and 1976 the proportion rose from 45 per cent to 53 per cent for those with one dependent child, and from 35 per cent to 44 per cent for those with at least three dependent children. This increase is *not* restricted to low income families although there is evidence of the operation of economic incentives. In the U.K. today about 12 per cent of children under the age of one year and 37 per cent of those aged four years have a working mother (Bone, 1977); the proportion is still higher for those of school age (Davie et al, 1972). In both the U.K. and Denmark there is a similarly high proportion of women in the labour force, but in both countries about two-fifths work part-time (Central Statistical Office, 1978). In fact, in Britain the upward trend during the 1970s in the proportion of children with working mothers has been largely due to an increase in those working part-time, with little change in those working full-time. In France and Germany fewer women work but of those that do the great majority work full-time. The Netherlands stands out as different from most other European countries in the very small proportion of married women with jobs outside the home.

The trend for an increasing proportion of working mothers applies equally to the U.S.A. (Bronfenbrenner, 1976). In 1948 only a quarter of women with school age children were in the labour force, whereas in 1974 half were. As in the U.K., the increase applies to women with children and not to those without dependent offspring. The most recent and most rapid increase has applied to mothers of young children. One-third of all married women with children under six years were working in 1974, a rate three times that in 1948. Mothers of infants were not far behind; 3 out of 10 mothers of children under three years had a job outside the home. Whatever the age of the children, the great majority (two-thirds) of the mothers with jobs were working full-time. These figures apply only to families in which the husband was present. In single parent families the proportions of women in the labour force are much higher still—54 per cent of those with youngsters under six and 45 per cent of those with children under three years, with 80 per cent and 86 per cent respectively working full-time.

The increase in working mothers has been accompanied by parallel changes in the numbers of preschool children in full-time day care. The number of children aged two to four years in maintained schools in England and Wales rose from 203,000 in 1961 to 340,000 in 1976; and those all day with registered child-minders from 48,000 in 1970 to 65,000 in 1976 (Central Statistical Office, 1978). Similarly, in the U.S.A. the number of children enrolled in day-care centres has doubled since 1965.

Professionals concerned with child care have frequently deplored the increasing tendency for mothers to go out to work and have exhorted women to remain at home with their children. However, this plea appears misplaced. In the first place, it seems inevitable that more women will want careers simply because most will have many working years after their children grow up. Many jobs will require women to keep their hand in on a part-time basis and this means more working mothers. Secondly, research findings have been consistent in showing that children over the age of two or three years who have working mothers (less is known about infants) develop just as well as those brought up by mothers who remain housewives tied to the home—provided that the arrangements for the care of the children are equally satisfactory (see Pilling and Pringle, 1978; Rutter, 1979c).

Nevertheless, the findings do not mean that children's upbringing is unaffected by the mother going out to work, nor does it mean that we should be indifferent to the trend for more mothers to take jobs outside the home—as the results for the children depend on both the effects of employment on mothers

Changes in society and the family

and on the ways in which the children's needs are met while the mothers are away from the home.

It appears that when the mother goes out to work, fathers tend to take a more active role in family life, children tend to take on more household responsibilities, and it is more likely that someone outside the family will be involved in child care (Hoffman, 1974). This may affect children's perceptions of sex roles but there is no evidence that the differences result in damage or disorder. Indeed, one study (Stacey et al, 1970) found that children who were used to being looked after by people other than their parents were *less* likely than other children to be upset by hospital admission. It seems that carefully graded happy separations in a family environment may actually have a beneficial *protective* effect—but the circumstances and the quality of care provided during the separation are likely to be crucial.

A further point with respect to working mothers is that the consequences for the child depend not only on the child's response but also on what having a job means to the mother. Yarrow et al (1962) found that child rearing provided most difficulties for women who wanted to work but yet remained at home out of a sense of duty. Brown and Harris (1978) found that the period when there were several preschool children at home was a particularly stressful one for working-class women in the inner city and that for some of them going out to work served as a protection against depression. Clearly, what remaining at home or having a job does for the mother's mental state is likely to make a big difference to the children (Hoffman, 1974). It is likely to be more important to have a satisfied happy mother than to have a mother at home all day. Whether maternal employment is a good thing for the family depends very much on whether the mother wants to work. Presumably, too, it matters whether the job proves to be a satisfying one and not so tiring as to lead to role strain or conflict. Many mothers of young children prefer part-time work, and stress and fatigue may be the result if full-time employment is the only alternative which is available.

Of course, the conclusion that having a working mother does not harm, and in some circumstances may even benefit, the children is highly dependent on the quality of care provided during the day while the mother is out (see Pilling and Pringle, 1978; Rutter 1979c). It is not enough that the child's physical needs be met, there must also be good opportunities for play and conversation, as the characteristics of adult–child interaction will influence the child's development. Moreover, there must be consistency in caretakers—children suffer from 'pillar to post' arrangements which do not enable the child to develop stable attachments to those who look after him. These are not very demanding criteria but frequently they are not met. Many children looked after by childminders spend a low level, under-stimulated day in cramped surroundings; some do not get the love and attention they need; and some experience frequent changes of minder (Mayall and Petrie, 1977). Obviously, this is not an acceptable situation.

A concern regarding the often poor quality care provided by informal arrangements has led to pressure for more day centres to be provided by the State (Tizard et al, 1976). At one time it was feared that day-care would lead children to be less attached to their parents. However, several studies (see Pilling and Pringle, 1978; Belsky and Steinberg, 1979; and Rutter, 1979c) have shown that this does not usually happen. Moreover, although they differ somewhat in their behaviour, most children in day care appear generally well adjusted. Nevertheless, some caution is needed in the interpretation of these reassuring findings (Rutter, 1979a). In the first place, not many children in day-care have been studied. Secondly, the day nurseries studied have tended to be particularly good ones. Thirdly, even in these nurseries occasional disadvantages have been reported for children who have experienced day-care from infancy. Data are too few for the topic to be closed. However, a few conclusions are possible. Clearly, the quality of care (including continuity in caretaking) is vital. Also, the advantages and disadvantages of any kind of day-care can only be assessed in relation to the realistic alternatives (that is what is provided at home or through unofficial minding arrangements). Nursery provision for children over the age of three years may often be beneficial. Infant day-care, too, has a place but probably it is less easy to attain the requisite standards for the very young. Also, it may be that, especially with disadvantaged families, parents need to be included in the activities provided and to do so in a way which enhances rather than detracts from their self-confidence and responsibilities (Bronfenbrenner, 1974).

Marriage

As discussed in chapter 2, from the time just after the First World War up to 1970 there was a progressive trend towards earlier marriage; the average age of first marriage for men dropping from 27·6 in 1921 to 24·4 in 1970, and for women from 25·6 in 1911 to 22·5 in 1970 (Central Statistical Office, 1972). In parallel with this trend there was an increasing tendency for a higher proportion of the population to marry—so that for women aged 30 to 44 years the proportion who were married rose from 73·2 per cent in 1901 to 88·8 per cent in 1971; and for men of the same age from 77·4 to 86·2 per cent. Similar trends were apparent in most other western nations. However, during recent years the pattern has changed with both a rise in the average age at first marriage (to 25·0 for men and 22·8 for women in 1976—Central Statistical Office, 1978), and a drop in the proportion of men and women married in all age groups up to about 29 years.

The increase in teenage marriages which had occurred up to the early '70s almost certainly carried with it sizeable disadvantages and the recent rise in the average age at marriage is probably to be welcomed. Marriage during the teenage years has regularly and consistently been associated with a very greatly increased rate of marital breakdown and later divorce (Rutter and Madge, 1976). Presumably, this is because teenagers are less mature and less ready to take on the responsibilities of marriage, and because people change and develop as they grow older and gain new experiences and meet different friends. Husbands and wives may develop in different directions after marriage and the partner who is most attractive at 17 years may not be the one who is most satisfying at 27—let alone 67! In addition, it may be that teenagers are not emotionally ready to cope with parenthood—an important factor as the birth of children so frequently follows soon after early marriage (Gibson, 1974). However, probably at least as important is the fact that people marrying in their teens tend to be at an economic disadvantage compared with those marrying later and may have difficulties finding suitable accommodation (Gibson, 1974). The problems of taut budgeting and over-crowding may well predispose to marital disharmony. In terms of providing the best basis for a satisfactory marital relationship which will continue it appears desirable that marriages should generally be delayed until the mid-20s.

The interpretation of the slight fall in overall marriage rate rather depends on its meaning. However, it may be that in part it reflects changes in people's attitudes to marriage. Nevertheless, it would be a misleading over-simplification to see the trend as meaning that marriage is becoming generally less popular. In the first place, the great majority of both men and women are con-tinuing to get married and the proportions are still well above those of the inter-war years. Secondly, although the divorce rate has greatly increased (see below), the proportion of remarriages has also risen markedly. Thus, in 1951, 18 per cent of marriages were remarriages whereas in 1976 31 per cent were second or subsequent marriages for one or other party (Central Statistical Office, 1978). Or put another way, in 1961 there were 18.8 thousand marriages of divorced men whereas in 1977 there were 71·5 thousand. Of course, in part these figures simply reflect the larger pool of divorced people who are eligible for remarriage. But even when this is taken into account the marriage rate for divorced persons has not fallen appreciably (a fall between 1961 and 1976 from 18·6 per cent to 16·5 per cent for men and a rise from 9·8 per cent to 11·5 per cent for women). The net effect is that the proportion of the population who are in their second marriage has greatly increased. Thus, of 30-year-old men born in 1948 41 per 1000 had remarried compared with 10 per 1000 for men of the same age born in 1930; the comparable figures for women are 57 and 19 (Leete, 1979). It is estimated that in the U.S.A., three quarters of all divorced women and five-sixths of all divorced men sooner or later remarry (Norton and Glick, 1976).

Although it would be wrong to consider that there has been a general turning against marriage, it seems clear (even if ill-documented) that people's attitudes to marriage have been changing in subtle ways. As discussed in chapter 2, although still a minority view, there has been an increase in the proportion of U.S. college students who express the view that marriage is obsolete (Yankelovich, 1974). Moreover, in 1973 only 41 per cent of college women and 62 per cent of non-college women in Yankelovich's survey said that they thought that having children without formal marriage was morally wrong. Taken together with the evidence (see chapter 2) of an increasing proportion of young people who are living together without getting married, it does imply that for many young adults sexual relationships, living together, and even getting married are not primarily for the purpose of having children. Moreover, the expectations are to a considerable extent in terms of the man–woman relationship rather than parenthood so that there may be a greater readiness to break the relationship if it is no longer satisfying. Thus, in a recent U.K. survey (McCann-Erickson, 1977) some three-fifths of young single people thought that divorce was something that might happen to them. How far this is likely to be helpful or harmful to the children depends on many factors (some of which are discussed below), but amongst other things on how high the needs of children come in the list of priorities to be considered in relation to the handling of marital difficulties and the arrangements following separation or divorce.

Another important trend during the 1970s has been the falling proportion of marriages in which the bride was pregnant (Thompson, 1976; Central Statistical Office, 1978). For women under the age of 25 years the number of premarital conceptions resulting in a birth after marriage fell from 61·5 thousand in 1971 to 31·3 in 1976; and for women 25 years and over from 5·8 thousand to 4·1 thousand over the same period of time. This means that the cumulative rate per 1000 women aged 21 years for first births in marriage premaritally conceived dropped from 128 for those 21 years in 1973 to 80 for those 21 in 1978 (Leete, 1979). The reason for the drop in 'forced marriages' is likely to reside as much in the changing public attitudes to illegitimacy and to the desirability of marrying someone purely to legitimize the birth as in the spread of birth control. This is implied by the fact that illegitimacy rates have not fallen to the same extent.

Changing patterns of married life

In both the U.K. and the U.S.A. the marriages of pregnant brides carry a much increased risk of later marital breakdown (Gibson, 1974; Christensen and Meisner, 1953; Coombs and Zumeta, 1970). The reasons for the high rate of marital disruption are probably varied (Thornes and Collard, 1979). In part, it is likely to be a consequence of the youth of most of the pregnant brides so that many are immature and not yet prepared for marriage; in part a consequence of a lack of commitment to their spouse when the marriage has been precipitate and unplanned; in part a lack of kin support; in part a result of the economic disadvantages of early child bearing; and in part that the abrupt introduction of a child may sometimes interfere with the formation of solidarity between husband and wife which otherwise tends to develop in the early years of marriage.

Because marriages forced by pregnancy tend to have a worse outcome than other marriages, it is to be hoped that the recent reduction in their number may improve the chances of a greater number of marriages working out successfully.

Divorce and one parent families
The divorce rates in Britain have been going up steadily since 1857, but there was a big rise after the Second World War and a further surge in 1972 following the Divorce Law Reform Act (Leete, 1976). Thus, the divorce rate per 1000 population rose from 25·4 in 1961 to 74·4 in 1971, leaped to 119·0 in 1972 and has continued to rise more slowly up to a rate of 129·1 in 1977 (Office of Population Censuses and Surveys, 1979). Thus, for women born in 1930, 25 per 1000 had been divorced by age 30 years whereas for those born in 1949, 101 had been divorced by the same age—a four-fold increase (Leete, 1979). The number of children involved in divorce has risen even further because the increased divorce rate has particularly applied to marriages where there are dependent children (Leete, 1976). The divorce trends in other industrialized nations have been very similar although the absolute levels vary from country to country (Leete, 1979). Thus, between 1963 and 1969 the divorce rate (per 1000) rose from 2·2) to 3·16 in the U.S.A., from 1·30 to 2·56 in the USSR and from 0·49 to 0·71 in the Netherlands (Central Statistical Office,

215

1976). In the U.S.A. it is estimated that around 40 per cent of all current marriages will end in divorce if recent rates of divorce are sustained into the future (Leete, 1979). Again, as in the U.K., the rise in the rate of children involved in divorce has been disproportionately high because the spread of divorce to marriages with children has been particularly marked (Bronfenbrenner, 1976).

A consequence of the rising divorce rates (as well as of the high illegitimacy ratio) has been the increasing number of children brought up in single parent households. In the U.S.A. in 1974, one-sixth of children under the age of 18 years were living in a single parent family—a rate almost double that of a quarter of a century ago (Bronfenbrenner, 1976). This increase has been most marked for children under six years of age—from 7 per cent in 1948 to 15 per cent in 1974. In the U.K., the changes have been very comparable (Leete, 1978a and b). Since 1971 the number of one parent families has increased by about a third—i.e. an increase of some 6 per cent per year. In 1976, single parent households made up 11 per cent of all families with dependent children compared with 8 per cent in 1971. The increase has been mainly due to the rise in the number of children of broken marriages but there has also been an increase in the number of unmarried women keeping their illegitimate children.

There has been a slight fall in the number of widowed lone mothers. About half of all mothers bringing up dependent children on their own go out to work.

The socio-economic disadvantages suffered by one parent families are very great indeed (Finer, 1974; see also Rutter and Madge, 1976). One-third rely on supplementary welfare benefits as their main source of income; a quarter live in shared accommodation and they constitute the group with much the highest likelihood of being homeless. Not surprisingly, children reared in these circumstances show increased problems in educational attainment, behaviour and social adjustment (Finer, 1974; Ferri, 1976). As a result, there must be a serious concern about the adverse effects on children and adolescents of the rising number of one parent families.

The overall effects of the rising divorce rate on the psychological well being of adolescents are difficult to evaluate. Clearly, how far the increasing use of divorce is a good thing or a harmful influence depends on just what it means and on what changes in family life it reflects. In so far as it represents any increase in the extent of marital discord and disharmony obviously it constitutes a serious hazard about which we should be very worried. However, there are no satisfactory data upon which to base any judgement of whether marital difficulties are becoming more or less common. Nor indeed is it possible to determine whether overt marital breakdown is becoming more common in that there are no reliable data available on desertions and separations and it seems reasonable to suppose that these accounted for a substantial number of marriage breakdowns in times past when divorce was not easily available (Thornes and Collard, 1979). McGregor (1967) has argued that the increase in divorce is nothing more than a shift from informal separation, largely due to the availability of financial assistance in the form of legal aid. However, although part of the recent increase in divorce can be attributed to legal and financial charges and to wartime disturbance these factors by no means account for the rise in divorce (Chester, 1972). Also it is clear from the examination of historical trends in divorce in different countries that divorce rates have gone on rising independently of alterations in the law. It must remain uncertain whether more marriages are breaking down or whether it is merely that more broken marriages are ending in divorce. So far as it can be judged, both are occurring.

In so far as divorce represents a rational solution to a marriage which is no longer viable, of course, it may be beneficial in its effects. The evidence indicates that it is *not* desirable for warring parents to remain together for the sake of their children. The damage stemming from family discord and disharmony is too great for that to be a sensible decision (Rutter, 1972c, 1979e). Obviously it is best if parents can resolve their difficulties and remake a harmonious marriage and family life, but if they cannot do that it may be better for them to part.

Nevertheless, although sometimes the best available alternative, divorce can never be viewed with equanimity. It is always an emotionally charged event for the children as well as the parents and not something to be embarked on lightly. People often assume that marital conflict ceases at the time of divorce but studies show that often this is not the case (Hetherington et al, 1978; Wallerstein and Kelly, 1979). A substantial proportion of families remain as turbulent and conflicted following the divorce as during the marriage, and bitterness between divorcing parents sometimes escalates rather than diminishes following separation. Moreover, disagreements over custody of the children may lead parents to involve them actively in forming hostile alliances against the other parent which precipitate feelings of confusion, conflict, guilt, and hostility in the children. Children must cope not only with the restructuring and new stresses in the household but with loss and separation from a parent and also the concomitant family turmoil which surrounds the marriage break-up. In view of these factors it is not surprising that research findings indicate that members of divorced families exhibit *more* disrupted psychological and social functioning and more emotional distress one year after the divorce than they do two months after divorce (Hetherington et al, 1978). In the first year following divorce, children in divorced families function *less* well than children in high discord nuclear families which remain together. But, during the second year after the divorce, there is a dramatic improvement in coping and in psychosocial adjustment. The findings suggest that in the long run it is not a good idea for parents to remain in a severely discordant marriage for the sake of the children, in that after two years marital discord is associated with more adverse outcomes for the children than is divorce. On the other hand, the short-term picture appears rather different. In the transition period of family disequilibrium and reorganization following divorce, children's problems may be exacerbated before they decline. The same findings show that the adverse impact of both marital discord and divorce appears more pervasive and more long lasting for boys than for girls. Clearly, although divorce may well improve things in the long-term, it carries with it substantial hazards. For this reason, it is not a solution which should be turned to lightly and it is evident that most children need a good deal of support and understanding at the time of break-up of their parents' marriage. Because of the many unknowns with respect to possible changes over time in the frequency of marital discord, it is not possible to be sure whether the balance of effects of the rising divorce rate are likely to be good or bad. However, it is evident that there are likely to be losses as well as gains and that the continuing increase in divorce cannot be regarded with equanimity.

Much the same applies to the very high rate of parental remarriage, where it remains rather uncertain how far this helps or hinders the child's psychological development. As already noted, mothers bringing up children on their own suffer very considerable economic and social disadvantages, and it is likely that in most instances remarriage will improve the family's financial circumstances. This should benefit the children. Also, too, a single parent will often lack the emotional support usually provided by the spouse. In addition a child brought up by just one parent lacks the opportunity of seeing how two adults live together in a close and harmonious relationship—a lack which may make marital relationships more difficult for him later. Moreover, if the same-sexed parent is missing from the home the child will lack an important model of sex-appropriate behaviour and the opportunity parents present for same-sexed identification. Parental remarriage should improve matters in relation to all these considerations. On the other hand, children may find the arrival of a step-parent stressful because it alters the balance of family relationships, because it brings about a change in patterns of child-rearing or discipline, or because it introduces a discordant relationship between step-parent and child or between step-brothers and sisters into a previously harmonious home. The balance of advantages and disadvantages is likely to be influenced by the child's age at his mother's remarriage (the suggestion is that adolescents find it more difficult to adjust), by the quality of the mother–child relationship, by the mother's attitude to the step-parent and by the characteristics of the man the mother marries (or the woman the father marries). Not surprisingly, studies of parental remarriage vary in their findings; some show adverse effects on the children's behaviour and adjustment whereas others find that a step-parent makes little or no difference (Murchison, 1974; Biller, 1974; Pilling and Pringle, 1978). We may conclude that the high rate of parental remarriage following divorce may well improve circumstances for the lone parent but for the child there are both advantages and disadvantages.

Finally, it is necessary to take notice of the fact that various other alterations in society as a whole have consequences for parents and children, and for patterns of family life. Such changes have been many and various and it is possible only to pick out a few to illustrate some of the implications.

Patterns of immigration

International migration on a substantial scale was common to all western European countries during the 1950s and 1960s (Little, 1978). Official estimates suggested that in 1973 migrant workers constituted 6 per cent of the working population in the EEC. However, two features made the pattern in the U.K. somewhat different. Firstly, many migrants had an automatic right of entry and were settlers rather than guest workers. Secondly, many were identifiable by the colour of their skin. Between 1931 and 1971 the proportion of the population born in the New (mainly black) Commonwealth increased seven-fold from 0·3 per cent to 2·1 per cent—with over half of Asian origin and a third from the West Indies. Ethnic minorities still make up a relatively small proportion of the total population (although a rather larger proportion— about 7 per cent—of the child population). However, there is a considerable concentration of black people in relatively few areas so that places such as Bradford, Birmingham, and London have a fifth or more of their school entrants born to women from the New Commonwealth. These areas tend to be ones of urban decay and social disadvantage. Of the 12 urban areas with the greatest incidence of urban blight, nine were among those with the highest proportion of immigrants. At first many of the children in immigrant families had been born abroad and had come with their parents, or more commonly joined them later. That is no longer the case; most children of black parents are British born and bred. Hence for them the difficulties they experience are not those of immigration but rather are those stemming from cultural differences with their parents, from social disadvantage, from differences in upbringing, and from racial discrimination.

Alan Little (1978) has described the growth during the 1960s and '70s of public fears concerned with immigration—fears arising from both the rapidity of the growth of immigration and from its visibility as a result of skin colour. The result was legislation to severely restrict entry from the New Commonwealth. At the same time, it became clear that racial discrimination was widespread in relation to both employment and housing (Daniel, 1968). More recent studies have shown that these forms of discrimination have diminished (McIntosh and Smith, 1974), but young black people leaving school still face substantial discrimination in the job market; black school-leavers require four times as many interviews in careers offices to obtain jobs as do white school-leavers of similar educational qualifications, and unemployment among black teenagers is much higher than among their white counterparts (Rutter and Madge, 1976; Little, 1978). The experience of racial hostility and discrimination is clearly something which makes life different for adolescents from ethnic minority backgrounds, and it is something which requires an effective response to eliminate this slur from our society.

Culture differences with parents also make their teenage years somewhat different from those of other young people. James (1974) described the strong family ties of Sikh families in the U.K. and the constraints on children which stemmed from religious or cultural duties and rituals. Arranged marriages are still common, there are restrictions on the social life of teenagers (especially of girls) and home upbringing for girls tends to be seen as largely a preparation for marriage and motherhood. Children's questioning and explanations are actively encouraged but many children have to be bilingual because Punjabi continues to be spoken at home. On the other hand, Taylor's (1967) study of young Indians and Pakistanis in Newcastle showed that they did better educationally than their white contemporaries and achieved substantial equality in employment. Although these young men from Asian families had experienced racial hostility and had cultural concepts which differed from those of their parents this had not stopped them from making considerable advances on a broad front.

Patterns of upbringing also tend to be somewhat different in families of West Indian or African origin (see Rutter and Madge, 1976). Thus, Holman (1973) found that West African students were much more likely than indigenous or other immigrant groups to make use of private fostering arrangements for pre-school children—arrangements that did not always provide high quality care. It has been found, too, that West Indian children in the U.K. are frequently discouraged from touching and playing with objects at one year (Hood et al, 1970), make less excursions, have less toys and play fewer games with parents than white children of indigenous origin at three years (Pollak, 1972), and at 10 years are more disciplined and controlled than their white peers (Rutter et al, 1975b). It is not at all that the West Indian parents are unconcerned but it does appear that they do not always appreciate the developmental importance of play, communication, and parent–child interaction in the early years. More West Indian mothers go out to work when their children are young, and more use private child-minding arrangements which may be of poor quality. Somewhat more mothers lack the support of a husband and West Indian families are two or three times as likely to have at least four or five children. Single parenthood, large family size, and an absence of extended family support (because grandparents often remain in the West Indies) make it more difficult for West Indian families to cope on their own at times of crisis, and perhaps because of this, more children are admitted into the care of the local authority (Fitzherbert, 1967; Yudkin, 1967).

The situation with respect to social disadvantage is somewhat complicated and differs markedly between ethnic minority groups. Asian fathers tend to include a particularly high proportion of self-employed, salesmen, and shopkeepers with considerable entrepreneurial success (Taylor, 1976), whereas West Indian fathers are more likely to be found in unskilled or semi-skilled manual jobs of lower status than those they held prior to immigration (see Rutter and Madge, 1976). All surveys have shown that a higher proportion of black people, compared with the indigenous white population, live in poor quality housing. For all too many, overcrowding, multiple occupancy, and a lack of basic household amenities characterize their homes. On the other hand, faced with grave difficulties in obtaining local authority rented accommodation, West Indian parents have shown considerable drive and initiative in buying their own homes, and home ownership is more common than among native white families (Richmond, 1973; Rutter et al, 1975b). Unfortunately, many of the properties bought have been in poor repair and on short-term leases, so that the ultimate benefits remain rather uncertain.

U.S. studies of white immigrants have shown higher levels of crime in second (but not third) generation immigrants and consistently high levels among black people. However, the social and racial situation in the U.K. differs from that in the U.S.A. in many crucial respects, and the pattern in the U.K. may prove to be different. So far the evidence suggests that first generation black immigrants are more law abiding than the community as a whole, and crime rates among Asian families are particularly low (Lambert, 1970). However, domestic disputes involving violence may be particularly common among black immigrants (Bottoms, 1967). The data on adolescence are less satisfactory but as the unemployment rate among West Indian teenagers has risen (being twice that of white youngsters) more have got into problems with the police; some are homeless and have broken with their parents (Community Relations Commission, 1974). Thus, it may be that delinquency rates among black adolescents are rising but it is uncertain how far any rises which have occurred are due to strained relations between the young black community and the police with tensions arising from both misunderstandings and differences in expectations (Banton, 1973).

Several surveys using teacher questionnaires have suggested that children of West Indian parents have rates of behavioural difficulties at school which are rather above those found in indigenous white children (Rutter and Madge, 1976). The more detailed interview study of ten-year-olds undertaken by Rutter et al (1974) showed that the higher rate of problems at school was confined to those involving socially disapproved conduct; there was no excess of emotional disturbance or of difficulties getting along with other children, nor did the children differ in terms of disorder shown at home. Varlaam's (1974) findings suggested that in many cases the behavioural disorders resulted from the children's reading difficulties. The other striking difference between West Indian children and their native white counterparts concerns the pattern of problems in girls, where conduct disorders predominate in much the same way as they do in boys. This contrasts to the pattern in white girls in whom emotional disturbance is more frequent. The reason for this difference is not known.

The last issue to be discussed with respect to ethnic minority children concerns their educational performance (see Rutter and Madge, 1976, and Little, 1978, for a fuller discussion of this matter). Asian children who have received all of their education in this country show scholastic attainments which are generally comparable to the white indigenous population. However, many studies have shown that this is not the case with children of West Indian origin. They tend to be developmentally disadvantaged at age three years (Pollak, 1972); they show lower vocabulary scores at school entry and in infants school (Barnes, 1975); their reading attainments are lower at age 10 years (Yule et al, 1975); and their disadvantages with respect to literacy are just as great at age 15 years (Little, 1978). Clearly, the educational difficulties experienced by black adolescents are very considerable. The reasons for this state of affairs and hence the choice of remedies remain matters for controversy. It is most unlikely to be a consequence of any lack of motivation as Rutter et al (1975b) found that West Indian families were just as likely as others to take their children to the library, to buy books for them and to help with homework. Moreover, both the earlier study by Townsend and Brittan (1972) and the more recent investigation by Gray (1979) have shown that West Indian adolescents are more likely to stay on at school into the sixth form. Gray (1979) also found that they had better attendance rates at secondary school. It is evident that black teenagers show a determination to succeed in education despite their relative underachievement.

Also it is unlikely to be simply a result of inferior genetic endowment or racial discrimination as black children adopted into white families, or reared in good children's homes, fare much better (Rutter and Madge, 1976,—see also Scarr and Weinberg,

1976). It may well be that less than adequate schooling plays a part, in that Yule et al (1975) found that West Indian children were more likely to attend disadvantaged schools and Little (1978) has pointed out that the response of education authorities to the needs of West Indian children has generally been less helpful than their response to Asian immigrants whose native language was other than English. But, this cannot be the whole explanation as studies show that the children are cognitively disadvantaged even before they enter school.

Social disadvantages, large family size, and poor quality over-crowded housing are all likely to play a part. These handicaps to learning are all very much more common among West Indian children. On the other hand, this too is an insufficient explanation as West Indian children fully educated in the U.K. have reading scores below those of white children from an unskilled working-class background (Little, 1978). It seems likely that on top of the difficulties posed by racial discrimination, by social disadvantage, and by indifferent schooling, there may be something about the pattern of upbringing in the early years which puts the children from a West Indian background at an educational disadvantage. Certainly, that possibility warrants further study. However, it is important in exploring this issue to be aware of the value of different cultural styles and of the danger of imposing our own particular set of values without appreciation that others may be just as good.

In connection with schooling, one further point requires mention. Both the general public and politicians express fears from time to time that a high proportion of ethnic minority children in any one school will create educational problems and will hold back the scholastic progress of the other (white) children in the school. In fact, studies of both primary (Mabey, 1974) and secondary schools (Rutter et al, 1979) show that this fear is largely without substance. The ethnic and social balance within a school seems to make very little difference to educational outcome, however measured. However, intellectual balance does appear more important, even if it matters little how this is distributed in social or ethnic terms. In short, although undoubtedly black adolescents face more than their fair share of educational problems,

Changes in society and the family

there are no special disadvantages faced by the white youngsters going to school with them.

Religions

The next example of a general change concerns the diminishing influence of organized religion—at least in the U.K. Thus, Christian Church membership figures fell from 10·582 thousand in 1970 to 9·695 thousand in 1975 and the proportion of civil marriages went up from 41 per cent to 50 per cent between 1971 and 1976 (Central Statistical Office, 1978). The proportion of infants baptised at birth fell from 60·2 per cent in 1956 to 46·6 per cent in 1970; and the proportion of 12- to 20-year-olds confirmed in church dropped from 3·5 per cent to 2·0 per cent over the same period of time (Central Statistical Office, 1974). In the U.S.A., too, there is some evidence that Christian religious commitment has decreased, at least among college students (Hastings and Hoge, 1970). In both countries, however, there may have been some increase in young people's adherence to Eastern religions and to some of the new religious sects. Accurate data on this matter are lacking.

The effects of this change are not known. The loss of reliance on moral laws laid down by the Church may have brought greater flexibility and freedom, but also it is likely to have greatly increased the need for young people to establish their own set of values and ideals. This may well provide its own stresses, as it is usually much easier to rely on rules already laid down even though their restrictions are resented.

However, there is another less obvious effect of the reduced role of the Church. In the past the Church has created a social milieu as well as a religious setting. When people moved to a different community it has often provided a ready means of meeting new people, as well as providing solace, comfort, and practical support at times of crisis. If the Church no longer does this for many people, their needs are nevertheless still there and will have to be met in other ways. It is uncertain how far alternative sources of social contact and support have in fact been established.

Urbanization

Throughout the world, the rapid urbanization which has taken place over the last 150 years has been one of the most striking and dramatic changes in recent times (Davis, 1973; Basham, 1978). Moreover, it is a change which has brought with it many psychosocial problems, especially in developing countries. Even in advanced nations, though, adolescent problems tend to be more frequent in inner city areas, as discussed in chapter three. Urbanization first took place in the U.K. In 1801, when the Industrial Revolution was still getting under way, although the U.K. was then the most urbanized nation in the world it had only one city (London) of more than 100,000 inhabitants. This city, the largest in Europe if not in the world, accounted for only 4·7 per cent of the U.K. population. Half a century later the U.K. had twelve cities of over 100,000 and they housed 17·1 per cent of the population. By 1901 there were thirty-five such cities containing 25·9 per cent of the population, and altogether over three-quarters of the population was then classed as urban. Comparable changes took place in the U.S.A. somewhat later, with urbanization continuing right up to the present time. Urbanization in Japan and the U.S.S.R. has been much more recent, with huge increases in the middle years of the twentieth century. Most recently of all, nonindustrial nations in the developing world have begun to show similar changes during the years following the Second World War.

Without doubt this rapid pattern of urbanization has had immense implications for patterns of life generally and for psychosocial functioning in particular. However, although of great relevance to adolescents in many parts of the world, it is of little consequence with respect to the changes which have taken place in the U.K. over the last quarter of a century. The figures show that urbanization in the U.K. has increased very little since the 1930s and it cannot be held responsible for any changes now taking place in adolescent behaviour.

Prosperity, employment and housing

During this century there have been major reductions in poverty and in poor housing conditions. Thus, Rowntree's studies of poverty in York (Rowntree and Laver, 1951) showed that in 1899 about 10 per cent of the population were in poverty, whereas in 1950 only 1·7 per cent were judged to be severely poor. This dramatic improvement in standards of living for large numbers of people was attributed to rising employment and the role of the welfare state. The trend towards increasing prosperity and decreasing poverty has continued during the last 25 years. The Royal Commission figures in the U.K. (Diamond, 1978) showed that the average real net income (i.e. its true purchasing power) of the bottom 30 per cent of the population (in terms of income) increased by about 25 per cent between 1961 and 1974, with a slight decline in 1975–6. That rate of increase was about the same as that for the population as a whole. It is evident that people in the U.K. over the course of the last 80 years have become more prosperous in the very real sense that they have been able to buy more goods and to enjoy a higher standard of living. This improvement has been experienced by the lowest income groups as well as by those earning wages in the average range.

In parallel with the rise in prosperity there have been considerable gains in the general level of housing conditions and of basic household amenities. For example, in 1911 about one-third of households were overcrowded to the extent of having more than one person per room; but by 1961 the proportion had fallen to 11 per cent; by 1971 to 4·8 per cent; and by 1977 it had dropped to 3·2 per cent (Hole and Pountney, 1971; Central Statistical Office, 1978). Even between 1967 and 1971 the proportion of dwellings lacking an internal W.C. fell from 19 per cent to 12 per cent and those lacking a fixed bath from approximately 13 per cent to 8 per cent (see Rutter and Madge, 1976). Similarly, the proportion of dwellings regarded as physically unsatisfactory fell from 17·9 per cent to 10·0 per cent between 1971 and 1976 (Central Statistical Office, 1978).

It might be thought that this very marked and widespread improvement in living conditions over this century should have had very considerable benefits for children and adolescents. Indeed, it probably has, but the picture as just given is a misleadingly rosy one for several rather different reasons. Firstly, the figures for households or for adults misrepresent the circumstances of young people because poverty and overcrowded housing are particularly likely to be experienced during the period of family life when there are dependent children. Thus, although in 1961 only 3 per cent of the population was overcrowded to the extent of 1·5 persons per room (Hole and Pountney, 1971), the National Child Development Study (Davie et al, 1972; Wedge and Prosser, 1973) showed that *one in six* children had experienced this degree of overcrowding at either 7 or 11 years of age. Secondly, there is another source of bias in that poverty is strongly associated with family size. Whereas only one in eight families with one dependent child are in the lowest quartile of income distribution, one half of those with four or more children are in the bottom quartile (Diamond, 1978). As, for obvious reasons, the proportion of children in large families is considerably greater than the proportion of large families, there will be more *children* in poverty than there are *families* in poverty. Thirdly, poverty is very much commoner in one parent families than in two parent families (half are in the lowest quartile of net family incomes compared with a fifth of two parent families—Diamond, 1978). As an increasingly high proportion of children are being brought up—at least for a time—in a one parent home, it is likely that the number of children experiencing poverty may be increasing relative to the general population.

Fourthly, although the general level of prosperity has risen greatly during this century the *distribution* of incomes has changed surprisingly little (see Diamond, 1978). As a result, the proportion of people feeling relatively poor (in terms of their incomes being more than a certain amount below the average) has not changed much over the years. If the most relevant issue is how a person fares relative to other people, rather than how well off he is in absolute terms, things have not altered much. Fifthly, it is likely that people's expectations and their assessments of what they 'need' have increased greatly over the course of this century. This is apparent, for example, in relation to household technology. At the turn of the century there were no TV sets, cars were still a rare curiosity, and automatic washing machines were not yet available. Accordingly, the question of their purchase did not arise. But today, most people would regard a TV set as a 'necessity' and cars and washing machines are increasingly coming into that category. As a result, people are now needing a higher real income than hitherto in order to avoid poverty.

Sixthly, it may be that people's feelings of security and prosperity are related at least as much to their power to control their own destiny as to their absolute level of income. In that connection, two factors have served to make things worse—the 'poverty trap' and rising unemployment. In the U.K. the systems of welfare and other benefits has resulted in a situation whereby, over a range of earnings from £30 per week to £54 per week, any increase in wages is entirely offset by the loss of benefits (Diamond, 1978). Even up to £70 per week, there is very little increase in net spending power with any rise in gross earnings. The consequence is that over this range of earnings people have no power to increase their income—the more they earn, the more they lose. The evidence suggests that this poverty trap has so far had a remarkably small effect on decisions on jobs or earnings. Nevertheless, it would be surprising if it had not led to some feelings of resentment and impotence—which may have adverse psychological consequences. In this connection it should be noted that the poverty trap has its greatest effect in the case of large families with dependent children.

Throughout the world, unemployment rates have risen very greatly over the last decade (Central Statistical Office, 1978). Between 1971 and 1977 the rates in France increased from 2·8 per cent to 5·2 per cent and in the U.K. from 3·9 per cent to 6·9 per cent. Between 1977 unemployment rates in the U.S.A. doubled to reach 7 per cent. In the U.K. the unemployment rate went up *five-fold* between 1966 and 1977 (Diamond, 1978). Moreover, the increase in unemployment has disproportionately affected young people so that the numbers of young men out of work in the 18- to 20-year age group went up from 14,000 to 75,000 between 1966 and 1978 and for the under 18s from 11 per cent to 67 per cent. The comparable figures for females (8000 to 65,000 and 7000 to 68,000 respectively) show that they have been even more affected. The duration of unemployment has also gone up most markedly in the 'school leaver' age group. Not only is unemployment associated with low income (half the male unemployed are in the lowest income quartile), but also it is likely to be associated with loss of self-esteem.

So far as housing is concerned there is no doubt that homes have become less crowded and better supplied with amenities. However, there is more uncertainty on the extent to which these changes have improved the psychological environment provided by living accommodation (see Rutter and Madge, 1976). Firstly, the large scale redevelopment programmes designed to clear slums have often meant that people have had to leave the district to which they had formed attachments, and that people have had to move home just because the whole area was being demolished irrespective of whether or not they wanted to leave. Various studies (e.g. Hartman, 1963; Vereker et al, 1961) have shown how people's ties to an area influence their satisfaction with their housing, whatever its condition. Secondly, rehousing frequently means the break-up of neighbourhood friendships and altered patterns of social interaction. Sometimes, too, kinship ties may be adversely affected as two-generation households are split up (Jennings, 1962). Thirdly, the physical design of housing and housing estates may influence people's response to their environment (Newman, 1973, 1974). Large anonymous estates with high-rise dwellings in which many housing units share the same entrance to the building seem to increase the likelihood of vandalism because there is so much public area for which no one feels responsible and because so many people have access to the buildings that strangers are not easily identifiable. Perhaps this leads big city dwellers to lose their sense of mutual obligation and helps explain the repeated observation that, compared with small town inhabitants, they are less likely to give aid to strangers and less likely to respect other people's property (Zimbardo, 1969; Milgrim, 1970). For these and other reasons, the material advantages of improved physical amenities may to some extent be offset by some of the psychological disadvantages associated with rehousing in the ways that it has often occurred. *How* people are rehoused and the design of the estates to which they are moved are likely to have an impact on their life and behaviour, but so far we have only an extremely limited understanding of the crucial elements in this process. Perhaps it is because we know so

Changes in society and the family

little on what to compare with what in the field of housing that the studies of the effects of housing on psychiatric morbidity, extent of delinquency and levels of educational achievement have been so generally inconclusive (Rutter and Madge, 1976).

For all these reasons it would be wrong to conclude that young people have steadily increased in prosperity and that this should have clear-cut psychological benefits. There *have* been real gains and these should not be underestimated but to some extent their effect has been offset by the problems associated with a rising number of one parent families and sharply increasing unemployment. Moreover, the changes in housing have included both advantages and disadvantages with the balance between them rather unclear.

Televisions, cars and telephones

As part of the pattern of increasing prosperity, there have been huge increases in the numbers of people with television, cars, and telephones (Central Statistical Office, 1972, 1976, 1977 and 1978). Thus, TV licences rose from 2 million in 1951 to 17 million in 1978 and in 1974 there were over 300 TV receivers per 1000 population. Moreover, among those with TV sets the weekly hours of viewing have also gone up steadily—from 18 hours in 1967 to 24 hours in 1978 for 5- to 14-year-olds, and from 15 to 18 hours for 15- to 19-year-olds. The number of telephones and of passenger cars has also gone up enormously, so that in 1976 53 per cent of households owned a car and in 1975 there were well over 300 telephones per 1000 population, a rate over twice that in 1960.

Adequate data are lacking on the effects of these changes on adolescents and on patterns of family life. However, it is obvious that the great spread of private cars and of telephones must have substantially facilitated communication and contact between families and their extended kin network. Although it is probable that grandparents are now more likely to live further away than in previous eras, it may well be that families remain as much in touch by telephone and by visiting as they ever were. Unfortunately, we lack indicators for historical changes in kin contact. It is often supposed that intergenerational ties are weakening but

Conclusions

the findings from recent epidemiological studies in both London and the Isle of Wight cast doubt on this assumption (Quinton, 1979). In both areas the vast majority of mothers had supportive relationships with relatives and/or friends.

The impact of television is difficult to assess and opinions differ on the net effect of the various advantages and disadvantages. On the one hand it provides a powerful medium for education and for communicating both ideas and factual information. Its potential in this connection is great but data are lacking on how much it actually achieves. On the other hand, it provides a most influential set of models of behaviour and concern is frequently expressed about the extent to which these models portray aggression and violence. Undoubtedly, TV programmes do include a good deal of violence and there is evidence that to some extent these may serve to increase the likelihood of violent behaviour in the adolescents who view the programmes (Berkowitz et al, 1978; Belson, 1978; Surgeon-General, 1972). However, there is also a very different reason for concern about the possible effects of television—in terms of its inhibiting effect on family conversations (Bronfenbrenner, 1976). Maccoby (1951) found that most families had no conversation while television was on and that the TV set tended to dominate and determine family life while it was in operation. As Bronfenbrenner put it: 'The primary damage of the television screen lies not so much in the behaviour it produces as the behaviour it prevents—the talks, the games, the family festivities, and arguments through which much of the child's learning takes place and his character is formed'. The danger is clear, but again data are lacking on how much this actually occurs.

CONCLUSIONS

Many changes for the better have taken place in society. Life expectancy has greatly increased as fewer children die in their infancy; young people are taller and better nourished; perinatal hazards have been reduced and very small babies are now much more likely to survive without major handicaps; fewer children are orphaned; more grandparents are living on to be available throughout the whole of young people's period of development;

233

the average family size has been reduced and effective contraceptive techniques have become available to prevent the birth of unwanted or rejected children; the emancipation of women has brought them greater rewards; poverty has been much reduced; housing has improved and basic household amenities have become generally available. Obviously there is much for which to be thankful. Yet the nagging doubt remains. There are other items to be put in the negative side of the balance and it is clear that not all the gains have been free of disadvantages. The extension of education to the late teens some time after young people reach physical maturity carries with it the potential for family stresses; surprisingly, hospital admissions have increased rather than decreased; the reduction in deaths of parents has been more than offset by the vast increase in divorce so that far more children are experiencing broken homes and more are being brought up (at least for a while) in a single parent household; it is unclear whether we have yet developed satisfactory means of day care for young children while their parents go out to work; children of ethnic minorities face a variety of hazards, not least of which is the disgrace of racial discrimination; and increased prosperity has not necessarily brought about greater family harmony or more happiness for young people. It is obvious that we have not yet got things right, although unfortunately it is less clear what remedies need to be applied. However, that is the question to which we must now turn in the last chapter.

5

Services: implications and speculations

INTRODUCTION: SUMMARY OF THE ISSUES

Adolescent problems

Three main questions have constituted the focus of this review of adolescent development and disorder: are there definable psychosocial problems in adolescence?, are such problems getting worse or changing in character?; and how should we deal with them? Before attempting some sort of answer to the last of these, it is necessary to draw together the threads on the issues relevant to the planning of services which derive from considerations of the first two questions.

As we saw in chapter 1, there are indeed a variety of features which mark adolescence as a period of development which to some extent differs from both earlier and later stages. Physical growth is then more rapid than at any time since infancy and it is during the teenage years that bodily configurations change to an adult pattern. Puberty, of course, marks the reaching of sexual maturity with all the psychological connotations that that implies. As one component of the emergent sexuality, there is a marked change in hormone production—a change which has implications with respect to assertiveness, sex drive, and emotions. Psychosexual development during adolescence is accompanied by greater changes in the patterns of peer relationships than at any other stage of development; and this is the age period when depressive feelings become much more common. Also, these 'in-between' years in western societies constitute the time when various crucial life-hurdles have to be overcome—such as critical examinations with career implications, and the transition to either further education or employment. There can be no doubt that many changes take place during adolescence and that some of these are unique to that period of development. It is for all these,

235

and other, reasons that adolescence is rightly regarded as a distinctive developmental phase.

On the other hand, it does not constitute any kind of 'break' in the course of development and for most teenagers it is not a period of either psychological disturbance or social alienation. Certainly, important changes take place but they are not usually accompanied by gross behavioural disruption or marked emotional disequilibrium. With all these bodily and social changes during the second decade of life, one might expect more disturbance than actually occurs. Three factors are probably relevant in any explanation of why this does not happen in most individuals. Firstly, many of the changes represent increased *capacities* of various kinds; cognitive skills become both more complete and more flexible as powers of abstraction and logic make new problem-solving easier than it was when younger; social skills increase in range and complexity and the powers of love and friendship expand and mature; also emotional development includes an enhanced ability to appreciate other people's feelings and to understand their point of view. Secondly, substantial continuities in development are apparent. The crises of adolescence are not wholly new and to a considerable extent the patterns of psychological functioning which emerge during the 'teens represent a growth and maturation of patterns already established in earlier childhood. The coping mechanisms developed when younger in relation to other life crises continue to have some relevance and the changes during adolescence build on what has gone on before. Thirdly, not all the changes take place at the same time. Adolescence spans some half-dozen years or more and for most young people puberty, the first love affair, critical school examinations, transition to employment, leaving the family, and the various other life crises do not coincide. Rather they come in series so that the success in coping with the first gives both greater confidence and improved skills for dealing with the second.

Nevertheless, even if the *sturm und drang* concept of adolescence has proved to be a considerable distortion of the usual course of development, for many youngsters the transition from childhood to adulthood *is* marked by an upsurge in depressive feelings, an uncertainty about the future and an increased risk of

psychosocial disorder. Delinquency is typically a teenage phenomenon and crime rates reach their peak then, with a fall-off as
adult life is reached. Drug abuse increases markedly during the
teenage years; alcoholism also first becomes a problem at this
time; and attempted suicide reaches its highest rate during late
adolescence. Emotional disorders show a marked alteration in sex
ratio over the adolescent period, with the female preponderance
typical of adult disorders first becoming evident then. Depressive
conditions become much more common during and after puberty
to reach a peak during late adolescence or early adult life. There
can be no doubt, then, that major changes take place in the pattern
of disorders.

On the other hand, once again, there is little indication of any
developmental discontinuity and the psychiatric disorders occurring in adolescents have a course and outcome broadly comparable to disorders of similar severity and diagnosis occurring in
other age groups. With respect to the planning of services three
factors are particularly important. Firstly, many disorders of
adolescence begin in earlier childhood and are already well-
established chronic conditions by the time teenagers come or are
brought to clinics for treatment of their psychosocial problems.
These conditions are not disorders of adolescence in the sense that
they arise then—rather they represent the persistence of disorders
stemming from a much earlier phase of development. Measures
to prevent these conditions would have to be applied to younger
children and not to teenagers.

Secondly, the psychiatric disorders which do arise for the first
time during the years of adolescence differ in some important
respects from those persisting from earlier childhood. Most
obviously they are not associated with educational retardation in
the way that is so characteristic of the disorders of the pre-
pubescent period. Also, they show a much weaker association
with almost all indices of family psychopathology, although this
appears to be a function of their lesser severity as much as the age
of onset. However, while it is fairly clear what the disorders
arising in adolescence are *not* due to, it is much less clear what
aetiological factors *are* important. This is a matter which is greatly
in need of further study, but in the meanwhile we are left with a

very weak data base from which to plan preventive services for this group of conditions.

Thirdly, although it is true that many adolescent disorders first arise at a much earlier stage of development, that does *not* mean that they are impervious to influences during adolescence. To the contrary, there is every indication that experiences during the teenage period have a considerable impact on young people's behaviour. Research findings show that this is evident not only with the general run of pupils at ordinary secondary schools but also with recidivist delinquents receiving institutional care. Accordingly, there is every reason to include environmental manipulations during adolescence in the list of interventions to be considered, even though many disorders arise earlier than that.

The second question on whether disorders are getting worse or changing in character has to be answered separately with respect to its two parts. There is no indication that the nature of adolescent disorders is changing in any fundamental way; to the contrary, the problems that exercise us most today are largely the same ones that exercised our predecessors several generations ago. The emergence of an adolescent drug culture in the U.K. is, however, something of an exception to that statement. Before the 1960s narcotic addiction in the U.K. was largely restricted to adults connected in some way with the medical or nursing professions and it was virtually unknown in adolescents. The picture then changed markedly during the mid-1960s, not only with the increase in opiate addiction among young people, but also with the spreading use of marihuana, stimulants, and hallucinogens.

The question of whether adolescent disorders are increasing in frequency is more difficult to answer with certainty in view of the lack of truly comparable data for different eras. However, although some of the more alarmist views appear to be unwarranted, there are definite indications that certain adolescent problems are on the increase. These include delinquency, attempted suicide, anorexia nervosa, alcoholism, and drug abuse— in short, many of the psychosocial problems most characteristic of the adolescent age period. It seems less likely that educational standards have fallen to any substantial degree but nevertheless all is not entirely well in secondary schools. Scholastic attainments appear to have ceased increasing; a worryingly high proportion of secondary school children fail to attend regularly; many young people drop out of education at 16 years (in the U.K. more so than a few years ago); and standards vary greatly between schools. These trends do not all reflect the same problems and, although it provides some leads, the survey in chapter 4 of the changes taking place generally in society does not give a satisfactory answer to the question of why some adolescent problems seem to be getting worse. But the very observation that things are not improving immediately raises the further question of what we should do about it. No easy answers are readily available, as is all too clear from the recent deliberations of both national and international committees (Court, 1976; WHO, 1977). However, the remainder of this chapter represents an attempt to grapple with the issues and to sort out which avenues are worth further exploration, even if we do not know as yet quite where or how far they will lead.

Causes and remedies

Before discussing possible remedies for the problems experienced and shown by adolescents we need to consider the levels and types of intervention which are possible. This issue naturally turns on the question of causes and influences—a complicated matter as evident in the brief discussion of concepts of causation in the introduction to chapter 3. Clarke's (1978) conceptualization of the groups of variables contributing to an explanation of vandalism provides a useful model which, with appropriate modifications, may be applied more generally to most forms of adolescent behaviour (see fig. 5.1).

Firstly, there is the matter of individual predisposition, as it is shaped by genetic variables and by influences in the physical and psychosocial environment. Thus, this would include hereditary factors as they apply to personality, intelligence and mental illness. It would also include the effects of perinatal complications, of post-natal head injury or of current physical illness. A person's liability to behave in particular ways may be affected both by handicaps, such as cerebral palsy, which he has carried from birth, and also by the results of concurrent illness (e.g. the depression

239

Simplified Model of Causative Influences

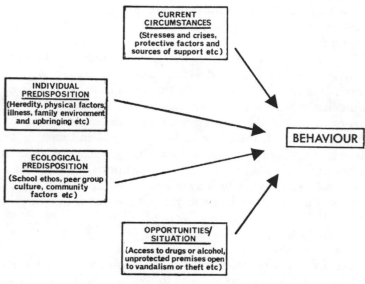

FIGURE 5.1

often associated with infectious mononucleosis or hepatitis) or by its treatment (e.g. the mood alterations which may accompany the use of reserpine or corticosteroids). In addition, an individual's predisposition is likely to have been powerfully influenced by the form of upbringing he has received—by the environmental stresses and traumata experienced as a child, by the kinds of love and discipline provided by his parents, by the values he has been taught and by the social skills he has acquired. All of these variables play a part in making an adolescent the sort of person he is and hence serve to determine the personal characteristics which predispose him to behave in particular ways. This is the case whether we are talking about normal variations in behaviour (such as whether a person is assertive or timid) or whether we are dealing with psychopathology (e.g. the development of schizophrenia or manic-depressive psychosis), although obviously the relative importance of different influences on individual predisposition will vary according to the 'outcome'· being considered.

Secondly, there is a different set of predisposing influences of a kind which apply to groups rather than to individuals. These may be subsumed under the general heading of ecological predisposition. This would cover, for example, the effects of the social environment provided by schools. As discussed in chapter 3, there is good evidence that children's behaviour is quite strongly influenced by the ethos of the school they attend. Some schools provide a setting which predisposes adolescents to attend regularly, work hard, get on well with their peers and their teachers, and generally to respond with interest and enthusiasm. But in others, youngsters who were apparently similar at the time they entered the school become prone to truant, to vandalize school premises, and to learn little in class. Within each school, huge individual differences remain but the group predisposition is influenced in ways which make the overall levels of good behaviour and scholastic attainment in different schools quite disparate. Much the same applies to other social settings. Thus, young people's behaviour is much influenced by the characteristics of the peer group of which they are a part, and by the social role expectations relevant to the situations in which they find themselves. We saw this effect, for example, in the findings of the 'Robbers' Cave' experiment and the simulated prison study described in chapter 3. Also included under this heading are the whole range of community and subcultural influences, together with the effects of the mass media in increasing or decreasing the acceptability of particular forms of behaviour.

Thirdly, a person's current circumstances must also be taken into account in terms of the stresses and supports for the individual. This heading would cover those acute life events such as the death of a parent; the loss of a job; a quarrel with a girlfriend; or a public humiliation at school which may precipitate depression or a suicidal attempt, or an act of vandalism. Also, however, it would include those protective factors and sources of support (such as a good confiding relationship at home or the satisfactions and high self-esteem associated with accomplishments at school or on the sports field) which may enable the adolescent to survive the crises and cope successfully with the life stresses he is experiencing.

Lastly, there is the situation prevailing or the opportunities available at the time. Thus, a girl may have become depressed because of her genetic predisposition, her susceptibility as a result of attending a low morale school in a disintegrating neighbourhood, and the precipitant of the death of her best friend in a road accident. However, whether this results in suicide may also be influenced by whether or not lethal drugs are readily accessible to her at the time. Similarly, whether a troubled teenager becomes an alcoholic will be influenced by the cost and availability of alcohol; and whether a potentially disruptive adolescent engages in vandalism may depend on his being in the vicinity of a poorly lit street with an empty building left unsupervised and already identified as being a suitable target by the existence of broken windows left unrepaired.

Of course, these four sets of variables are not truly separate (as the same factor may be considered under more than one heading) and there are complex interactions between them (not shown in fig. 5.1). Nevertheless, they provide a convenient way of considering possible modes of preventive intervention, and they will be used as a general structure for the discussion of service implications in the rest of this chapter.

PREVENTIVE POLICIES DIRECTED AT INDIVIDUAL PREDISPOSITION

Preventive policies have frequently been community wide in their application (as, for example, with immunization or the delivery of babies in hospital) but generally their action has been intended to affect individual predisposition. In the field of psychosocial disorders the aim has usually been to provide some kind of experience which it is hoped will give the child strengths to counter the chronic stresses and disadvantages with which he has to cope in growing up. The unsuccessful attempts to prevent juvenile delinquency by means of personal counselling (see chapter 3) provide one example of this approach. More recently the introduction of compensatory preschool education and day-care provides another. There is continuing uncertainty and controversy on the question of how far they succeeded in raising the cognitive performance of poor children from a seriously disadvantaged background. The initial conclusion of complete failure (Jensen, 1969) now seems to have been both premature and too negative, as follow-up studies suggest some modest medium-term benefits from some (but not all) programmes (Bronfenbrenner, 1979). Even so, clearly the results have fallen far short of the grand hopes with which the schemes were introduced. A critical appraisal of the preventive policies so far evaluated can only lead to the conclusion that our knowledge of effective primary prevention measures for psychosocial disorders of adolescence is extremely limited and that there are very few interventions of proven value (Court, 1976; WHO, 1977; Graham, 1977). Nevertheless, as each of these reports shows, possibilities for effective prevention do exist.

There are several key problems in carrying out successful primary preventions. Firstly, there is a considerable gap between identifying a damaging factor and knowing how to eliminate it or reduce its effect. Thus, it has long been clear that severe family discord and tensions put children at a markedly increased risk for conduct disorders and delinquency. But it is quite another matter to know what can be done to increase family harmony. Secondly, it is evident that with but a few exceptions, short-term change in a chronically depriving situation will rarely have long-term benefits. To be effective in influencing ultimate levels of development, either the interventions must involve a lasting change (as is the case, for entirely different reasons, with both immunization or adoption), or the improved experiences will need to be available throughout the child's period of growth. The very best of summer camps for preschool children cannot be expected to have any worthwhile long-term benefits. Thirdly, even when an effective measure is available there may be problems in ensuring that it reaches all target populations. For example, effective means of contraception have been available for some years and their use has led to major changes in patterns of family building (see chapter 4). On the other hand, there has been much less success in reducing unwanted births among teenagers (see chapter 2).

Fourthly, although for the most part 'critical periods' of development do not exist (Clarke and Clarke, 1976; Rutter, 1979e) and hence it is never too late to intervene, nevertheless patterns of disadvantage and failure tend to persist once established and therefore there is a need to start interventions early in children's lives.

Lastly, all programmes of prevention must take into account the cost/benefit ratio (WHO, 1977). This requires an assessment of the importance of the behaviour or disorder they are meant to influence; the likelihood of the measure making a real difference; the number of people who can be reached by the method of intervention; the disadvantages that come as side-effects (almost no effective intervention is free of these); political and ethical considerations (such as the loss of personal freedom in the imposition of remedies) and the cost of the preventive measures in terms of finance, resources and personnel. With these considerations in mind let us turn to the various possibilities of action which are open to us.

General health measures

As noted in chapter 3, there is good evidence that young people with any form of organic brain dysfunction (such as cerebral palsy, epilepsy, or encephalitis) or with mental retardation have a much increased rate of psychosocial disorders. It is also apparent that children with chronic physical handicaps of a kind that do not involve brain damage have a somewhat increased rate of mental health problems, although the increase is much less than that with brain disorders. Accordingly, any measures that reduce the incidence of these physical conditions, and especially of brain pathology, should have psychosocial benefits. In this connection, improved social conditions and improved maternal and obstetric care (see W.H.O., 1976) should ultimately lead to a reduction in the incidence of both cerebral palsy and severe mental retardation, although it remains uncertain how far this has occurred up to now (Alberman, 1979). A reduction in accidents would also be of value. Not only are accidents a principal cause of death in children but also survivors may be left with brain damage from head injuries. Steps to reduce accidents, as through the imposition of speed limits on roads, the use of safety belts in cars, road-sense training and the provision of adequate play space for children should be worthwhile. Better care of the chronically handicapped, antenatal screening to detect the presence of spina bifida or Down's syndrome in high risk individuals, effective immunization on a community-wide basis, and adequate nutrition are also among measures which could play a part in reducing the number of young people suffering physical handicaps (Court, 1976; Graham, 1977; W.H.O., 1977).

Prevention of unwanted births

Children whose birth was not wanted by their parents, who were born to teenage mothers, who are brought up in single parent households, and who grow up in very large families, are all subject to a substantially increased risk of psychosocial problems. Much could be done to reduce the disadvantages experienced by all these groups, but also it is important to reduce the number of unwanted births. This is no straightforward matter. The free availability of family planning services is one important step but it is not enough. Those most likely to produce unwanted children (young single people and those with personal and social problems) are just those least likely to avail themselves of services. Usually it is not that they positively wish to conceive a child or that they have ethical objections to contraception, but rather that their difficulty in planning a family is merely one facet of a general feeling of hopelessness and inevitability or of a pervasive lack of foresight in planning all aspects of their lives. Conflicts over sexuality and socio-cultural attitudes (including a male antagonism to female autonomy) also play a part in the lack of take-up of services. For these reasons, family planning must form part of a wider community service that is educational in the broadest sense (Court, 1976; W.H.O., 1977). Greater use needs to be made of informal and formal publicity through the press, TV, and other sources of communication (Allen, 1974); discussions in schools and talks to youth groups can also be of value; the puerperium needs to be used as an opportunity for nurses to discuss family planning with both mothers and their consorts; terminations of pregnancy need to be linked with contraception counselling; and domiciliary family planning services have a place with high risk groups who are reluctant to seek advice from clinics or family practitioners. It must be said that little is known on the cost-benefits of these various approaches and further monitoring and evaluation are obviously essential. However, what can be stated is that a successful family planning service will need to be broad-based in its approach and will have to pay as much attention to questions of take-up and utilization as to the development of safe and effective methods of birth control. Terminations of pregnancies, too, play a role in the prevention of unwanted births and it is important that these be readily available to all sections of the population. However, abortion is a distasteful procedure, which is relatively expensive in its use of medical resources, and which is far from psychologically neutral in its effect on the woman. Accordingly, it seems essential to educate the public to rely on abortion only if appropriate contraceptive techniques have been used and have failed. Abortion should be a last resort and not a first solution in family planning. Also, it appears desirable that counselling should be available as part of abortion services—although once again little is known on its value either in reducing the need for a second abortion or in limiting psychological disturbance at the time or during a later pregnancy (see Kumar and Robson, 1978).

Provision of continuity in good quality parenting
Children who repeatedly go in and out of Children's Homes or foster homes or who live with their own parents in a severely unstable and unsettled family environment tend to have a high rate of psychosocial problems in adolescence: the same applies to young people who are reared in institutions with multiple changing caretakers (see chapter 3). Those from a similar background who are adopted (Hersov, 1977b) or who receive long-term fostering in an ordinary family environment (Triseliotis, 1978) are much more likely to develop normally.

Accordingly, in the case of young children whose parents seem unlikely ever to be able to look after them at all adequately, an *early* decision should be taken with respect to adoption or long-term fostering. It is not in the child's interests for there to be vacillation and indecision while he shuffles to and from his parents into the care of the local authority; nor is it in his interests to remain for long periods in an institution in the forlorn hope that the parents who abandoned him and who now only visit sporadically will one day take him back. Children require stability and continuity in parenting and it is important that their needs should be paramount in such circumstances, as they now are as the result of recent legislation in the U.K. Adoption is the one intervention in early childhood which clearly makes a major environmental change which is often of long-term benefit to the child. Obviously, there must be stringent legal safeguards to ensure that children are not compulsorily removed from their parents without it being shown in court that this is a necessary step to ensure the child's well-being. Also, such removal should not take place (unless essential to preserve life) until strenuous and well thought out efforts have been made to improve family circumstances and to help the parents in their task of child-rearing. Such safeguards are essential both because of the difficulties in making state provision of a quality which is up to even the average conditions in the ordinary family, and to protect parents from discriminatory intervention. Nevertheless, it is not helpful for children to remain with parents who reject them, who cannot look after them properly, and who repeatedly give them up to the local authority for short periods when they can no longer cope. In these circumstances it may well be better to recognize that things are not going to improve and that it would be preferable for the child to receive long-term fostering or to be adopted.

A related issued is the need to improve the quality of Children's Homes as environments which can meet the young children's psychosocial needs (Rutter, 1979e). It has proved possible to make residential nurseries for preschool children stimulating and interesting places with plenty of joint activities between staff and children. No longer need there be any intellectual impairment associated with an institutional upbringing. However, it has proved much more difficult to ensure any kind of continuity in parenting. All too frequently the pattern is of a very large number of different and changing caretakers concerned with any one child during the preschool years. This is not a pattern conducive to normal social development and ways must be found to improve this aspect of institutional life for young children. Of course, an institutional upbringing should never be a first choice but regrettably it is likely that there will always be circumstances when no other alternative is available. We should strive to find better ways of dealing with problems of family break-down, but also we must take steps to ensure that, for those children who experience it, being brought up in a Children's Home is as positive and beneficial in its effects as we can make it.

Admission to hospital

Repeated hospital admissions, especially in young children already experiencing chronic family adversity, is associated with an increased risk of psychosocial problems in later childhood and adolescence. While the precise mechanism whereby this leads to long-term disorder remains uncertain, four steps seem likely to diminish the likelihood of psychological damage (see Rutter, 1979c). First, the conditions during the admission should be improved by, for example, allowing unrestricted visiting (and by making it possible for parents to be admitted in order to accompany very young children); by adequate provision of toys and supervised play; by keeping unpleasant medical and nursing procedures to a minimum; by counselling; and by ensuring that each child should be looked after by only a few staff who have a special responsibility for him rather than by a large number of changing staff who deal with the total ward group. Secondly, recurrent admissions should be avoided whenever possible. Every effort should be made to treat ill children as out-patients or day-patients unless there are strong reasons for admitting them to hospital. Thirdly, the fact that repeated admissions often arise for social as much as for medical reasons should be used as an indicator of risk. When children are experiencing their second or third admission, hospital staff should be alert to the possibility that there may be chronic family stresses or disadvantage requiring and susceptible to treatment. Fourthly, it seems that many of the difficulties shown after return home from hospital arise because parents do not understand the meaning of their child's clinging, irritating behaviour and respond with punishment when comfort is needed. Explanations and guidance could do much to help parents respond more appropriately at this time of stress.

Day-care and working mothers

As discussed in chapter 4, both in the U.K. and the U.S.A. over recent years more mothers of young children have been going out to work and more young children have been experiencing various forms of day-care. Professionals have reacted to this trend in different ways—some wanting to reverse the trend by paying mothers to stay at home with their children and some wanting to meet the needs by a major expansion in the state's provision of day care facilities. Yet others have seen the need as one of bringing fathers more into child-care or of providing more part-time work for women. The available research data do not allow any empirical basis for a choice between these and other alternatives with respect to children under three years of age. With older preschool children, research findings indicate that no ill-effects need stem from either mothers going out to work or from day-care—the issue is simply one of *quality* of care. Obviously, the quality of care is also crucial with the youngest children but less is known on the advantages and disadvantages of divided care. The matter requires further study.

However, in the meanwhile there is everything to be gained from efforts to improve children's experiences in day-care facilities of all kinds, whether they be day-nurseries, play-groups, nursery schools or private child minders. Thus, it is important that there be continuity in the staff who care for the children so that each child has only a quite limited number of primary caretakers. But also there needs to be a sufficient number of staff to provide the children with play and conversation and with an adequate range of experiences and learning opportunities. The second immediate need is to ensure that the day-care experiences enhance, rather than diminish, the qualities of parent-child interaction at home (see Bronfenbrenner, 1974 and 1979). This is not just a matter of including parents in the day-care activities—this may not be possible with working parents and indeed their presence at the centre or nursery may detract from their effective functioning if they are made to feel inexpert by the professionals looking after the children. Rather it is a recognition that day-care needs to be viewed in terms of its effects on family life as a whole and not merely as an experiential 'input' to the child. Also, it needs to be seen as an opportunity, if properly taken, to help parents better enjoy their children, understand their needs, and know how to play and talk with them. Many studies provide valuable leads on what may be done in this connection but the merits and demerits of different approaches have still to be evaluated.

Mentally ill and criminal parents
It is well established that children being reared by mentally ill or criminal parents have a considerably increased risk of psychosocial problems in adolescence. Doubtless, in part, the risk is influenced by genetic factors but also it seems that much of the risk stems from the family difficulties, discord and disturbance associated with the parental problems. Obviously, this provides an opportunity for preventive action and it is highly desirable that those professionals looking after parents with personality disorders, chronic psychiatric conditions, or recidivist criminality, should be aware of the need to consider the children in such families. In particular, they should be alert to the ways in which the adult's problems may be causing some impairment in parental functioning. A developmental and a family perspective is necessary even though the adult patient or client comes for help with just their own illness or difficulties. However, while the preventive opportunity is inherent in the situation, it must be added that no means of intervention (with respect to the children) are known to be effective. The situation is important because of its potential and because of the need to develop preventive strategies rather than because solutions are immediately to hand.

Educational retardation
The link between educational retardation and psychiatric disorder (also delinquency) applies with respect to conditions arising in childhood and persisting into adolescence, although not to those arising for the first time during the teenage period. The mechanisms involved are ill-understood but are certainly multiple. In part, it is likely to be because both educational and psychiatric

problems have their roots in the same set of temperamental features and family adversities. Also, however, it seems that to some extent severe reading difficulties predispose to emotional and behavioural problems through the experience of scholastic failure and its accompanying stigma. In so far as that is the case, the effective prevention or remediation of reading (and other scholastic) difficulties should have psychosocial benefits—although that has yet to be demonstrated. Services for children with reading difficulties are generally rather unsatisfactory at present and there is a need both to extend and improve the provision (D.E.S., 1972; Bullock, 1975). Regrettably little is known on the best means of remedial treatment for children with severe reading retardation and further research is much needed in this area.

Education for parenthood

It is obvious from all that has gone before that we should aim for an enhanced public awareness of children's needs and that in particular we should do more to improve parental skills and sensitivities (Court, 1976; WHO, 1977). Many parents fail to enjoy their children because they do not know how to play and talk with them; and discipline is a cause of strain and discord because parents set about it in the wrong ways. However, while that is generally recognized and accepted, there is considerable uncertainty and disagreement on just what to do about it. Clearly there is no one 'right' way. The two most striking features of child care manuals over the years have been, firstly, that the professionals have usually expressed considerable certainty at any one time on the best method of child rearing and, secondly, that their recommendations alter each decade or so! Rather than a 'best buy' on the techniques to follow, it is a question of appreciating the implications of individual differences; of understanding the meaning of children's sensitivities and signals; of developing coping strategies, of learning when to persist and when to desist; of monitoring what is done to see if it works and if not why not; and most of all of maintaining harmonious relationships in the home with respect for the different personalities and different ways of doing things in the family (Rutter, 1975).

How should that be accomplished? No tested answer is available and one can only speculate about possible solutions. But, perhaps the first point needs to be that numerous opportunities for education for parenthood already exist and full use should be made of these before we try to create new situations or opportunities. The second point is that it seems unlikely that book knowledge as such would help to any extent. Putting on academic 'courses' in parenthood would not achieve much. The third point is a corollary of the second—that because parenthood constitutes one special aspect of the broader issue of social relationships, much of the learning will need to be by 'doing' rather than by reading or listening. Lastly, as with all learning, it is likely to be most successful if it takes place at a time when the individuals concerned are receptive and see the point of the learning.

In this connection the idealism and the human concern felt by most adolescents is relevant. It is also pertinent that most teenagers today (see chapter 1) spend time looking after young children; either through baby-sitting or caring for younger sibs or cousins at home. This provides a valuable opportunity for learning at a time when they are first having to try out a type of parental skill. Pre-adolescent children, too, (both boys and girls), are usually very interested in infants and love to share in their care. Parents could be helped to take advantage of these situations to enable their children to learn from their experiences. Schools, too, could provide time to discuss these matters and could provide supervised experiences in child care. For some years, Bronfenbrenner (1979) has advocated the adoption of a *curriculum for caring*. Its purpose:

... would be not to learn *about* caring, but to engage *in* it. Children would be asked to take responsibility for spending time with and caring for others—old people, younger children, the sick and the lonely. It would be essential that such activities be carried out under firm supervision ... (and) ... the supervisors should be drawn from persons in the community who have experience in caring—parents, senior citizens, volunteer workers and others who understand the needs of those requiring attention and the demands on those who would give it.

Bronfenbrenner goes on to argue that such caring activities could

252

not be restricted to the school and that the children should come to know something of the circumstances in which their charges live and of the people in their lives. He also rightly emphasizes the need to evaluate what might be achieved in this way. No evidence is available on its value but the principles seem right and the experiment worth making. Of course, the suggestion is not new and many schools already do something of this kind but so far there has been little attempt to integrate such activities into a meaningful programme.

In the same way, opportunities exist in terms of sex education in schools, psychosexual counselling in clinics, 'parentcraft' classes as part of antenatal care, health visitor or child health clinic contacts with families during the preschool years and interactions with parents as part of the provision of play care. The two pilot studies mentioned in chapter 4 on primary health care counselling offer some hope that something useful might be achieved but knowledge on the value of these approaches remains fragmentary and inconclusive.

Conclusions

In this section of the chapter I have tried to draw attention to possible opportunities for prevention. It does not need emphasizing that in all cases evidence is lacking on the efficacy of the suggested measures in terms of their power to reduce adolescent problems. However, the measures are based on reasonably good evidence of 'risk' situations in which effective intervention should bring benefits. The emphasis throughout has been on improving the quality of services which already exist, rather than on instituting new services—both because this is likely to prove more practicable and because the costs should be minimal. That is not to say that new and costly programmes should not be introduced. If their benefits are sufficiently worthwhile in relation to their costs then clearly the programmes should be undertaken. But before doing that some evidence is needed on efficacy and such evidence is not yet available. The main focus of this section has been on interventions in childhood rather than in adolescence itself, because the roots of many of the most severe adolescent disorders are to be found in the earlier years. However, in considering ecological interventions we now turn attention to the teenage period.

ECOLOGICAL INTERVENTIONS

At its most general, human ecology simply refers to the study of the mutual interactions between man and his environment. However, as a theoretical approach its distinctive features are that it deals with systems rather than with individuals; it focuses on the *mutuality* of social interactions; it is essentially comparative in orientation in its interest in how the effects of experience in one environment may influence a person's response to another environment; and it involves a study of the characteristics of environmental settings and of the dynamic interplay between people and their environments (Bronfenbrenner, 1974 and 1979). As such, it is concerned with social groups in terms of their features as *groups*, rather than as collections of unconnected individuals. The implication is that groups have a life and force of their own which is both more than and different from the sum of the separate effects of the individuals in them (see Rutter et al, 1979; and Bronfenbrenner, 1979, both for evidence supporting this point and for a discussion of its consequences). Ecological interventions, in turn, are those which are most usefully considered in terms of their impact on groups and on the interactions of those groups with environmental settings. It will be appreciated that the distinction from individual interventions is far from an absolute one but, nevertheless, the difference in emphasis is useful with respect to the planning of services.

Schools
Perhaps the most obvious application of this approach is to schools, because they constitute social organizations with recognizable boundaries and purposes. It was noted in chapter 3 that research findings have shown that schools have important effects on young people's behaviour and attainments. As all adolescents are expected to attend school, the possibility of improving the quality of schooling provides a major opportunity for effective preventive action. Before discussing what might be needed in order to take

advantage of this opportunity, it is necessary to consider just what sort of effect the school represents. Is it simply a matter of schools providing more or less opportunities for misbehaviour (an issue of importance in its own right discussed further below), or could it be just that some schools 'run such a tight ship' that adolescents' supposedly inherent tendency to be disruptive is kept in check within the school buildings only to erupt elsewhere in the community? Or yet again, is it a matter of school teachers directly shaping the behaviour of many individual children? Doubtless all these factors operate but it is clear from a study of the research findings that none constitutes the main explanation for the mode of operation of the school effect. Rather, it is necessary to utilize a concept of some sort of school ethos or climate. There are three main reasons for arguing that there is likely to be a broader institutional effect of some kind (Rutter et al, 1979).

First, in our own study of secondary schools most of the individual measures of school functioning had only a most indirect connection with the pupil outcome with which they were statistically associated. Thus, a host of school factors correlated significantly with attendance but many of them did not involve any kind of teacher or school response to absconding or truanting as such. Moreover, some school variables were significantly associated with adolescent behaviours completely outside the school itself—as was the case, for example, with delinquency. The implication is that the style and quality of life at school was having a relatively pervasive effect on children's behaviour—an effect which went well beyond any kind of immediate shaping by direct rewards and punishments.

Secondly, it appeared that the *same* teacher actions sometimes led to quite *different* results in different schools. For example, if children were left alone in lessons to get on with their own work, in some schools they did just that. In others any relaxation of direct control led to an increase in disruptive behaviour. The observation echoes the much earlier findings by Lewin, Lippitt and White (1939; White and Lippitt, 1960) on the consequences of three contrasting leadership styles in experimental groups of 10- to 11-year-old boys. The effects of 'authoritarian', 'democratic' and *laissez-faire* leadership styles were examined under conditions of both the presence and absence of the leader. With the 'authoritarian' style, productive behaviour was high when the leader was present but fell off markedly when he was away. With the so-called 'democratic' style, on the other hand, productivity was equally high in both conditions, suggesting that *that* group climate had had a more enduring effect. It seems that there can be something about the way young people are dealt with in general which influences their behaviour even when there is no direct supervision by staff.

Thirdly, many of the school variables in our study of secondary schools did not refer to actions which bore directly on individual children. Some were concerned with conditions in the school generally (such as good care of the buildings). Others were involved with the management of groups (for example, the *dis*advantage of frequent individual interaction in class-oriented teaching) or concerned teacher behaviours which were not focused on any individual (e.g. the disruptive effects of ending lessons early or beginning them late). It is important to recognize that the way of responding to an individual child will have an effect on the *rest* of the class. This was probably relevant, for example, in the observation that unofficial slapping or cuffing of children by teachers was associated with high rates of behavioural disruption (even after taking into account the behaviour of the children at the time they entered the school). Experimental studies provide ample demonstration of the fact that punishment can be a most effective way of controlling behaviour (see Walters and Grusec, 1977). But in a school context the ways in which punishment is used and the frequency with which it is given will carry messages to *other* children, and create an atmosphere which may run counter to the intended effect on the offending individual. Taken together, these three findings suggest that it is necessary to regard the school as having an overall ecological effect which goes beyond the consequences of particular teacher behaviours for individual children.

The particular features of schools with beneficial effects on pupils' behaviour and attainments were outlined in chapter 3. Here, we need to turn attention to the policy implications of these findings. The first issue arises from the observation that pupil outcomes tended to be worse (and especially that delinquency tended to be more frequent) in schools with a particularly high proportion of intellectually less able children. This is not just another way of saying that outcomes were usually less good for less able children (although obviously they were) but rather that for children of *any* level of ability, outcomes tended to be less good if the bulk of the school population consisted of children in the lowest ability band (as determined *prior* to secondary transfer). In other words, it was a group rather than an individual effect, and one which seemed to operate on a school-wide basis.

The implication is that there are considerable disadvantages in an educational system which allows such an uneven distribution of children that some schools have intakes with a heavy preponderance of the intellectually less able. It will be appreciated that the findings apply to schools operating within a supposedly non-selective system, so that the mere existence of 'comprehensive' schooling does not in itself provide a solution if either parental choice or matters of geography result in some schools getting a majority of less able children. The findings point to the major drawbacks of either a community school system (if the distributions mean that some communities include a preponderance of disadvantaged children) or an open-market system (if a combination of parental choice and school acceptance of applications can result in a severe imbalance between the intakes to different schools). Forced bussing of children to schools outside their district has not proved a particularly good solution either (see Rutter and Madge, 1976), in view, amongst other things, of the resentments it can arouse, of the problems of long periods spent in travel to and from school, and of the difficulties in linking school friendships with out-of-school activities. There can be no dodging the need to ensure a reasonable balance of intakes between schools but it is not obvious what is the best way of achieving this. In the long run it is likely to be best to ensure that communities are sufficiently socially mixed so that community schools would fairly automatically get a reasonable balance of intakes. Socially deprived ghettoes have many other disadvantages and, quite apart from the benefits for schooling, it seems highly desirable that towns be planned to avoid their development. In the shorter term, there is no alternative to local authorities maintaining a degree of control over admissions to schools to ensure a fair parity between intakes. So far as possible this should be done in a way which is in keeping with parental and child choice. This cannot happen so long as some schools are markedly inferior to others and the most urgent requirement is to improve the quality of schooling generally and especially to upgrade the worst schools. If this happens, parental choice is unlikely to work against the need to make intakes to different schools comparable.

It should be added that the findings on balance of intake also have implications for the political question of selective versus comprehensive schooling. While the two systems have not been directly compared in this connection, the results clearly suggest that although a selective system may well have advantages for the 15 per cent or so children in the academically selective schools, it will almost certainly have great disadvantages for the 85 per cent or so children in the non-academic (so-called secondary modern) schools. For this reason alone it does not appear a sound solution. On the other hand, there is an onus on those who support a comprehensive system to ensure that the most able youngsters do not suffer. As indicated in chapter 2, the official statistics are not organized in a way which allows any assessment of the attainments of the groups separately and it seems highly desirable that information be obtained not only on whether standards are rising or falling for this group of adolescents but also on how they fare in different types of schools. The key question is likely to be what should be done to ensure the best education for 16- to 18-year-olds taking academic courses in the sixth-form. If schools have an even balance of intake it may be that in the more socially disadvantaged inner city areas, the size of sixth-forms will be too small to support a proper range of courses. If this is the case it will be essential for several schools to pool resources at the sixth-form level (as is already being done in many areas).

The next issue concerns the allocation of resources. Several studies have shown that the pupil/teacher ratio within the ranges studied is unrelated to either behavioural or academic outcomes. The qualification 'within the ranges studied' is important as many of the investigations (like our own) concerned authorities with rather favourable staffing ratios and with above average levels of educational expenditure. The results definitely do *not* justify severe cuts in expenditure (as some politicians have proposed), nor do they mean that the pupil/teacher ratio is of no importance. It may be that there are educational advantages in having *very* small classes which allow a different approach to teaching (although this has yet to be demonstrated), but with the general run of pupils there seems to be little to gain from cutting class sizes by just a few pupils—from say 30 to 25. If extra funds are available for schools there are probably better ways of spending them.

The finding of no significant association between school class size and pupil outcomes (within the ordinary range of sizes) sometimes gives rise to negative reactions among teachers who feel that the implication is that teaching conditions do not matter and therefore that their classes can be loaded still further. Not only is this implication false, as noted above, but also the finding is better seen as having a liberating influence (Rutter, 1979h). For example, rather than struggle to reduce the size of all classes equally, it may be preferable to allow the regular classes to increase by a few children in order to make possible a really effective cut in the size of remedial classes. The results of group remedial teaching are not very encouraging (see Rutter and Yule, 1973) and it is clear that ways need to be found to improve things. The limited available evidence suggests that a really low pupil/ teacher ratio (four to one, or less), maximal instruction time, and intensive teacher/child interaction are the necessary (but not sufficient) ingredients for success (Guthrie, 1978). If remedial classes were reduced from their present average of 15 or so to say four children that certainly would allow a more individualized approach for youngsters with severe learning disabilities—a shift which might have sizeable educational benefits. Of course, the benefits have yet to be determined but the experiment would be worth undertaking. Alternatively, or in addition, regular class sizes could be increased marginally to free junior teachers to observe other classes and to receive fuller practical in-service training in classroom management.

That constitutes the third major issue which arises from studies of schools. Our research (Rutter et al, 1979) indicated not only that the skilled management of classroom groups constituted one crucial element in successful schooling, but also that schools varied greatly in the support and guidance provided to teachers and that probationary teachers in all schools had a rather difficult time during their first year. The difference in the better functioning schools was that teachers gained the necessary skills with further experience, whereas in the least successful schools they did not. There are implications here for teacher training in the need to focus more on the practical management skills involved in 'the craft of the classroom', as Michael Marland (1975) calls it, as well as on pedagogy as more narrowly understood. However, essentially these are skills learned on the job, so the main implication is for better in-service training in which probationers could both observe their more senior colleagues at work and benefit from the comments and advice of those who have observed them teach. The benefits to be gained from opportunities to observe and to be observed in the ordinary classroom have been noted with respect to courses for primary school teachers (Yule et al, 1977) and doubtless the same will apply at secondary school level.

However, the need for in-service training does not only apply to the skills of the classroom. Senior teachers tend to be involved as much in the management of the whole school organization as in classroom teaching itself. They need to ensure that it runs smoothly with clear decision-making, efficient communication, and good opportunities for consultation with staff at all levels. It is important that there be agreed policies on the curriculum and on discipline and there has to be the means for this to develop. An eye has to be kept on the maintenance of good working conditions for both teachers and pupils, on the appropriate balance of rewards and punishments, on opportunities for students to participate in school life and to take appropriate responsibilities. In-service training is required for senior teachers to enable them to acquire these wider school management skills.

Both types of in-service training raise the related issue of the role of external school inspectors and advisors. Currently, advice tends to be more readily available with respect to the teaching of specific subjects such as English, mathematics or languages.

Ecological interventions

There is a need for similarly skilled advice to be available on the various school and classroom management issues. However, for this to be most useful it will also be necessary for the external advisors to have the opportunity of freely observing everyday school functioning.

Finally, there is the most crucial question of all—that of implementing change and maintaining success. Given that we have a notion of *some* of the features that make for successful schooling (obviously more knowledge is needed on this topic and so far all that are available are useful guidelines), what needs to be done to ensure that the right kind of changes are brought about in schools which are currently in difficulties? The issue is a complicated one and no very satisfactory answers are available as yet. In the first place, there is no *one* formula for success; what is needed will depend not only on the circumstances and history of each school but also on its particular aims and values. Secondly, in a situation of failure and trouble the strong tendency is to close one's eyes to the awfulness of it all, or to believe that the difficulties are outside one's control, or to get out. To remain in a situation in which you accept that something needs to be done but nothing is done is just too painful. Thirdly, often it is the case that many of the difficulties have arisen as a result of attempted solutions to some other problem. It is not that there is a lack of will to change but rather that the absence of any long-term strategy means that one is constantly making a series of unconnected changes, each of which tends to undo any good stemming from the change before. Fourthly, knowledge of what is needed is not enough—there must also be the 'know-how' on how to bring the changes about and the right order and sequence of actions required to make the implementations of change a success. Lastly, the most appropriate strategy for improvement when there is a major change of key personnel (as with the coming of a new Head) may not be the same as that required when no alterations in staffing are possible. It is obvious that research is needed into the very process of change and into the ways to bring it about successfully and harmoniously. In the meanwhile, it seems that if schools are to have the will to change and the determination to succeed, self-monitoring will be needed so that staff can be properly aware of their pattern of success and failure. Also, they need to be able to appreciate what can be done. In this connection greater contact between schools might well be helpful. Most schools have got some things they do well and teachers are often surprisingly out of touch with the good ideas implicit in what is going on in the school up the road.

In this discussion of schools, it has been necessary to focus on both the problems and the need to improve things in schools experiencing difficulties. However, it is important to end this section by correcting the perspective. The very reason for picking on schools as an appropriate area for ecological intervention is just because it has been found that even schools serving a disadvantaged inner city area can function successfully and can be a force for the good. The challenge now is to take steps to ensure that so far as possible *all* schools approach the standards of the best.

Other institutions

The issues raised in connection with schools apply similarly to other forms of institution for adolescents; as shown by studies of probation hostels, schools for delinquents, units for autistic or mentally handicapped individuals, and colleges of further education (see Rutter et al, 1979, for references). However, in these more specialized residential institutions the problem of generalization to other environments is a more critical one, both because of their residential character and because the units provide a setting which is deliberately rather different from that in the outside world. This point is returned to briefly when considering therapeutic interventions (see below).

Community interventions

The idea of involving 'the community' in preventive and therapeutic interventions of various kinds has become somewhat fashionable in recent years. There are several roots to the concept. First and foremost, there has been an appreciation of the positive potential in community influences. They represent both the force inherent in a strong interest group and an untapped resource of ideas and of people. Alan Little (1978) noted the importance of this aspect of the community in his discussion of the needs of ethnic minority groups. Secondly, several studies of preschool day-care or education have observed what appeared to be 'diffusion' in terms of a spread of effects beyond the target groups. Interventions focused on the child have resulted in life style changes in mothers, or the 'experimental' families have interested their neighbours in the suggested new activities with the children (Bronfenbrenner, 1974 and 1979). Thirdly, community influences can operate as a counter to otherwise effective interventions. Delinquent or multi-problem subcultures may reject any form of help as not applicable to their needs and not acceptable because of its origin in an alien 'authority' organization.

The British Community Development Projects to deal with poverty and social deprivation (see Rutter and Madge, 1976), 'Intermediate Treatment' for delinquents (DHSS, 1973) and the Educational Priority Areas Projects (Halsey, 1972) represent community interventions in this philosophy. In all cases it is uncertain how much has been achieved but certainly they include examples of constructive community involvement. The Wincroft project (Smith, Farrant and Marchant, 1972) for detached delinquent youths, described in chapter 3, represents a rather different approach in which there was the aim of helping particular individuals by bringing resources into their own territory, being prepared to meet initially in coffee bars, and to join in their social activites. The various police initiatives with community groups (discussed under the heading of 'surveillance' in a later section of this chapter) also involve some of the same ideas. Few of these initiatives have been adequately evaluated, the concept of a 'community' is rather imprecise and assumes greater neighbourhood cohesion than is often the case (Quinton, 1979), and both the scope and content of the interventions has varied greatly between projects. The principles of engaging community support and of utilizing community resources seem sensible and the approaches deserve further trial and evaluation, but the ultimate value of this style of intervention remains to be determined.

Area influences

As discussed in chapter 3, there is good evidence indicating the importance of area influences in determining levels of child and adolescent psychopathology. In general, rates of problems tend to be high in inner city areas and lower in small towns but there are exceptions to this tendency and it is not yet known what are the key variables. The main impact seems to be on the parents and through them to the children. As a result the main area difference in adolescent disorders concerns those persisting from earlier childhood, rather than those arising for the first time during the teens. However, little is known about the ways in which some cities predispose to mental disorder and family discord. The opportunity for primary prevention is undoubtedly present, but until the mechanisms or key variables can be identified the opportunity for effective intervention remains potential rather than actual. Research to take the matter further is urgently needed. Needham (1977) and others have argued for an ecological systems approach to cities but so far there has been little attempt to apply this to the question of why and how city life increases the propensity to family problems.

Housing

Newman (1975) in his study of housing estates showed that the social characteristics of the resident population were stronger predictors of crime rate than the physical characteristics of design. However, he went on to argue that the *concentration* of high-risk families (e.g. low-income groups, single-parent households, families on welfare, fathers unemployed, etc.) in any particular estate affected the overall crime rate. In other words, a teenage boy from a high-risk family, Newman suggested, was more likely to be delinquent if living in an estate with a conglomeration of similar families than if he lives in a more mixed housing development. His data do not seem to allow an adequate test of the hypothesis but they point in that direction. Similarly, Gath et al (1977) found that children whose fathers held a semi-skilled or unskilled job were more likely to be referred to Child Guidance Clinics if they lived in a socially disadvantaged district than if they lived in a more mixed neighbourhood. This finding is in keeping with an ecological view that the *density* of disadvantaged families in the community as a whole affects individuals' behaviour over and above the effect of the characteristics of the family itself.

Ecological interventions

However, the inference is a weak one because social-class was the
only family variable available and it is quite likely that the families
in the high-risk and low-risk districts would differ on other
variables not taken into account. Clarke (1978) showed that the
child density of a housing block was the single most powerful
predictor of vandalism. On the other hand, the rate of recorded
vandalism *per child* was actually lower with increasing child
density. This does not necessarily contradict Newman's hypothesis both because only rates of vandalism and not levels of overall
crime were measured and because there may be a limit to the
level of damage possible in a particular block. Moreover, it could
be that the rate of reporting and of carrying out repairs may slow
down once levels of vandalism reach a certain point.

It is apparent that the ways in which families with problems are
distributed among housing estates may well influence the behaviour of teenagers in those families, but there is a paucity of
adequate empirical data on which to base policy recommendations.
Certainly, it is important to carry out further research to
determine the relative merits and demerits of policies of concentration or dispersal of high-risk families. Taken together with the
school findings, it is clear that a concentration policy makes it
almost certain that those housing blocks will become centres of
problem behaviour. A dispersal policy may make the difficulties
more manageable but whether it will affect overall rates of
problems (whether vandalism, delinquency or psychiatric disorder)
is much more uncertain. Nevertheless, the monitoring of natural
experiments in terms of varying housing policies should provide
both an answer and a guide to future housing policies.

The media, propaganda, and legislation
There can be little doubt that, if skilfully employed, propaganda
can have sizeable effects on both attitudes and behaviour. It would
be reasonable to suppose that it ought to be possible to harness
this power in the interests of health education. However, up to
now the results have been noticeably unsuccessful. For example,
the attempt by the Cummings (Cummings and Cummings, 1957)
to educate a community in greater understanding and tolerance
towards mental patients seemed paradoxically to reduce acceptance

265

of psychiatric disorder. More recently an appraisal of U.K. anti-smoking campaigns among adolescents attending secondary schools showed that they, too, were unsuccessful (Bewley, Day and Ide, 1974). The reasons why these various health education campaigns have achieved so little are unclear but obviously this is an area of action where greater expertise must be developed.

In contrast, the mass media do appear to have had effects—albeit undesired effects—in increasing violence among adolescents and possibly in precipating suicidal actions. Of course, aggressive and destructive behaviour has many origins and it would be both foolish and wrong to regard television as one of the major determinants. On the other hand, the evidence that it has *some* effect is quite strong (see chapter 3) and the inference is that an appropriate modification of TV programmes should have benefits. As the content of TV programmes is something which can readily be altered, there seems every reason to take action. However, it is not an easy matter to decide either how much of what kind of change is needed or how best to bring it about. The television companies have an obvious responsibility in this regard and the best solution is likely to be voluntary action on their part to make a major alteration in the violence content of TV programmes and then to systematically monitor the effects.

The last item to discuss under the heading of ecological interventions is that of legislation to enforce or prohibit some behaviour. Certainly this has a place as an appropriate mode of action. However, to be effective the legislation usually has to have fairly general public support. But even when the general principle has wide acceptance, it is not self-evident that compulsion (or prohibition) constitutes the most effective way of achieving the desired end result. The apparent effect of the raising of the school leaving age in the U.K. is a case in point. As discussed in chapter 2, it was immediately folowed by a massive *drop* in the proportion of young people staying on at school into the sixth-form. The lesson, surely, is that ultimately if we want young people to behave in a certain way we must create conditions such that they wish to do so because it proves rewarding or worthwhile. If legislation is not followed by the results we intend we need to ask ourselves whether we have created the right conditions for it to come about. Perhaps we have not yet achieved that with sixth-form education—especially for less able youngsters.

PREVENTION THROUGH INFLUENCES ON OPPORTUNITY AND SITUATION

The field of prevention through interventions designed to affect opportunities for particular forms of behaviour is one which has long been part of police thinking with respect to crime. The fitting of burglar-proof locks and the provision of security guards are both well-established examples of this approach. However, until recently the main emphasis has been on the more obvious forms of overt protection. It is now clear that in fact the range of possible preventive actions is very much wider than that, and moreover that the approach applies to a variety of non-delinquent behaviours as well as to crime. The several different types of intervention will be considered under the headings of access, diversion, physical design, maintenance, and surveillance.

Access

The recent Royal College of Psychiatrists (1979) report on alcoholism drew attention to the evidence from historical trends that the cost of alcoholic drinks bears a quite strong relationship to the per capita annual consumption of alcohol, which in turn is strongly linked to the extent of alcoholism and of alcohol-related diseases (such as cirrhosis of the liver). For example, at the turn of the century the per capita annual consumption of alcohol in the U.K. was equivalent to 4·2 gallons of spirit and the index of alcohol-related mortality was 182. By the mid-1930s alcohol consumption had fallen to 1·6 gallons and the index of mortality to 42. In more recent times both trends have reversed: thus, the per capita annual consumption of alcohol rose from 5·2 litres in 1950 to 9·7 litres in 1976. Over the same years the rate of alcohol-ism has also climbed steadily, as discussed in chapter 2. There are many reasons for supposing that the correlation represents a causal link. As the general level of alcohol consumption goes up, so the proportion of the population who suffer from alcoholism rises in parallel.

Of course, many factors will influence how much alcohol people consume but both economic influences (pricing) and formal controls (licensing) seem to play a part. There is a mass of evidence from data in many different countries that the price of alcohol is a major determinant of how much people drink. For example, in the U.K. when the price of a bottle of whisky was equivalent to some 40 per cent of the mean weekly per capita disposable income the annual consumption of whisky was less than a tenth of a proof gallon. When the price fell to the 20 per cent level, the annual consumption more than doubled to a fifth of a gallon. Alcohol consumption seems to be responsive to price in roughly the same manner evident with many other marketed commodities. The implication is that if taxation is used to ensure that alcoholic drinks are relatively expensive, it is likely that this will limit the amount of alcohol people consume and in turn will limit the extent of alcoholism.

The evidence on the effect of licensing controls is less clear-cut but it appears that *major* relaxations or tightening up of controls probably do have some impact on alcohol consumption. The Royal College report instanced the 50 per cent increase in per capita alcohol consumption in Finland between 1968 and 1970 when extremely restrictive licensing controls were very abruptly relaxed. Conversely, alcohol consumption in the U.K. fell by a half during the First World War when government restrictions were increased in an attempt to deal with the harm to the nation's productivity which seemed to stem from excessive drinking. It is uncertain whether the recent growth in the U.K. of supermarket sales of alcoholic drinks has encouraged their purchase as part of routine weekly shopping and hence has increased consumption, but it may have done so. The Royal College report concluded that if alcoholism is to be controlled there should be no further relaxation in the broad range of licensing provisions and that government revenue policies should be intentionally employed to keep alcohol costs sufficiently high so that alcohol consumption does not increase further and that by stages consumption should be brought back to an agreed lower level. These recommendations appear well justified and actions of this type might play a part in dealing with the growing problem of alcoholism in young people.

In much the same way, access to drugs is likely to be of some importance in relation to the levels of drug abuse, successful and attempted suicide—all of which have been increasing among adolescents. The very substantial reduction in toxicity of domestic coal-gas led to a dramatic fall in suicides due to coal-gas poisoning and in the population as a whole it probably also led to an overall reduction in deaths due to suicide (Hassell and Trethowan, 1972). Since the early 1960s there has been a marked fall in self-poisoning by barbiturates and a three-fold increase in poisonings by psychotropic drugs—almost certainly reflecting changing patterns of prescribing habits (Kreitman, 1977). There does not seem to have been any increase in the *proportions* of parasuicides by prescribed as compared with non-prescribed drug, so that the increase in parasuicide cannot be directly attributed to more liberal prescribing. Nevertheless, over two-thirds of self-poisonings are a result of prescribed drugs. Accordingly, the present extremely high rate of prescribing of drugs acting on the central nervous system may well make self-poisonings more likely both as a result of potentially toxic drugs being left lying around in a large proportion of households and through the creation of an attitude of relying on drugs to solve personal problems. Moreover, the extent to which prescribed drugs kill if taken in excess may well constitute one factor which plays a part in deciding whether a parasuicide becomes a suicide. The greater safety of many of the more modern drugs has probably been an advantage in this connection. Both steps to persuade doctors to reduce levels of prescribing to a more acceptable level and steps to increase the safety of drugs would be likely to be of benefit.

The availability of drugs of dependence is likely also to be of importance in the spread of drug abuse (de Alarcón, 1972). International comparisons indicate that the rates of use and abuse of any particular drug tend to follow the availability of the drug in that country. Moreover, strict drug legislation has been effective in some cases. For example, the introduction in Ireland of restrictions on the importing, distribution, and sale of amphetamines was followed by a marked decrease in their use by delinquents—as shown by urine tests in remand home boys (Wilson, 1972). Similarly, de Alarcón (1972) showed that the U.K. action in 1968 to reduce production of methylamphetamine and to withdraw the drug from retail pharmacists was immediately followed by a virtual disappearance of its abuse. Methylamphetamine users reverted to taking amphetamines by mouth or gradually transferred their preference to cannabis, LSD, and the hypnotics. Clearly, it is important in actions of this kind to consider which drug or activity may take the place of the one being eliminated. Nevertheless, effective control of the availability of drugs of dependence should help to limit drug abuse. However, while the aim is straightforward enough, the practical implications are more complicated as the U.S. National Commission on Marihuana and Drug Abuse (1973) pointed out. There is both the issue of controlling medical prescribing and there is the rather different issue of preventing illegal production and distribution. In both cases effective control of one drug may achieve little if it is then replaced by another which is equally noxious and still readily available. However, if strict control of the most damaging drugs shifts use to less dangerous substances this could be worthwhile in its own right. Discussion of the many factors which must be taken into account in deciding the cost-benefits attached to particular policies in drug control is beyond the scope of the present review, but it is clear that the control of access to drugs should constitute one element in any plan of action to reduce drug abuse.

Mayhew et al (1976) note that the recent memorandum on crime prevention by the Scottish Council in Crime argues that stricter control over the availability of dangerous weapons in Scotland might significantly reduce the incidence of violent crime. The much tighter restrictions on firearms in the U.K. compared with the U.S.A. probably plays a part in keeping crimes involving shooting to a relatively low level. Although not demonstrated by systematic studies, it is also clear that restrictions on access to unoccupied buildings is likely to reduce the possibility of vandalism. The Home Office Study Committee on Crime Prevention (1975), for example, listed some of the anti-vandalism practices available to the building industry. These include perimeter fencing of the building site during the course of construction work, the securing of all sheds during non-business hours and storage of mechanical plant in locked compounds. Similarly, local authorities may be able to limit vandalism by ensuring that vacated dwellings are firmly secured and by keeping unoccupied property to a minimum.

Diversion

As noted in earlier chapters, not much evidence is available on the value of diversionary measures. While it has been found that boys who spend their free time hanging around the streets in the company of a 'tough group' are much more likely than other boys to engage in vandalism (Clarke, 1978), it does not necessarily follow that better leisure facilities would reduce vandalism. The provision of more youth clubs might just draw more boys on to the street, so that travel to and from the clubs added yet another opportunity for destructive mischief. On the other hand, high delinquency areas are often those with a striking lack of leisure facilities (see Bagley, 1965; Central Policy Review Staff, 1978); delinquency rates go up during periods when adolescents are out of school and have nothing organized to do; and unemployed adolescents are particularly likely to become involved in crime. People of all ages need something to do in their spare time and if there are no facilities for socially acceptable activities, it would seem that vandalism and other forms of mischief may take their place. Accordingly, although the benefits remain unproved, it appears desirable that adequate leisure facilities should be available in all areas where young people live and congregate. School premises are a particularly under-used community asset and more use could be made of buildings such as empty warehouses or church-halls. Of course, there are problems in the multiple use of buildings and effective supervision and maintenance is essential. Nevertheless, opportunities exist and should be taken up by both voluntary organisations and local authorities.

Physical design

Several examples of the protective efficacy of physical design features were given earlier. These included the reduction of car thefts brought about by steering wheel locks (Mayhew et al, 1976) and the limiting of telephone call-box vandalism through the extensive strengthening of equipment (Post Office Telecommunications, 1979). Although their value may not have been experimentally demonstrated, there are many building features designed to provide a protection against vandalism (see Clarke, 1978; Central Policy Review Staff, 1978; Stone and Taylor, 1977; Home Office Standing Committee on Crime Prevention, 1975). These include 'target hardening' measures as through the use of glass substitutes; of more robust finishes which are impervious to crayons, felt tip pens, and the like; of stippled paint surfaces rather than plain ones; and of moulded fibreglass instead of upholstery of the most vulnerable seats (especially rear seats in the upper deck) of buses. Measures to reduce the accessibility of objects especially subject to vandalism may also be helpful—as by the use of concealed fixing-screws in door bolts or inaccessible interior fittings in lifts.

It is unknown how far adequate protective measures of this kind would merely serve to 'displace' vandalism from one site to another. Clearly, not much is likely to be gained if one part of a public area is made vandal-resistant while the immediately adjacent public area is left unprotected. However, in this connection it is relevant that most damage on housing estates is to stairs, corridors, walkways and other public or communal facilities rather than to personal dwellings. Also in the community as a whole, personal dwellings are the least likely of all buildings to be vandalised. Thus, in the Home Office Manchester Survey (Clarke, 1978) there were 19·2 incidents per property for schools, 7·8 for telephone kiosks, 3·4 for shops but only 0·04 per property for private dwellings. Hence the main need for protection is limited to particular areas and if all these are dealt with it is not likely that there would be substantial displacement to personal property. Moreover, there seems to be a strong opportunistic element in vandalism committed by adolescents and if the opportunities are not readily available damage may not take place. Mayhew et al's (1976) conclusion seems justified: that

... the various means of protecting public property ... have much to commend them, despite problems of public

272

acceptance, cost-effectiveness, and displacement of damage. More evidence about the effectiveness of these measures including target-hardening, rapid repair of damage and surveillance by employees would, however, be useful.'

Nevertheless, one caveat is necessary. As discussed further below, the provision of a pleasant, attractive environment is also important in reducing damage. If the physical protection creates an austere prison-like environment it may, by virtue of the atmosphere it establishes, predispose to the very behaviours it aims to discourage. However, a middle road is possible and there is no reason why a reasonably robust housing estate or group of public buildings should not also be attractive to the eye and conducive to good behaviour.

Maintenance

The research on schools (see chapter 3) showed that vandalism tended to be less in those where the buildings were well maintained and where the decorations were kept in good condition (see Pablant and Baxter, 1975; Rutter et al, 1979). Comparable data are lacking for public buildings and housing estates but derelict or neglected buildings seem particularly likely to be vandalized and adolescents seem most likely to cause damage to property which has already been damaged or which appears abandoned or uncared for. For example, Zimbardo (1973) found that an abandoned car in a run-down inner city area was quickly reduced to scrap by a combination of theft and vandalism. The Central Policy Review Staff (1978) noted that when a London Underground station which had been free of damage for years had a ceiling panel broken, thirty more were broken in the following three weeks. Satisfactory evidence is lacking but the strong impression is that neglect leads to vandalism and that the rapid repair of damage may prevent further destruction. As a result, the advice of those who have looked into these matters is that the maintenance of public buildings is vital and should not be made to bear the brunt of expenditure cuts; derelict areas should be rapidly cleared and put in good order; streets should be kept clean and tidy; building sites should be protected and rubble should not be kept lying around; graffiti should be promptly removed; and damaged street lighting or street furniture should be rapidly repaired (Home Office Standing Committee on Crime Prevention, 1975; Central Policy Review Staff, 1978; Clarke, 1978).

Surveillance

Finally, under the general heading of influences on opportunity there is the crucial matter of surveillance. Its importance with respect to crime has long been recognized by the police and there are many indications that properties and areas which are subject to continuous vigilance have less crime and vandalism (Home Office Standing Committee on Crime Prevention, 1975; Central Policy Review Staff, 1973). Thus, British Transport police secured a marked improvement in the behaviour of young people on 'football special' excursion trains through the extensive use of police escorts. Similarly, twenty-four hour coverage by police foot patrols sometimes seems to have played a part in reducing delinquency in selected high crime areas. Efficient supervision of schools and housing estates by resident caretakers seems to serve to reduce the rate of vandalism (DOE, 1977). Also the use of conductors on buses provides a degree of supervision which is sufficient to reduce significantly the amount of vandalism (Mayhew et al, 1976). All of these steps have been shown to be worthwhile and doubtless there are many other ways in which efficient supervision could limit delinquency and damage.

However, all these types of surveillance involve 'officials' of one sort or another. Recently, it has become clear that this is far too narrow a view of surveillance and it may be that the role of the general public will prove to be at least as crucial. Several rather different factors appear important.

Firstly, there is the question of design. As already noted, all studies have shown that it is the public and semi-public areas of housing estates which are most liable to be damaged and where most robberies take place. Adequate surveillance by the inhabitants of the estate is unlikely both because no-one identifies the territory as their responsibility and because of the impossibility of distinguishing strangers. As Newman (1975) put it:

In a high-rise building in which over a hundred families share an entry it is virtually impossible to distinguish neighbour from intruder or for anyone to attempt to enforce an acceptable code of behaviour or to feel comfortable about questioning the presence or activities of others.

The key physical variable seems to be the *number* of people involved in sharing a defined environment.

The smaller the number of families sharing a facility, whether it is a demarcated portion of a project's grounds or the access and circulation space within a circumscribed portion of a multi-family building, the stronger are their feelings of possession and, ultimately, of concern and responsibility.

It should be appreciated that the main issue here is not space (although space helps) but design. Quite high density estates can be built in a way that ensures that the street and grounds are linked to specific dwellings (rather than left in the public domain), and that the building entries and accompanying play spaces serve only a limited number of families.

Secondly, there is the matter of ownership. Insofar as it is *public* property which is most vulnerable to damage it might be advantageous for a much higher proportion of the population to own their homes rather than to rent them from the local authority. This could result in people feeling more responsible for the property in which they live and hence in their providing better surveillance of the premises. Certainly steps to this end are worth consideration—although the design of many public housing estates would make it difficult for people to provide much effective surveillance however much they wanted to do so. But, for a shift to private ownership to make any real difference it would have to involve a substantial number of families. This would only be possible if people with a low income and little savings could buy the houses or apartments they now rent. This poses a severe obstacle at present in view of the high cost of housing and the lack of any agreed means of financing which would include those on a very low wage. However, the problem is not inherently insoluble. For example, apparently Singapore has a scheme by which people can borrow against their pension contributions (which are compulsory) and in that country most apartments are owned—even those lived in by low income families. Graffiti appear less common on housing estates there than on comparable estates in the U.K. or the U.S.A. but whether this is due to private ownership or one of the host of other differences is not known. It should be added that if any scheme to increase private ownership by the selling of local authority housing to tenants is not to curtail severely the authority's ability to provide homes for those most in need, it is important (especially in the early stages) for the local authority to build or buy new homes. If this does not happen, the overall consequences could be to make the housing situation substantially worse for those who cannot buy their own homes. Until there are political answers to deal with these difficulties, the selling-off of local authority housing seems unlikely to be of general benefit.

Thirdly, there is the effect of getting people in the community to take more interest in and responsibility for the care of the public facilities available to them. The Central Policy Review Staff (1978) document gives some examples of local efforts which appear to have had success in reducing delinquency. In one a local community council was established and police officers who were qualified leaders took an active role in running youth clubs and sports teams. In another, the police were instrumental both in organizing groups of young people to clear up debris and remove graffiti and in obtaining premises for a community centre. Taylor (1978) has described the use of a contingency contract in a school as a means of dealing with vandalism in the toilets. The pupils' side of the bargain was to keep the toilets free of damage and graffiti for the whole of a summer term; in return if they succeeded in doing that Capital Radio would provide a Disco. To most people's surprise the scheme seemed to succeed. Clarke (1978) reported a similar experiment in Liverpool where young people received financial support for a youth centre in exchange for reducing vandalism. He also gave an American example of a school which provided the student body with a set sum of money to cover window breakage, with the agreement that the student body could keep whatever was left over after window repairs were paid for. The result was a dramatic reduction in window breakage. This 'contractual' approach has very obvious limitations in terms of the difficulties of instituting negotiations with those either responsible for vandalism or able to provide effective control of the vandalized areas. Nevertheless, although reliable evidence is lacking on the efficacy of community surveillance, this appears to be an avenue well worth further exploration.

Lastly, there is the matter of lighting of public areas. The argument is that vandalism is less likely to occur if it has to be done in the full glare of adequate lighting, so bringing the activities of destruction to the attention of everyone in the neighbourhood. Once more good data on how far this is effective are not available, but on the general principle of the value of surveillance it would seem to be likely to be of some value.

It is clear from this summary appraisal of the value of preventive policies which act through their effect on opportunities, that very little systematic evaluation has been undertaken so far. Moreover, of course, the interventions do not affect individual predispositions to behave in particular ways. Nevertheless, even from the slender leads so far available, it does appear that these approaches contain the possibilities of actions which could make a worthwhile (although quite limited) impact on certain forms of adolescent problems. The leads are worth following further.

CURRENT STRESSES AND STRENGTHS

The fourth potential area of intervention concerns adolescents' current circumstances with respect to the level of stresses experienced, the coping mechanisms they possess and the protective or ameliorating factors which are available. It might be thought that this would be the major area for preventive action in that (at least in theory) it has the most direct connection with the development of disorders. However, as we have seen, surprisingly little is known on the role of current stresses as precipitants of adolescent problems of any type and hence there is no ready point on which to obtain leverage for action. There is no doubt that further research is needed both into the role of stresses and into the influence of protective factors but no immediate policy recommendations can be made with respect to preventive interventions. The implications for therapeutic actions are considered as part of an overall discussion of this form of intervention.

THERAPEUTIC INTERVENTIONS

The question of the organization of health services for children and adolescents was considered at some length by the Court Committee as recently as 1976 and no attempt will be made here to cover the same ground. Nevertheless, there are some general issues which warrant brief discussion; also there are some therapeutic concerns which require consideration because they were outside the scope of that Committee.

Clinical skills

Because much has still to be learned about the most effective means of influencing adolescent behaviour and of alleviating their problems (see chapter 3) it is particularly important that those clinicians engaged in therapeutic services should include a good proportion of the most experienced and most able members of the caring professions. In this connection there must be concern over the relatively low status and salaries in the nursing and social work professions afforded to those who remain in day-to-day contact with patients (or clients). It is accepted that the salary scale was developed in order to provide an adequate career structure and to ensure that the very responsible senior administrative posts were filled by the best people, but the balance is now badly wrong. It cannot be right that a profession whose *raison d'etre* is personal care should heavily penalize those individuals who wish to continue in personal care, the main work for which they were trained and which probably provided the reason for their entering the profession. The salaries of nurses who remain on the wards now compares most unfavourably with all sorts of jobs requiring little or no training and in the long-run this is bound to be to the disadvantage of the continuing development of nursing skills.

As the Court Report (1976) stated:

There is great need to modify the salary structure to enable the best nurses to remain in clinical work (if they wish to do so) without loss of pay or status (original italics). The Briggs Report (1972) recognized that some ward-sisters (often in specialized fields) already have consultancy functions, exercise advanced clinical teaching skills, and participate in clinical research. It is recommended that these abilities and responsibilities should be accorded increased status and financial reward. The Halsbury Report (1974) went some way toward this end by suggesting the introduction of a higher level of ward-sister. This constituted a very important step in its provisions for recognizing higher clinical skills. If child psychiatric nursing is to develop its own expertise and advance its own subject it is necessary to attract able people into the work and to provide facilities and career structure for them to develop clinical research and teaching.

Much the same issues apply to social-work where again higher status and salaries are largely dependent on leaving field work to take on administrative responsibilities. As with nursing, these senior posts often involve supervision of junior colleagues who are seeing clients, but a supervisory role becomes less and less meaningful if the supervisor is not in practice himself. Providing advice on the basis of practical experience some years past is not a good model. A further issue in social-work is the very variable level of training (also the still large proportion of untrained workers) and the need for specialized courses after generic training for selected social-workers who will carry responsibility in working with adolescents and their families (and similarly also with other fields of social work). The current trend to extend this training provision, supported by the DHSS Working Party on Manpower Training for the Social Services (1976), is much to be welcomed. However, as the Court Report (1976) stated, it is also necessary to:

recommend the further development of field work posts with teaching and consultative responsibility so that senior social workers of high calibre can remain in direct practice without loss of salary or status (original italics). This is an essential requirement if social workers are to provide a good service, to expand clinical understanding, and to develop new and better ways of providing help.

Levels of training

A further issue in relation to staffing stems from the prevalence of psychosocial problems in adolescence. As discussed in chapter 1, some 10 to 15 per cent of adolescents experience significant mental health problems and with that level of disorder in the community it is clearly impractical, as well as undesirable, for all adolescents with emotional or behavioural disorders to be treated by psychiatrists. Rather, as the recent WHO Expert Committee (1977) pointed out, treatment should be carried out by those with the least training necessary to do the job really well. There is no point in using expensively trained medical personnel when this is not necessary. Two schemes to train carefully selected nurses to undertake specialized forms of treatment provide good models to follow in this connection. Isaac Marks (Marks et al, 1977) has pioneered the training of nurse-therapists to undertake the behavioural treatment of psychological disorders in adult patients. The demonstrated success of the scheme relies on a careful delineation of those problems which are within and those which are outside the range of skills expected of the nurses, together with clear educational objectives on the diagnostic and therapeutic skills to be acquired. John Newton (Newton et al, 1976 and 1978) has similarly provided a valuable lead in training nurse specialists in family planning who can prescribe oral contraceptives, undertake some forms of health screening, and fit intrauterine devices, tasks hitherto regarded as requiring medical skills. A follow-up of the patients treated showed excellent results, every bit as good as those achieved by doctors. These two examples concern very different forms of therapy (but both relevant to adolescents) and demonstrate how much can be achieved once the therapeutic task and skills can be accurately described and taught. There is much scope for the application of these approaches to other forms of treatment.

However, it must be added that the medical profession has been very slow to accept the value of this form of training for paramedical professionals and very reluctant to recognize their competence. It is to be hoped that in the future doctors will come to appreciate that far from being a threat, these developments free doctors to undertake work which only they can carry out. A further need is for a proper career structure and adequate financial rewards for specialist nurses of this kind—a point which has already been emphasized in the preceding section of this chapter.

Access to services

With psychosocial disorders generally, there is a need to ensure that services are readily available to those who need them and that they are provided in a manner which makes them acceptable (Court, 1976). The issue is a particularly important one in the case of adolescents, some of whom may be wary of services catering for children or requiring the presence of parents. Yet also they may not be at ease in clinics for adults where their problems may not be so readily understood. As the Court report (1976) argued, adolescents warrant consideration as a distinct group for health-care provision, even if total specialization in adolescent care is not to be recommended. This means that all professionals dealing with teenagers should have a training which not only provides a developmental perspective but also which covers the special problems and needs of adolescents.

However, in addition there are implications for the organization of services. Adolescents ought to be able to refer themselves for help and opportunities for consultation should be available in settings where teenagers work and meet. The most obvious site in this connection is the school and it is evident that teachers need to be receptive to young people's needs and to be willing to be consulted about personal problems relevant to school (see Rutter et al, 1979). The provision of counselling services in schools is a more extended attempt to provide help of this kind and there is some evidence that it may be beneficial to those individuals who receive it (Rose and Marshall, 1974). However, there are at present several, sometimes competing, developments in counselling and comparative evaluations are required. Views differ on whether counsellors should be practising teachers, how far it should be linked to careers guidance, whether it should cover families as well

281

as pupils, and on the extent to which its function should be directly therapeutic rather than coordinative (Court, 1976). Nevertheless, even though further studies are required to resolve these issues and to determine how much can be achieved through this approach, it is clear that counselling has a valuable role to play in secondary schools and that coverage on a much wider scale is needed.

Clinics specifically planned for adolescents also have a place. Thus, youth advisory clinics have been found to be helpful in meeting the particular needs of teenagers with respect to birth control and to psychosexual counselling (Cossey, 1978). So-called 'walk-in' advice centres, where there is informality, easy access and privacy, may be valuable as a means of providing consultation on psychosocial problems. Such clinics may be particularly useful in areas where homeless, rootless young people congregate, since they are particularly likely to shun organizations smacking of authority (Court, 1976). Evaluations of walk-in counselling services are still required to determine their merits and limitations but something of this kind would seem to be a worthwhile development.

Community based treatments for psychiatric disorder

The research findings on evaluations of different methods of treatment for psychiatric disorders in young people were reviewed in chapter 3 and the service implications have been discussed in Rutter (1975), the Court report (1976), and the WHO Expert Committee report (1977). While it is obvious that further studies of therapeutic efficacy are required and that all is far from well with psychiatric services, nevertheless it is also clear that some effective techniques are available. This is not the appropriate place to discuss the details of therapeutic strategies and tactics but it is perhaps worth drawing attention to a few of the more important trends offering hope for improvements in the future. Firstly, counselling has become more focussed and problem oriented, in keeping with the evidence that this is generally superior to the more traditional lengthy open-ended style. Secondly, with both the dynamic and behavioural psychotherapies there has been a shift away from the exclusive treatment of individuals to a focus on the family as a group of interacting members and on the child in his social context at home and at school. Thirdly, there has been a move away from the rigid application of treatments deriving from some all-encompassing theory to a more pragmatic approach based on an analysis of what works in a particular case. Fourthly, there is an increasing appreciation of the need to find ways of helping adolescents and their families develop coping mechanisms and social skills. That is, there has been a realization that the suppression of deviant behaviours is often inadequate on its own; more positive strategies, responses and adaptive mechanisms must be developed to take their place. Fifthly, it has become accepted that treatments need to be devised to improve young people's environment and not just help them adapt to disadvantage. There is value in a concern for intrapsychic mechanisms but this should not be at the expense of a neglect of the remediation of current real life problems.

Tariff or treatment for delinquency

In the U.K., the 1969 Children and Young Persons Act sought to make society's response to delinquency both more humane and more effective by making the main responsibility of Juvenile Courts that of enabling children's needs to be met (see Morris et al, 1980). Protecting society from delinquents and helping delinquent children's development were seen as complementary. The precise form of treatment provided for delinquents was to be largely left to those with the relevant specialist skills; the Court's role was to make the necessary orders to allow such help to be provided; and the duration of the orders was to be largely determined by the length of time required for effective treatment. Also, when circumstances changed, different treatments were to be tried as they might be in any ordinary clinic setting.

The approach sounds eminently reasonable and indeed it is easy to point to evidence which supports many of the underlying principles. For example, it is well established that minor un-detected delinquent acts are committed by many normal boys (e.g. Belson, 1975; Clarke, 1978), supporting the view expressed in *Children in Trouble* (Home Office, 1968) that delinquent behaviour is often no more than an incident in the pattern of

283

normal development and therefore does not warrant the operation of Criminal Court proceedings. It is also easy to show that the problems and backgrounds of children appearing before Juvenile Courts are often closely similar to those of children attending child guidance clinics (see e.g. Tennant, 1970); that persistently delinquent behaviour tends to be part of a pervasive life pattern (see e.g. West and Farrington, 1977); that this is often associated with severe family problems and parental difficulties (see e.g. West and Farrington, 1973); and that these family adversities are related to the likelihood of delinquency continuing (see e.g. Power et al, 1974; West and Farrington, 1977). Nevertheless, as Morris et al (1980) eloquently argue, not only have the principles of the Act never been put into operation in any meaningful fashion, but also the strategy itself is suspect. They have many criticisms to make of the treatment approach which underlies the 1969 Act, but the three most damaging are: (1) that there is no evidence that treatment works; (2) even worse, there are research data showing that court appearances may actually perpetuate delinquency (see Farrington, 1977); and (3) that the notion that involuntary treatment is not punishment is not a view shared by the delinquents themselves. They suggest that these drawbacks are so serious that they totally undermine the entire philosophy of the Act. Their solution is to transfer the problems into the public domain through a variety of community actions (which have much in common with some of those suggested in earlier sections of this chapter), and to adopt a 'tariff' system of justice by which both the scope (e.g. the use of residential placements) and duration (e.g. the length of supervision orders) of judicial responses are directly related to the seriousness of the delinquent acts, rather than to any supposed therapeutic needs. The crux of the argument is that if the assumptions underlying a treatment approach are suspect and if treatment does not in any case achieve what it sets out to do, it is better to 'protect' offenders from well-meant but unhelpful interventions and to replace futile attempts at cure by a system which is at least fair and predictable.

Undoubtedly there is a need for some sort of tariff in that there must be an adequate justification for society to intervene in the way that it does. Suppose that it could be shown that *the* effective treatment for occasional truancy or stealing of milk bottles was a minimum of ten years in-patient hospital care with continuous heavy medication. Everyone would agree that in this case the treatment is so totally out of keeping with the seriousness of the behaviour that it would not be acceptable for it to be enforced. Of course, the example is absurd but it serves to make the point that there must be limits to society's right to intervene and some sort of general tariff would be useful in making these explicit. However, it seems much more doubtful whether a tariff approach could be adequate in itself. Surely, at some point it is necessary to evaluate the effects of the judicial actions (be they therapeutic, punitive, or custodial)? Some delinquent acts are so trivial that it matters little whether or not they recur, but this is not the case with many others. For example, society cannot be indifferent to the frequency with which its citizens are subjected to violent assault or to robberies in which they lose their life savings. Nor should we be indifferent to the subsequent development of persistently antisocial adolescents. Robins' studies (1966 and 1979), as well as those of others, clearly document the greatly increased risk of a wide range of serious personal, psychiatric, and psychosocial troubles in adult life. These young people will not thank us if we cease to search for effective means of remediation and just abandon them to their fate. I suggest that, with *both* a tariff system and a treatment system, it is essential to determine the consequences of what we do. In this connection, of course, the results must include both community prevention, in terms of success in making it less likely that other people will engage in delinquent acts, and personal outcome in terms of the effects of the action in improving the chances of normal psychosocial development of that particular offender (this would include but not be restricted to a reduction in his delinquent behaviours). In short, the judicial response should be determined both by what is justifiable in terms of the seriousness of the offence and by what is known to be effective. However, two further points need to be made here. Firstly, at present the utility of the latter criterion is severely limited by a lack of treatments or punishments of proven efficacy. Not only must more effective responses be developed but also there must be an expansion of evaluative research.

Secondly, as emphasized in earlier sections of this chapter, it is by no means self-evident that the most effective actions will prove to be individual or family based. The range of possible interventions must extend to the community as a whole.

Residential placements

There has been a substantial growth in U.K. psychiatric in-patient facilities for children and adolescents over the last fifteen years but there is a continuing demand for more places for adolescents (see Court, 1976). Clinical experience suggests that the need is genuine but there is a paucity of evidence on either the appropriate indications for psychiatric care or the effects of this treatment approach (Hersov and Bentovim, 1977; Barker 1974). The WHO Expert Committee (1977) suggested that the need mainly arose when the young person's behaviour was too disturbed to be managed elsewhere (as with some psychotic disorders in adolescents); when psychiatric problems were associated with severe medical conditions (as in some cases of intractable asthma or epilepsy); when there was a life-threatening condition (as in some cases of anorexia nervosa or suicidal depression); when intensive intervention was required in conditions not manageable at home (as with some instances of severely disordered parent-child interaction); when the problem required a controlled separation of the adolescent from his family (as in some severe cases of school refusal); and when the main therapeutic action required manipulation of the total environment. These indications appear reasonable but the need for systematic evaluation and for comparison with other treatment approaches is great. This is particularly the case because the majority of youngsters leave hospital only to go on to some other kind of special facility. As Barker (1974) put it: '... in-patient care was thus often a passport to further help rather than a complete treatment in itself'. This is not necessarily because the individual problems are so intractable (although sometimes this is the case). Rather it may be that the very 'specialness' of the environment which underlies the in-patient unit's success in improving the adolescent's problems may also be responsible for the long-term limitations of this form of treatment. Perhaps the two main needs are firstly to help young people develop the coping mechanisms required to deal with the environmental stresses to which they may have to return (and this may require them to be in that environment) and, secondly, to involve parents in the treatment of a youngster removed from home in a way which maximizes the possibility of a return to the family (Holbrook, 1978).

Rather comparable issues arise with respect to residential placements for delinquents, with the additional concern that a boy's identification with a delinquent subculture may be strengthened by causing him to live entirely in the company of other delinquents. The reconviction rates following all forms of residential treatment are depressingly poor (Home Office, 1970; Clarke and Cornish, 1978) with some three-quarters of adolescents returning to court because of further delinquent acts. This has been so with more or less all forms of residential provision (approved schools, borstals, detention centres, etc.) with little evidence that any one type is better than any other. This does not mean that it is of no consequence what sort of regime is provided. To the contrary, as discussed in chapter 3, there is evidence that the qualities of the institution do matter, but the crucial features concern social structure and interpersonal relationships rather than the ostensible purpose or theoretical orientation of the establishment. Cawson (1978), in her study of residential staff in Community Homes, provides a helpful discussion of the issues and of the ways in which many of the difficulties stem, at least in part, from the organizational structure of the Homes and from the traditions of staff behaviour. However, as Clarke and Cornish (1978) point out, there is another consideration which limits the utility of residential treatments. It is just because the environment *is* such an important determinant of a person's current behaviour that the benefits are so evanescent. When boys move from Community Homes into their home environment their behaviour becomes subject to a different set of situational stimuli. The adaptive patterns of response which may have been acquired in the institution will be of limited use in the very different environment outside. Residential staff have relatively few opportunities to intervene in the home environment (and often do not regard it as part of their role to do so). For all these reasons there must be doubts on the wisdom of relying on residential care as any kind of general answer to delinquency. Nevertheless, residential placements will always be needed for some delinquent youths and it will continue to be necessary to try to improve the quality of the care they experience. At least as important, however, is the need to develop better links between institutions and the community and to extend the treatment goals beyond the individual to the home environment.

Secure provision

The debate over the need for social control has gone on for very many years and there is a long history of isolating and locking up severely recalcitrant children (Millham et al, 1978). However, in recent years there has been an increasing demand for more secure provision to deal with severely disruptive adolescents and to protect society from their actions. This demand stems from both the evidence of a marked increase in violent crimes (see chapter 2) and from the frustrations inherent in the lack of any effective way of coping with those who persistently abscond from community homes. The evidence that boys are now being admitted to secure units at an earlier age (32 per cent under 14½ years in 1964–8 but 62 per cent in 1975—Millham et al, 1978) may also be interpreted as a sign of things getting worse. Undoubtedly the problem is a real enough one. Three-quarters of those in secure units are persistent delinquents with a history of recurrent breakdowns of residential placements as a result of persistent absconding and socially provocative behaviour; 16 per cent are grave offenders guilty of offences such as rape, violent robbery, or arson; and 8 per cent have severe and often bizarre behaviour problems with spasmodic violence to staff and attempts at suicide—these boys are deeply disturbed but not necessarily particularly delinquent. About half the boys who have been in secure units regard their stay there as having been enjoyable and most feel that they have gained by the experience. Nevertheless, a quarter go on to other custodial settings and of the remainder only 24 per cent commit no further offences during the next two years. Not very good results by any criterion.

There has been a tendency to view the problem as one of severe individual problems, and certainly there is something in this—many of the adolescents who land up in secure units both come from a very disturbed background and show severe personal maladjustment. On the other hand, it is also evident that some residential facilities send more boys on to secure units than do others. High rates of absconding, of transfer and of failure tend to go together and it appears that, to some degree, the extent of the need for secure units will be influenced by the quality of other placements.

Undoubtedly, there is a need for some secure units and it is important that they be provided. However, as Millham et al (1978) argue, it may be that in many cases only relatively short spells of security are required because the crisis of control wanes and as it does so other methods of response become possible. The point is that the behaviour of adolescents is influenced by the environment in which they live and long periods of physically enforced security may not be the best means of providing rehabilitation. Substantial degrees of security may also be provided by generous staffing ratios, by intensive care, and by close relationships between staff and boys; moreover, the need for security may be reduced by appropriate training in social and community skills and by other steps to help the boys develop more effective coping strategies for dealing with their problems.

Special educational treatment

It has been estimated on the basis of several epidemiological enquiries that about one child in five is likely to need some kind of special educational provision (not necessarily at a special school) at some point during his school career (Warnock, 1978). The needs are many and various and have been well summarized in the Warnock report (1978). Many of the issues already discussed with respect to residential placements arise similarly in the field of special education and once again there is a lack of good empirical data upon which decisions on the indications for boarding-school might be based. Undoubtedly, there are children who require a total setting which encompasses both school and home because of the severity or complexity of their disabilities or because poor social conditions or disturbed family relationships contribute to exacerbate the child's educational difficulties in a major way. But as with other residential facilities there is the need for close liaison between school and the home.

A particular issue with respect to special education concerns the merits and demerits of 'mainstreaming' or integration, as against special schooling or segregation. In other words, how far should children with educational disabilities be taught alongside other disabled children and how far should they be intermingled with ordinary children who have no special needs? The first point is that the question is not 'whether?' but 'when?'. This is because the vast majority of young people with special educational needs will ultimately take their place in the community at large and at that time they will *have* to be integrated. So the issue is what needs to be done in terms of schooling to prepare them better for that stage. The main advantages of integration are that the child grows up in the community of ordinary children with whom he must eventually live and compete; that it is supposed to avoid the problem of labelling (but of course the handicapped can still be labelled in ordinary schools); and that it may be cheaper (although if the special provision in ordinary schools is of a quantity and quality comparable to that in special schools this will only sometimes be the case). The disadvantages are that integration can be made an excuse for just dumping handicapped children in ordinary classes without any special provision (although of course this should not happen); and that it may be very difficult to provide for a very wide range of needs in one setting (this is a real difficulty so far as the most severely disabled youngsters are concerned). The pro's and con's of segregation are largely the opposite side of the same coin. However, the main argument in its favour is the concentration of expertise needed to develop new and better methods of teaching and the doubt that as much would be achieved (for example, with the teaching of the blind, deaf, or autistic) if there had been integration from the outset. The other need for segregation reflects the fact that special needs do not refer only to pedagogy but also concern the setting or social milieu. What is best for the ordinary child is not necessarily best for the special child. It is obvious from just stating these issues that both segregated and integrated schooling is required. Integration should be the norm, provided that this involves no loss in the quality of education, but special schools will continue to be needed in order to provide adequately for some groups of young people. In this connection, it should be added that there are different degrees and types of integration—involving location, social contacts outside the classroom, and formal teaching (Warnock, 1978).

One other general issue concerns adolescents—the transition from school to work. Of all aspects of special education this is probably the one which is least adequately dealt with at the moment. In the first place, it is noteworthy that when the school-leaving age was raised for ordinary children it was not raised for those at special schools. Doubtless this was because it already stood at 16 years for them and indeed it may be right for many to leave at that age. But also it is evident that many handicapped adolescents would benefit from further schooling and it is most important that it be possible for them to remain at school until 17 or 18 years if it is in their interests to do so. A related point is that the association between reading difficulties and psychiatric disorder means that many special schools lack the facilities to help the academically able child with severe emotional or behavioural problems. Most special schools do a good deal to prepare their pupils for work, and both careers guidance and links with industry are helpful in this connection. However, less is available for handicapped adolescents who may eventually become able to hold a job but who cannot do so at the time of school leaving. For example, it is clear that autistic individuals who are not also mentally retarded sometimes improve substantially in the late-teens and early-twenties (Rutter, 1970a). For these and for other groups with similar needs training facilities are required to bridge the gap between school and employment.

FINAL THOUGHTS

In this final chapter of the monograph many suggestions have been made on what might be useful leads to follow in the development of preventive and therapeutic services for adolescents with psychosocial problems. I have drawn freely on the ideas of colleagues in a variety of disciplines and it seems that there is no shortage of good ideas about. However, there is a grave shortage of systematic data. My approach throughout has been empirical rather than theoretical, so that recommendations have been based on research findings and on established knowledge whenever these have been available. But it will have become all too apparent that in many instances they have been conspicuous by their absence. Throughout all chapters I have drawn attention to some of the more important research needs as they arose in relation to specific issues. But, this chapter has served to emphasize that research on therapeutic methods and services has been particularly neglected. If we are to develop better means of dealing with the manifold problems which present during adolescence, some priority must be given to evaluative research in the future. If this does not happen there is a danger of continuing to use ineffective measures. But there is also the even greater, but opposite, danger of abandoning measures that are in fact effective because their utility has not been empirically demonstrated.

Of course the evaluation of preventive and therapeutic interventions is difficult, and often inconclusive, because of the many factors involved. However, certain lessons arise out of the evaluative research which has been undertaken in the past. Firstly, there is a need to assess the process and quality of the interventions being studied and to define and describe the therapeutic techniques involved. Findings that 'psychotherapy' or 'counselling' or 'Community Homes' are or are not effective are almost valueless as a guide to action without detailed knowledge about the specific interventions. Secondly, all the answers cannot be obtained at once. At the very least there are the two very different questions of (a) which methods are truly effective given optimal conditions, and (b) whether these methods can be applied successfully on a community-wide basis. The former requires intensive small-scale studies with a tight control over what is done, whereas the latter involves large-scale research with the necessarily looser control of a real-life application across a range of different community settings. If both are combined in one overall research design there is a danger that no unequivocal answer will be obtained to either question—as illustrated by the EPA and Head Start enquiries. Moreover, the two problems may be rather different. For example,

Final thoughts

the 'Achievement Place' research seems to demonstrate that the techniques are effective but also that it is not easy to apply the methods on a wide scale.

Thirdly, all research indicates the situation-specificity of much behaviour. The goal of intervention must be to generalize the benefits across situations and the methods of evaluation must be planned to determine how far this has occurred. Fourthly, there are difficulties in the choice of the most appropriate outcome measures. All too often there has been recourse to whatever has been most easily available—IQ scores or court convictions—without enough concern for the development of measures truly relevant to the goals of treatment. Lastly, both long-term and short-term benefits need to be assessed. Most of the drug studies with chronic disorders have examined changes over periods of only a few weeks—these provide little guide to the utility of pharmacotherapy with conditions in which the handicaps tend to last for years. Also, some interventions may take time to have an impact. For instance, it would not be expected that improved housing would have a significant short-term impact on mental health. Conversely there are some treatments of self-limiting disorders which may cut short the problems without affecting the ultimate prognosis—short-term as well as long-term evaluations are needed to examine this possibility.

In so far as there is evidence on the efficacy of different types of intervention, it is quite clear that there is no *one* grand strategy which will provide the answer to adolescent problems. Rather there is a variety of different interventions, none of which solves the problem but each of which might contribute to a partial solution. Traditionally, preventive and therapeutic strategies have tended to focus on the individual. These approaches are both useful and relevant but the review of interventions has demonstrated that a great deal (perhaps more) is to be gained through ecological and situational (or opportunity) type interventions. So far their utility has been explored with only a rather narrow range of outcomes (especially vandalism) but I have been forcefully struck by the parallels between developments in different areas and the need for cross-fertilization of ideas. Some of these interventions could be usefully exploited with other adolescent problems.

One related issue in this connection is that very few of the suggested solutions lie in some overall centrally imposed solution. Legislation can be very useful in facilitating change and it can be crucial in blocking action. However, at the present stage of knowledge it is evident that a reliance on local initiative must constitute an important element in whatever is done. Indeed, because it is likely that to some extent we will always be making changes in ignorance, small scale experimental attempts which constitute evaluated responses to local situations will always be needed.

Finally, in trying to adopt a rational, empirically based approach I have deliberately avoided the equally important problems of why more has not been done already. Part of the answer lies in ignorance of what might be effective and it is on that part of the issue that I have focussed. However, there are also the problems of resistance to change as a result of professional self-interest, of political dogma, and of financial constraints. These topics require an equally extended discussion but they must be the subject of a different essay.

REFERENCES

ABEL SMITH, B. AND TOWNSEND, P. (1965). *The Poor and the Poorest*, Occasional Papers on Social Administration No. 17 (London: Bell).

ADELSON, J. (1975). 'The development of ideology in adolescence', in Dragastin, S. E. and Elder, G. H. (eds), *Adolescence in the Life Cycle*, 63–78: *Psychological change and social context* (London: Halstead Press).

ADELSTEIN, A. AND MARDON, C. (1975). 'Suicides 1961–74', *Population Trends*, 2, 13–18.

ADLER, F. (1977). 'The interaction between women's emancipation and female criminality: A cross-cultural perspective', *Internat. J. Criminol. Penol.*, 5, 101–12.

ALBERMAN, E. (1979). 'The epidemiology of cerebral palsy', in Rose, F. C. (ed), *Clinical Neuro-Epidemiology* (Tunbridge Wells: Pitman Medical), (In press).

ALDOUS, J. AND HILL, R. (1965). 'Social cohesion, lineage type, and intergenerational transmission', *Social Forces*, 43, 471–82.

ALEXANDER, J. AND PARSONS, B. (1973). 'Short-term intervention with delinquent families', *J. abn Psychol.*, 81, 219–25.

ALLEN, I. (1974). *Birth Control in Runcorn and Coalville: a study of the F.P.A. Campaign*, vol. xl, Broadsheet 549 (London: PEP).

ARIÈS, P. (1962). *Centuries of Childhood* (London: Cape).

BACHMAN, J. (1970). *Youth in transition*, vol. 2 (Ann Arbor: University of Michigan).

BAGLEY, C. (1965). 'Juvenile delinquency in Exeter', *Urban Studies*, 2, 35–9.

BAKWIN, H. (1957). 'Suicide in children and adolescents', *J. Pediatrics*, 50, 749–69.

BALDWIN, J. A. (1968). 'Psychiatric illness from birth to maturity: an epidemiological study', *Acta Psychiat. Scand.*, 44, 313–33.

BANTON, M. (1973). *Police-Community Relations* (London: Collins).

BARKER, P. (1974). 'The results of in-patient care', in Barker, P. (ed), *The Residential Psychiatric Treatment of Children* (London: Crosby Lockwood Staples).

BARKLEY, R. A. (1977). 'A review of stimulant drug research with hyperactive children', *J. Child Psychol. Psychiat.*, 18, 137–65.

BARNES, J. (1975). *Educational Priority*, vol. 3 (London: HMSO).

295

References

DARRACLOUGH, B., SHEPHARD, D., AND JENNINGS, C. (1977). 'Do newspaper reports of coroners' inquests incite people to commit suicide?' *Brit. J. Psychiat.*, **131**, 528–32.

BARTAK, L. AND RUTTER, M. (1976). 'Differences between mentally retarded and normally intelligent autistic children', *J. Autism Child Schiz.*, **6**, 109–20.

BASHAM, R. (1978). *Urban Anthropology: the cross-sultural study of complex societies* (Palo Alto, Calif.: Mayfield).

BAUMRIND, D. (1975). 'Early socialization and adolescent competence', in Dragastin, S. E. and Elder, G. H. (eds), *Adolescence in the Life Cycle: Psychological change and social context*, pp 117–46 (London: Halsted Press).

BELL, R. R. (1971). *Marriage and Family Intervention*, third edition (Homewood, Ill.: The Dorsey Press).

BELLMAN, M. (1966). 'Studies on encopresis', *Acta Paediat. Scand.* Suppl. 170.

BELSKY, J. AND STEINBERG, L. D. (1979). 'The effects of day care: a critical review', *Child Develop.*, **49**, 929–49.

BELSON, W. A. (1975). *Juvenile Theft. The Causal Factors* (London: Harper & Row).

—— (1978). *Television Violence and the Adolescent Boy* (Farnborough: Saxon House).

BENGTSON, V. L. (1970). 'The generation gap: a review and typology of social-psychological perspectives', *Youth and Society*, **2**, 7–32.

BENNETT, S. N. (1978). 'Recent research on teaching: a dream, a belief and a model', *Brit. J. Educ. Psychol.*, **48**, 127–47.

BERGER, M., YULE, W., AND RUTTER, M. (1975). 'Attainment and adjustment in two geographical areas: II. The prevalence of specific reading retardation', *Brit. J. Psychiat.*, **126**, 510–19.

BERKOWITZ, L., PARKE, R. D., LEYENS, J. P., WEST, S., AND SEBASTIAN, J. (1978). 'Experiments on the reactions of juvenile delinquents to filmed violence', in Hersov, L. A., Berger, M., and Shaffer, D. (eds), *Aggression and Antisocial Behaviour in Childhood and Adolescence*, pp. 59–71 (Oxford: Pergamon).

BEWLEY, B. R., DAY, I., AND IDE, L. (1974). *Smoking by Children in Great Britain—A review of the literature* (London: SSRC/MRC).

BEWLEY, T. H. (1975). 'An Introduction to Drug Dependence', in Silverstone, T. and Barraclough, B. (eds), *Contemporary Psychiatry* (London: Royal College of Psychiatrists).

BILLER, H. B. (1974). *Paternal Deprivation: Family, School, Sexuality and Society* (London: D. C. Heath).

BIRCH, H. G. AND GUSSOW, J. D. (1970). *Disadvantaged Children: Health, Nutrition and School Failure* (New York: Harcourt, Brace and World).

BLAUG, M. (1970). *An Introduction to the Economics of Education* (London: Allen Lane).

BLOCK, J. (1971). *Lives Through Time* (Berkeley: Bancroft Books).

BLOOM, B. S. (1964). *Stability and Change in Human Characteristics* (New York: Wiley).

References

BLOS, P. (1970). *The Young Adolescent: Clinical Studies* (London: Collier-Macmillan).

BLUMBERG, H. (1977). 'Drug taking', in Rutter, M. and Hersov, L. (eds), *Child Psychiatry: Modern Approaches*, pp 628–45 (Oxford: Blackwell Scientific).

BONE, M. (1977). *Pre-School Children and the Need for Day-Care* (London: HMSO).

—— (1978). 'Recent trends in sterilization', *Population Trends*, **13**, 13–20.

BOTTOMS, A. E. (1967). 'Delinquency amongst immigrants', *Race*, **8**, 357–83.

BOWERMAN, C. E. AND KINCH, J. W. (1959). 'Changes in family and peer orientation of children between the fourth and tenth grades', *Social Forces*, **37**, 206–11.

BOWLBY, J. (1951). *Maternal Care and Mental Health* (Geneva: World Health Organization).

BRAUCHT, G. N., BRAKARSH, D., FOLLINGSTAD, D., AND BERRY, K. L. (1973). 'Deviant drug use in adolescence: a review of psychosocial correlates', *Psychol. Bull.*, **79**, 92–106.

BRAUKMANN, C. J. AND FIXSEN, D. L. (1978). 'Behaviour modification with delinquents', in Hersen, M., Eisler, R. M., and Miller, P. M. (eds), *Progress in Behavior Modification* (New York: Academic Press).

BRAUNGART, R. C. (1975). 'Youth and social movements', in S. E. Dragastin and G. H. Elder (eds), *Adolescence in the Life Cycle: Psychological change and social context*, pp 255–90 (London: Halsted Press).

BRIGGS, A. (1972). See DEPARTMENT OF HEALTH AND SOCIAL SECURITY, 1972,

BRITISH TRANSPORT POLICE (1979). Personal communication.

BRITTAIN, C. V. (1963). 'Adolescent choices and parent-peer cross pressures'. *Amer. Sociol. Rev.*, **28**, 385–91.

—— (1967). 'An exploration of the bases of peer-compliance and parent-compliance in adolescence', *Adolescence*, **2**, 445–58.

BRODERICK, C. B. AND FOWLER, S. E. (1961). 'New patterns of relationships between the sexes among preadolescents', *Marriage and Family Living*, **23**, 27–30.

—— AND ROWE, G. P. (1968). 'A scale of preadolescent heterosexual development', *J. Marriage and the Family*, **30**, 97–101.

BRODY, S. R. (1976). *The Effectiveness of Sentencing—A Review of the Literature* (London: HMSO).

BRONFENBRENNER, U. (1970). *Two Worlds of Childhood: U.S. and U.S.S.R.* (New York: Russell Sage Foundation).

—— (1974). *Is Early Intervention Effective? A report on the longitudinal evaluations of pre-school programmes* (Bethesda, Maryland: Office of Child Development, U.S. Department of Health, Education and Welfare).

—— (1976). 'Who cares for America's children?' in Vaughan, V. C. and Brazelton, T. B. (eds), *The Family—Can it be Saved?*, pp 3–32 (Chicago: Year Book Medical Publ. Inc.).

—— (1979). *The Ecology of Human Development: experiments by nature and design* (Cambridge Mass.: Harvard University Press).

References

BRONSON, W. C. (1967). 'Adult derivatives of emotional expressiveness and reactivity-control: developmental continuities from childhood to adulthood', *Child Develop.*, **38**, 801–17.

BROWN, G. W. AND HARRIS, T. (1978). *Social Origins of Depression* (London: Tavistock).

BROWN, J. D. (ed). (1967). *The Hippies* (New York: Time-Life).

BROWN, R. C. AND DODSON, D. W. (1959). 'The effectiveness of a boys' club in reducing delinquency', *Annals Amer. Acad. Polit. Soc. Science*, **322**, 47–52.

BULLOCK, Sir Alan (1975). See DEPARTMENT OF EDUCATION AND SCIENCE, 1975.

BURK, B. A., ZDEP, S. M., AND KUSHNER, H. (1973). 'Affiliation patterns among American girls', *Adolescence*, **8**, 541–46.

BURKE, R. J. AND WEIR, T. (1978). 'Sex differences in adolescent life stress, social support and well-being', *J. Psychol.*, **98**, 277–88.

BURT, C. (1925). *The Young Delinquent* (London: University of London Press).

—— (1937). *The Backward Child* (London: University of London Press).

CAMPBELL, E. H. (1939). 'The social-sex development of children', *Genet. Psychol. Mon.*, **21**, 461–552.

CAMPBELL, E. Q. (1969). 'Adolescent socialization', in Goslin, D. A. (ed), *Handbook of Socialization Theory and Research*, pp 821–60 (Chicago: Rand McNally).

CANTWELL, D. (1977). 'Hyperkinetic syndrome', in Rutter, M. and Hersov, L. (eds), *Child Psychiatry: Modern Approaches*, pp 524–55 (Oxford: Blackwell Scientific).

CAPES, M. (1973). 'Evaluating services for adolescents', in Wing, J. K. and Häfner, H. (eds), *Roots of Evaluation: the epidemiological basis for planning psychiatric services*, pp 167–74 (London: Oxford University Press for the Nuffield Provincial Hospitals Trust).

——, GOULD, E., AND TOWNSEND, M. (1971). *Stress in Youth* (London: Oxford University Press for the Nuffield Provincial Hospitals Trust).

CAPLAN, H. L. (1970). *Hysterical 'Conversion' Symptoms in Childhood*. M. Phil dissertation, University of London.

CARPENTER, R. G. (1959). 'Statistical analysis of suicide and other mortality rates of students', *Brit. J. prev. soc. Med.*, **13**, 163–74.

CARTER, C. O. (1959). 'A life table for mongols with the causes of death', *J. Ment. Defic. Res.*, **2**, 64–74.

—— (1977). *Human Heredity, second edition* (Harmondsworth: Penguin).

CARTWRIGHT, A. (1976). *How Many Children?* (London: Routledge & Kegan Paul).

CASTLE, I. M. AND GITTUS, E. (1957). 'The distribution of social defects in Liverpool', *Sociol. Rev.*, **5**, 43–64.

CAWSON, P. (1978). *Community Homes: A Study of Residential Staff*. DHSS Research Report, no. 2 (London: HMSO).

References

CENTRAL POLICY REVIEW STAFF, (1978). *Vandalism* (London: HMSO).
CENTRAL STATISTICAL OFFICE, (1972). *Social Trends*, no. 3 (London: HMSO).
—— (1974). Ibid., no. 5.
—— (1976). Ibid., no. 7.
—— (1977). Ibid., no. 8.
—— (1978). Ibid., no. 9.
CHANDLER, M. J. (1977). 'Social cognition: a selective review of current research', in Overton, W. F. and Gallagher, J. M. (eds), *Knowledge and Development*, Vol. 1, *Advances in Research and Theory*, pp 93–147 (New York and London: Plenum).
CHESTER, R. (1972). 'Current incidence and trends in marital breakdown', *Postgrad. Med. J.*, **48**, 529–41.
CHRISTENSEN, H. T. AND MEISSNER, H. M. (1953). 'Studies in child spacing: IV. pre-marital pregnancy as a factor in divorce', *Amer. Sociol. Review*, **18**, 641–4.
CLARKE, A. M. AND CLARKE, A. D. B. (eds), (1976). *Early Experience: Myth and Evidence* (London: Open Books).
CLARKE, R. V. G. (ed), (1978). *Tackling Vandalism. Home Office Research Study No. 47* (London: HMSO).
—— AND CORNISH, D. B. (1978). 'The effectiveness of residential treatment for delinquents', in Hersov, L. A., Berger, M., and Shaffer, D. (eds), *Aggression and Antisocial Behaviour in Childhood and Adolescence*, pp 143–59 (Oxford: Pergamon).
—— AND MARTIN, D. N. (1971). *Absconding from Approved Schools* (London: HMSO).
CLAUSEN, J. A. (1975). 'The social meaning of differential physical and sexual maturation', in Dragastin, S. E. and Elder, G. H. (eds), *Adolescence in the Life Cycle: Psychological change and social context*, pp 25–48 (London: Halsted Press).
COCKETT, R. AND MARKS, V. (1969). 'Amphetamine taking among young offenders', *Brit. J. Psychiat.*, **115**, 1203–4.
COLEMAN, J. S. (1961). *The Adolescent Society* (London: Collier-Macmillan).
——, et al. (1966). *Equality of Educational Opportunity* (Washington, DC: U.S. Government Printing Office).
COLEMAN, John C. (1974). *Relationships in Adolescence* (London: Routledge & Kegan Paul).
—— (1978). 'Current contradictions in adolescent theory', *J. Youth and Adolescence*, **7**, 1–11.
——, GEORGE, R., AND HOLT, G. (1977a). 'Adolescents and their parents. A study of attitudes', *J. genet. Psychol.*, **130**, 239–45.
——, HERBERT, J., AND MORRIS, M. (1977b). 'Identity in adolescence: present and future self-concepts', *J. Youth and Adolescence*, **6**, 63–75.
COMSTOCK, G. W. AND HELSING, K. J. (1976). 'Symptoms of depression in two communities', *Psychol. Med.*, **6**, 551–63.

References

COMMUNITY RELATIONS COMMISSION (1974). *Unemployment and Homelessness: a report* (London: HMSO).

CONGER, J. H. (1973). *Adolescence and Youth: Psychological Development in a Changing World* (New York: Harper & Row).

CONNELL, P. H. (1965). 'Suicidal attempts in childhood and adolescence', in Howells, J. G. (ed), *Modern Perspectives in Child Psychiatry*, pp 403–27 (Edinburgh: Oliver & Boyd).

COOMBS, L. C. AND ZUMETA, Z. (1970). 'Correlates of marital dissolution in a prospective fertility study: a research note', *Social Problems*, 18, 92–101.

COOPER, J. E., KENDELL, R. E., GURLAND, B. J., SHARPE, L., COPELAND, J. R. M., AND SIMON, R. (1972). *Psychiatric Diagnosis in New York and London.* Institute of Psychiatry Maudsley Monograph, no. 20 (London: Oxford University Press).

COOPER, S. F., LEACH, C., STORER, D., AND TONGE, W. L. (1977). 'The children of psychiatric patients: clinical findings', *Brit. J. Psychiat.*, 131, 514–22.

CORBETT, J. (1977a). 'Tics and Tourette's syndrome', in Rutter, M. and Hersov, L. (eds), *Child Psychiatry: Modern Approaches*, pp 674–87 (Oxford: Blackwell Scientific).

—— (1977b). 'Mental retardation—psychiatric aspects', Ibid, 829–58.

CORNISH, D. B. AND CLARKE, R. V. G. (1975). *Residential Treatment and its Effects on Delinquency* (London: HMSO).

COSSEY, D. (1978). *Safe Sex for Teenagers* (London: Brook Advisory Centres).

COURT, S. D. M. (1976). See DEPARTMENT OF HEALTH AND SOCIAL SECURITY, 1976.

COWEN, E. L., PEDERSON, A., BABIGIAN, H., IZZO, L. D., AND TROST, M. A. (1973). 'Long-term follow-up of early detected vulnerable children', *J. Consult. Clin. Psychol.*, 41, 438–46.

COX, A. (1976). 'The association between emotional disorders in childhood and neuroses in adult life', in Van Praag, H. M. (ed), *Research in Neurosis*, pp 40–58 (Utrecht: Bohn, Scheltema & Holkema).

——, RUTTER, M., YULE, B., AND QUINTON, D. (1977). 'Bias resulting from missing information: some epidemiological findings', *Brit. J. prev. soc. Med.*, 31, 131–36.

CRAIG, M. M. AND FURST, P. W. (1965). 'What happens after treatment?', *Social Service Review*, 39, 165–71.

CRISP, A. H., PALMER, R. L., AND KALUCY, R. S. (1976) .'How common is anorexia nervosa? A prevalence study', *Brit. J. Psychiat.*, 128, 549–54.

CRELLIN, E., PRINGLE, M. L. K., AND WEST, P. (1971). *Born Illegitimate* (Slough: NFER).

CROWE, M. J. (1978). 'Conjoint marital therapy: a controlled outcome study', *Psychol. Med.*, 8, 623–36.

CULLEN, K. J. (1976). 'A six-year controlled trial of prevention of children's behaviour disorders', *J. Paediat.*, 88, 662–66.

CUMMINGS, E. AND CUMMINGS, J. (1957). *Closed Ranks* (Cambridge, Mass.: Harvard University Press).

References

DALTON, K. (1977). *The Premenstrual Syndrome and Progesterone Therapy* (London: Heinemann Medical).

DANIEL, W. W. (1968). *Racial Discrimination in England* (Harmondsworth: Penguin).

DAVIDSON, W. S. AND SEIDMAN, E. (1974). 'Studies of behavior modification and juvenile delinquency: a review, methodological critique and social perspective', *Psychol. Bull.*, **81**, 998–1011.

DAVIE, R., BUTLER, N., AND GOLDSTEIN, H. (1972). *From Birth to Seven* (London: Longmans).

DAVIES, J. AND STACEY, B. (1972). *Teenagers and Alcohol: a developmental study in Glasgow*, vol. 2 (London: HMSO).

DAVIS, K. (ed) (1973). *Cities: Their Origin, Growth and Human Impact*, Readings from Scientific American (San Francisco: W. H. Freeman).

DE ALARCÓN, R. (1969). 'The spread of heroin abuse in a community', *Bull. Narcot.*, **21**(3), 17–22.

—— (1972). 'An epidemiological evaluation of a public health measure aimed at reducing the availability of methylamphetamine', *Psychol. Med.*, **2**, 293–300.

DEPARTMENT OF EDUCATION AND SCIENCE (1963). *Statistics of Education*, 1962, part 1 (London: HMSO).

—— (1964). Ibid, 1962, part 3 (London: HMSO).

—— (1969). Ibid, 1968, vol. 1 (London: HMSO).

—— (1972). *Children with Specific Reading Difficulties*. Report of the Advisory Committee on Handicapped Children, Chairman: Professor Jack Tizard (London: HMSO).

—— (1975). *A Language for Life*. Report of the Committee of Inquiry appointed by the Secretary of State for Education and Science, Chairman: Sir Alan Bullock (London: HMSO).

—— (1976). *Statistics of Education*, 1975, vol. 3, *Further Education* (London: HMSO).

—— (1977). Ibid., 1976, vol. 1, *Schools* (London: HMSO).

—— (1978a). Ibid., 1976, vol. 2, *School leavers CSE and GCE* (London: HMSO).

—— (1978b). *Special Educational Needs*. Report of the Committee of Enquiry into the Education of Handicapped Children and Young People, Chairman: Mrs. H. M. Warnock, Cmnd 7212 (London: HMSO).

—— (1979). Personal communication.

DEPARTMENT OF HEALTH AND SOCIAL SECURITY (1972). *Report of the Committee on Nursing*, Chairman: Professor A. Briggs, Cmnd. 5115 (London: HMSO).

—— (1973). *Intermediate Treatment Project: an account of a project set up to demonstrate some ways of providing intermediate treatment* (London: HMSO).

—— (1974a). *One-Parent Families*. Report of the Committee, Chairman: Hon. Sir Morris Finer, Cmnd. 5629 (London: HMSO).

—— (1974b). *Pay and Related Conditions of Service of Nurses and Midwives*. Report of the Committee of Inquiry, Chairman: Rt. Hon. Earl of Halsbury (London: HMSO).

References

—— (1976). *Fit for the Future.* Report of the Committee on Child Health Services, Chairman: Professor S. D. M. Court (London: HMSO).

—— (1976). *Report of the Working Party on Manpower Training for the Social Services* (London: HMSO).

DEPARTMENT OF THE ENVIRONMENT (1977). *Housing Management and Design.* Lambeth Inner Area Study, 1AS,1A,18 (London: DOE).

DESCHAMPS, J. P. AND VALANTIN, G. (1978). 'Pregnancy in adolescence: Incidence and outcome in European countries', in Parkes, A. S., Short, R. V., Potts, M., and Herbertson, M. A. (eds), *Fertility in adolescence. J. biosoc. Sci.,* suppl. 5, pp 101–16 (Cambridge: Galton Foundation).

DIAMOND, LORD (1978). See ROYAL COMMISSION ON THE DISTRIBUTION OF INCOME AND WEALTH, 1978.

DOHRENWEND, B. P. AND DOHRENWEND, B. S. (1976). 'Sex differences and psychiatric disorders', *Amer. J. Sociol.,* **81,** 1447–54.

——, —— (1977). 'Reply to Gove and Tudor's comment on "Sex differences and psychiatric disorders",' *Amer. J. Sociol.,* **82,** 1336–45.

DOLLERY, C. (1978). *The End of an Age of Optimism* (London: Nuffield Provincial Hospitals Trust).

DONNAN, S. AND HASKEY, J. (1977). 'Alcoholism and cirrhosis of the liver', *Population Trends,* **7,** 18–24.

DOUGLAS, J. W. B. (1973). 'Early disturbing events and later enuresis', in Kolvin, I., MacKeith, R., and Meadow, S. R. (eds), *Bladder Control and Enuresis,* Clinics in Develop. Med. Nos. 48/49, pp 109–17 (London: SIMP/Heinemann Medical).

—— (1975). 'Early hospital admissions and later disturbances of behaviour and learning', *Develop. Med. Child Neurol,* **17,** 456–80.

—— AND MANN, S. (1979). Personal communication.

——, ROSS, J. M., AND SIMPSON, H. R. (1968). *All Our Future: A longitudinal study of of secondary education* (London: Peter Davies).

DOUVAN, E. AND ADELSON, J. (1966). *The Adolescent Experience* (London: Wiley).

—— AND GOLD, M. (1966). 'Modal patterns in American adolescence', in Hoffman, L. W. and Hoffman, M. C. (eds), *Review of Child Development Research,* vol. 2, pp 469–528 (New York: Russell Sage Foundation).

DRYFOOS, J. G. (1978). 'The incidence and outcome of adolescent pregnancy in the United States', in Parkes, A. S., Short, R. V., Potts, M., and Herbertson, M. A. (eds), *Fertility in Adolescence, J. biosoc. Sci.,* suppl. 5, pp 85–99 (Cambridge: Galton Foundation).

DUDDLE, M. (1973). 'An increase of anorexia nervosa in a University population', *Brit. J. Psychiat.,* **123,** 711–12.

DUNLOP, A. (1975). *The Approved School Experience* (London: HMSO).

DUNN, J. (1979). 'Individual differences in temperament', in Rutter, M. (ed), *Scientific Foundations of Developmental Psychiatry* (London: Heinemann Medical). (In press).

302

References

Dweck, C. S. and Bush, E. S. (1976). 'Sex differences in learned helplessness: I. Differential debilitation with peer and adult evaluators', *Develop. Psychol.*, **12**, 147–56.
——, Davidson, W., Nelson, S., and Enna, B. (1978). Ibid., II. The contingencies of evaluative feedback in the classroom, and III. An experimental analysis. *Develop. Psychol.*, **14**, 268–76.
Dytrych, Z., Matejcek, Ü., Schüller, V., David, H. P., and Friedman, H. L. (1975). Children born to women denied abortion', *Family Planning Perspectives*, **7**, 165–71.

Edwards, G. (1974). 'Cannabis and the criteria for legalisation of a currently prohibited recreational drug: Groundwork for a debate', *Acta Psychiat. Scand.*, suppl. 251.
——, Kyle, E., Nicholls, P., and Taylor, C. (1978). 'Alcoholism and correlates of mortality', *J. Studies on Alcohol*, **39**, 1607–17.
——, Hawker, A., Hensman, C., Peto, J., and Williamson, V. (1973). 'Alcoholics known or unknown to agencies: Epidemiological studies in a London suburb', *Brit. J. Psychiat.*, **123**, 169–83.
Eggers, C. (1978). 'Course and prognosis of childhood schizophrenia', *J. Autism Child. Schiz.*, **8**, 21–36.
Eissler, K. R. (1958). 'Notes on problems of technique in the psychoanalytic treatment of adolescents', *Psychoanalyt. Study Child*, **13**, 223–54.
Elder, G. H. (1974). *Children of the Great Depression* (Chicago: University of Chicago Press).
—— (1979). 'Historical change in life pattern and personality', in Baltes, P. and Brim, O. (ed), *Lifespan Development and Behavior*, vol. 2 (New York: Academic Press).
—— and Rockwell, R. C. (1979). 'Economic depression and postwar opportunity: a study of life patterns in hell', in Simmons, R. A. (ed), *Research in Community and Mental Health* (Greenwich, Conn.: TAI Press). (Cited by Bronfenbrenner, 1979.)
El-Guebaly, N. and Offord, D. R. (1977). 'The offspring of alcoholics: a critical review', *Amer. J. Psychiat.*, **134**, 357–65.
Elkin, F. and Westley, W. A. (1955). 'The myth of adolescent culture', *Amer. Soc. Rev.*, **20**, 680–84.
Engel, M. (1959). 'The stability of self-concept in adolescence', *J. abn. soc. Psychol.*, **58**, 211–15.
Epperson, D. C. (1964). 'A re-assessment of indices of parental influence in "The Adolescent Society"', *Am. Sociol. Rev.*, **29**, 93–6.
Erikson, E. H. (1955). 'The problem of ego identity', *J. Amer. Psychoanal. Assoc.*, **4**, 56–121.
—— (1968). *Identity: Youth and Society* (New York: Norton).

References

EYSENCK, H. J. AND EYSENCK, S. B. G. (1975). *Manual of the Eysenck Personality Questionnaire (Junior and Adult)* (London: Hodder & Stoughton).

FARRELL, C. AND KELLAHER, L. (1978). *My Mother Said: The Way Young People Learn About Sex and Birth Control* (London: Routledge and Kegan Paul).

FARRINGTON, D. P. (1977). 'The effects of public labelling', *Brit. J. Criminol.*, **17**, 112–25.

—— (1978). 'The family background of aggressive youths', in Hersov, L. A., Berger, M., and Shaffer, D. (eds), *Aggression and Anti-social Behaviour in Childhood and Adolescence*, pp 73–94 (Oxford: Pergamon Press).

—— (1979). 'Longitudinal research on crime and delinquency', in Morris, N. and Tonry, N. (eds), *Crime and Justice—1978: An Annual Review of Criminal Justice Research* (Chicago: University of Chicago Press). (In press).

——, GUNDRY, G., AND WEST, D. J. (1975). 'The familial transmission of criminality', *Med. Sci. Law.*, **15**, 177–86.

FENDRICH, J. M. (1974). 'Activists ten years later: a test of generational unit continuity', *J. Social Issues*, **30**, 95–118.

FERBER, H., KEELEY, S. M., AND SHEMBERG, K. M. (1974). 'Training parents in behaviour modification: outcome of and problems encountered in a program after Patterson's work', *Behav. Ther.*, **5**, 415–19.

FERRI, E. (1976). *Growing Up in a One-Parent Family* (Slough: NFER).

FINER, M. (1974). See DEPARTMENT OF HEALTH AND SOCIAL SECURITY, 1974a.

FITZHERBERT, K. (1967). *West Indian Children in London*: Occasional Papers on Social Administration no. 19 (London: HMSO).

FLACKS, R. (1967). 'The liberated generation: An exploration of the roots of student protest', *J. Social Issues*, **23**, 52–75.

FLEMING, O. AND SEAGER, C. P. (1978). 'Incidence of depressive symptoms in users of the oral contraceptive', *Brit. J. Psychiat.*, **132**, 431–40.

FOGARTY, M. P., RAPOPORT, R., AND RAPOPORT, R. M. (1971). *Sex, Career and Family* (London: Allen and Unwin).

FOGELMAN, K. (ed) (1976). *Britain's Sixteen-Year-Olds* (London: National Children's Bureau).

—— (1978). 'School attendance, attainment and behaviour', *Brit. J. educ. Psychol.*, **48**, 148–58.

FORSSMAN, H. AND THUWE, I. (1966). 'One hundred and twenty children born after application for therapeutic abortion refused', *Acta Psychiat. Scand.* **42**, 71–88.

FREEMAN, R. (1977). 'Psychiatric aspects of sensory disorders and intervention', in Graham, P. (ed), *Epidemiological Approaches in Child Psychiatry*, pp 275–304 (London: Academic Press).

FREUD, A. (1958). 'Adolescence', *Psychoanalyt. Study Child*, **13**, 255–78.

References

FRIES, M. E. (1959). 'Review of the literature on the latency period', in Levitt, M. (ed), *Readings in Psychoanalytic Psychology* (New York: Appleton).

GALLOWAY, D. (1976). 'Size of school, socio-economic hardship suspension rates and persistent unjustified absence from school', *Brit. J. Educ. Psychol.*, **6**, 40–47.
—— (1979). Personal communication.

GAMER, E., GALLANT, D., GRUNEBAUM, H. U., AND COHLER, B. J. (1977). 'Children of psychotic mothers', *Arch. Gen. Psychiat.*, **34**, 592–97.

GATH, D., COOPER, B., GATTONI, F., AND ROCKETT, D. (1977). *Child Guidance and Delinquency in a London Borough*. Institute of Psychiatry Maudsley Monographs no. 24 (London: Oxford University Press).

GELFAND, D. M. AND HARTMANN, O. P. (1968). 'Behaviour therapy with children: A review and evaluation of research methodology', *Psychol. Bull.*, **69**, 204–15.

GENERAL HOUSEHOLD SURVEY UNIT (1978). 'The changing circumstances of women 1971–76', *Population trends*, **13**, 17–20.

GERSTEN, J. C., LANGNER, T. S., EISENBERG, J. G., AND SIMCHA-FAGAN, O. (1977). 'An evaluation of the etiologic role of stressful life change events in psychological disorder', *J. Health and Social Behaviour*, **18**, 228–44.

——, ——, ——, ——, AND MCCARTHY, E. D. (1976). 'Stability and change in types of behavioral disturbance of children and adolescents', *J. abn. Child Psychol.*, **4**, 111–28.

GHODSIAN, M. AND LAMBERT, L. (1978). 'Mum and Dad are not so bad: the views of sixteen-year-olds on how they get on with their parents', *J. Assoc. Educ. Psychol.*, **4**, 27–33.

GIBBENS, T. (1977). 'Treatment of delinquents', in Rutter, M. and Hersov, L. (eds), *Child Psychiatry: Modern Approaches*, pp 859–79 (Oxford: Blackwell Scientific).

GIBBENS, T. C. N. AND PRINCE, J. (1965). *The Results of Borstal Training*. Sociological Review Monograph no. 9: Sociological Studies in the British Penal System (Keele: University of Keele).

GIBSON, C. (1974). 'The association between divorce and social class in England and Wales, *Brit. J. Sociol.*, **25**, 79–93.

GILDEA, McL., GLIDEWELL, J. C., AND KANTOR, M. B. (1967) 'The St Louis school mental health project: History and evaluation', in Cowen, E. L., Gardner, E. A., and Zax, M. (eds), *Emergent Approaches to Mental Health Problems* (New York: Appleton).

GIORDANO, P. C. (1978). 'Girls, guys and gangs: The changing social context of female delinquency', *J. Criminal Law & Criminol.*, **69**, 126–32.

GLADSTONE, F. J. (in preparation). *Co-ordinating crime prevention efforts: a report of a demonstration project on school vandalism*. Home Office Research Studies Series (London: HMSO).

305

References

GOLDMAN, N. (1961). 'A socio-psychological study of school vandalism', *Crime and Delinquency*, 7, 221–30.

GORER, D. (1977). *Death, Grief and Mourning* (New York: Arno Press).

GOSSETT, J. T., LEWIS, S. B., LEWIS, J. M., AND PHILLIPS, V. A. (1973). 'Follow-up of adolescents treated in a psychiatric hospital, I. A review of studies', *Amer. J. Orthopsychiat.*, 43, 602–10.

GOVE, W. R. AND TUDOR, J. F. (1973). 'Adult sex roles and mental illness', *Amer. J. Sociol.*, 78, 812–35.

GRAHAM, P. J. (1977). 'Possibilities for prevention', in Graham, P. J. (ed), *Epidemiological Approaches in Child Psychiatry*, pp 377–97 (London: Academic Press).

GRAHAM, P. AND RUTTER, M. (1973). 'Psychiatric disorder in the young adolescent: A follow-up study', *Proc. Roy. Soc. Med.*, 66, 1226–29.

——, —— (1977). 'Adolescent disorders', in Rutter, M. and Hersov, L. (eds), *Child Psychiatry: Modern Approaches*, pp 407–27 (Oxford: Blackwell Scientific).

GRAY, G. (1979). Personal communication.

GURMAN, A. (1973). 'The effects and effectiveness of marital therapy: a review of outcome research', *Family Process*, 12, 145–70.

GUSTAFSON, B. (1972). *Life Values of High School Youth in Sweden* (Stockholm: Institute of Sociology of Religion). (Cited in Coleman, J. C., 1978.)'

GUTELIUS, M. F., KIRSCH, A. D., MACDONALD, S., BROOKS, M. R., AND McERLEAN, T. (1977). 'Controlled study of child health supervision: behavioral results', *Pediatrics*, 60, 294–304.

GUTHRIE, J. T. (1978). 'Principles of instruction: a critique of Johnson's "Remedial approaches to dyslexia"', in Benton, A. C. and Pearl, D. (eds), *Dyslexia: An Appraisal of Current Knowledge*, pp 423–34 (New York: Oxford University Press).

HAGBERG, B., OLOW, I., AND HAGBERG, G. (1973). 'Decreasing incidence of low birth weight diplegia', *Acta Paediat. Scand.*, 62, 199–200.

——, —— (1975). 'The changing panorama of cerebral palsy in Sweden 1954–1970', *Acta. Paediat. Scand.*, 64, 187–192.

HAGGERTY, R. J., ROGHMANN, K. J., AND PLESS, I. B. (1975). *Child Health and the Community* (London: Wiley).

HAIM, A. (1974) *Adolescent Suicide*, Translated by A. M. Sheridan Smith (London: Tavistock).

HALL, G. S. (1904). *Adolescence: Its psychology and its relation to physiology, anthropology, sociology, sex, crime, religion and education* (New York: Appleton).

HALSBURY, Lord (1974). See DEPARTMENT OF HEALTH AND SOCIAL SECURITY, 1974b.

HALSEY, A. H. (ed) (1973). *Educational Priority No. 1: EPA Problems and Policies* (London: HMSO).

References

HANEY, C., BANKS, C., AND ZIMBARDO, P. (1973). 'Interpersonal dynamics in a simulated prison', *Int. J. Criminology and Penology*, **1**, 69–97.

HARTMAN, C. W. (1963). 'Social values and housing orientations', *J. Soc. Issues*, **19**, 113–31.

HARTSHORNE, H. AND MAY, M. A. (1928). *Studies in Deceit. Vol. 1, Studies in the Nature of Character* (New York: Macmillan).

HARTUP, W. W. (1975). 'The origins of friendships', in Lewis, M. and Rosenblum, L. A. (eds), *Friendship and peer relations* (New York: Wiley).

—— (1979). 'Peer relations and family relations: Two social worlds', in Rutter, M. (ed), *Scientific Foundations of Developmental Psychiatry* (London: Heinemann Medical). (In press).

HASSELL, C. AND TRETHOWAN, W. H. (1972). 'Suicide in Birmingham', *Brit. med. J.*, **1**, 717–18.

HASTINGS, P. K. AND HOGE, D. R. (1970). 'Religious change among college students over two decades', *Social Forces*, **49**, 16–28.

HAZEL, N. (1977). 'How family placements can combat delinquency', *Social Work Today*, **8**, no. 23, 6–7.

—— (1978). 'Teaching family placement', *Adoption and Fostering*, **94**, no. 4, 31–5.

HEIDENSOHN, F. (1968). 'The deviance of women: a critique and an enquiry', *Brit. J. Sociol.*, **19**, 160–175.

HEISEL, J. S., REAM, S., RAITZ, R., RAPPAPORT, M., AND CODDINGTON, R. D. (1973). 'The significance of life events as contributing factors in the diseases of children. III. A study of pediatric patients', *J. Pediat.*, **83**, 119–23.

HENDERSON, A. S., KRUPINSKI, J., AND STOLLER, A. (1971). 'Epidemiological aspects of adolescent psychiatry', in Howells, J. G. (ed), *Modern Perspectives in Adolescent Psychiatry* (Edinburgh: Oliver & Boyd).

HERSOV, L. (1977a). 'School refusal', in Rutter, M. and Hersov, L. (eds), *Child Psychiatry: Modern Approaches*, pp 455–86 (Oxford: Blackwell Scientific).

—— (1977b). 'Adoption', Ibid., pp 136–62.

—— AND BENTOVIM, A. (1977). 'Inpatient units and day-hospitals', Ibid., pp 880–900.

HESS, R. D. AND GOLDBLATT, I. (1957). 'The status of adolescents in American society: a problem in social identity', *Child Develop.*, **28**, 459–68.

HETHERINGTON, E. M., COX, M., AND COX, R. (1978). 'Family interaction and the social, emotional and cognitive development of children following divorce', Paper presented at the Symposium on the Family, 'Setting Priorities', Washington, D.C., 17–20 May, 1978.

HILL, R. AND ALDOUS, J. (1969). 'Socialization for marriage and parenthood', in Goslin, D. A. (ed), *Handbook of Socialization Theory and Research*, pp 885–950 (Chicago: Rand McNally).

HINDE, R. A. (1979). 'Family influences', in Rutter, M. (ed), *Scientific Foundations of Developmental Psychiatry* (London: Heinemann Medical). (In press).

307

References

HOFFMAN, L. W. (1974). Effects of maternal employment on the child—a review of research', *Develop. Psychol.*, **10**, 204-28.

HOLBROOK, D. (1978). 'A combined approach to parental coping', *Brit. J. Social Work*, **8**, 439-52.

HOLDING, T. A., BUGLASS, D., DUFFY, J. C., AND KREITMAN, N. (1977). 'Parasuicide in Edinburgh—a seven year review 1968-74, *Brit. J. Psychiat.*, **130**, 534-43.

HOLE, W. V. AND POUNTNEY, M. T. (1971). *Trends in Population, Housing and Occupancy Rates*, 1861-1961 (London: HMSO).

HOLMAN, R. (1973). *Trading in Children: a study of private fostering* (London: Routledge & Kegan Paul).

HOME OFFICE (1968). *Children in Trouble* (London: HMSO).

—— (1970). *Care and Treatment in a Planned Environment* (London: HMSO).

—— (1977). *Criminal Statistics England and Wales*, 1976 (London: HMSO).

—— (1978a). *Criminal Statistics England and Wales*, 1977 (London: HMSO).

—— (1978b). *Offences of Drunkenness. 1977. England and Wales* (London: HMSO).

—— (1979). Personal communication.

HOME OFFICE STANDING COMMITTEE ON CRIME PREVENTION (1975). *Protection Against Vandalism* (London: HMSO).

HOOD, C., OPPÉ, T. E., PLESS, I. B., AND APTE, E. (1970). *Children of West Indian Immigrants: a study of one-year-olds in Paddington* (London: Institute of Race Relations).

HUENEMANN, R. L., SHAPIRO, L. R., HAMPTON, M. C., AND MITCHELL, B. W. (1966). 'A longitudinal study of gross body composition and body conformation and their association with food and activity in a teen-age population', *Amer. J. Clin. Nutrition*, **18**, 325-38.

INNER LONDON EDUCATION AUTHORITY (1975). *Report (ILEA 603) by the Education Officer on 'Non-Attendance and Truancy' to the Education Committee, Schools Sub-committee* (London: ILEA).

—— (1976). *Attendance at secondary schools in ILEA on 23 April 1975*, RS 656/76 (London: ILEA).

—— (1979). Personal communication.

IVIN, P. (1979). Personal communication.

JAHODA, G. AND CRAMOND, C. (1972). *Children and Alcohol: a developmental study in Glasgow*, vol. 1 (London: HMSO).

JAHODA, M. AND WARREN, N. (1965). 'The myths of youth', *Sociol. Educ.*, **38**, 138-49.

References

JAMES, A. G. (1974). *Sikh Children in Britain* (London: Institute of Race Relations,Oxford University Press).

JAMES, I. P. (1971). 'The changing pattern of narcotic addiction in Britain, 1959–69', *Internat. J. Addict.*, 6, 119–34.

JENCKS, C., SMITH, M., ACLAND, H., BANE, M. J., COHEN, D., GINTIS, H., HEYNS, B., AND MICHELSON, S. (1972). *Inequality: A reassessment of the effect of family and schooling in America* (New York: Basic Books).

JENNINGS, C., BARRACLOUGH, B. M., AND MOSS, J. R. (1978). 'Have the Samaritans lowered the suicide rate?' *Psychol. Med.*, 8, 413–22.

JENNINGS, H. (1962). *Societies in the Making* (London: Routledge & Kegan Paul).

JENNINGS, M. AND NIEMI, R. (1975). 'Continuity and change in political orientations: A longitudinal study of two generations', *Amer. Polit. Sci. Rev.*, 69, 1316–75.

JENSEN, A. R. (1969). 'How much can we boost IQ and scholastic achievement?', *Harvard Educ. Rev.*, 39, 1–123.

JENSEN, G. J. AND EVE, R. (1976). 'Sex differences in delinquency: An examination of popular sociological explanations', *Criminology*, 13, 427–48.

JONES, M. C. (1965). 'Psychological correlates of somatic development', *Child Develop.*, 36, 899–911.

JOSLYN, W. D. (1973). 'Androgen-induced social dominance in infant female rhesus monkeys', *J. Child Psychol. Psychiat.*, 14, 137–45.

JOSSELYN, I. M. (1954). 'The ego in adolescence', *Am. J. Orthopsychiat.*, 24, 223–37.

KAGAN, J. AND MOSS, H. A. (1962). *Birth to Maturity: A study in psychological development* (New York: Wiley).

KANDEL, D., SINGLE, E., AND KESSLER, R. C. (1976). 'The epidemiology of drug use among New York State high school students: distribution, trends and change in rates of use', *Amer. J. Publ. Hlth.*, 66, 43–53.

KELLAM, S. G., BRANCH, J. D., AGRAWAL, K. C., AND ENSMINGER, M. E. (1975). *Mental Health and Going to School: the Woodlawn Program of Assessment, Early Intervention and Evaluation* (Chicago: University of Chicago Press).

KELLEY, C. M. (1974). *Uniform Crime Reports from the United States—1973* (Washington DC: U.S. Government Printing Office).

KELVIN, P. (1969). *The Bases of Social Behaviour: An approach in terms of order and value* (London: Holt, Rinehart & Winston).

KENDELL, R. E., HALL, D. J., HAILEY, A., AND BABIGIAN, H. M. (1973). 'The epidemiology of anorexia nervosa', *Psychol. Med.*, 3, 200–3.

— —, WAINWRIGHT, S., HAILEY, A., AND SHANNON, B. (1976). 'The influence of child birth on psychiatric morbidity, *Psychol. Med.*, 6, 297–302.

KENISTON, K. (1967). 'The sources of student dissent'. *J. Social Issues*, 23, 108–38.

KENT, R. (1976). A methodological critique of 'interviewing for boys with conduct problems', *J. Consult. Clin. Psychol.*, 44, 297–9.

309

References

KESSEL, N. AND COPPEN, A. (1963). 'The prevalence of common menstrual symptoms', *Lancet*, **ii**, 61–4.

KETT, J. F. (1977). *Rites of Passage: Adolescence in America 1790 to the Present* (New York: Basic Books).

KIDD, C. B. AND CALDBECK-MEENAN, J. (1966). 'A comparative study of psychiatric morbidity among students at two different universities', *Brit. J. Psychiat.*, **112**, 57–64.

KINSEY, A. C., POMEROY, W. B., AND MARTIN, C. E. (1948). *Sexual Behavior in the Human Male* (Philadelphia: Saunders).

KLEIN, D. F. AND GITTELMAN-KLEIN, R. (1978). 'Drug treatment of separation anxiety and depressive illness in children', in Mendlewicz, J. and van Praag, H. M. (eds), *Childhood Psychopharmacology: Current Concepts. Advances in Biological Psychiatry*, **2**, 50–60.

KOHLBERG, L. (1969). 'Stage and sequence: the cognitive-developmental approach to socialization, in Goslin, D. A. (ed), *Handbook of Socialization Theory and Research*, pp 347–480 (Chicago: Rand McNally).

KOLVIN, I. (1973). 'Evaluation of psychiatric services for children in England and Wales', in Wing, J. and Häfner, H. (eds), *Roots of Evaluation: the epidemiological basis for planning psychiatric services*, pp 131–62 (London: Oxford University Press for the Nuffield Provincial Hospital Trust).

KOSVINER, A., HAWKS, D., AND WEBB, M. G. T. (1974). 'Cannabis use amongst British university students, I. Prevalence rates', *Brit. J. Addict.*, **69**, 35–60.

KREITMAN, N. (ed) (1977). *Parasuicide* (London: Wiley).

KREUZ, L. E., ROSE, R. M., AND JENNINGS, J. R. (1972). 'Suppression of plasma testosterone levels and psychological stress: a longitudinal study of young men in officer candidate school', *Arch. gen. Psychiat.*, **26**, 479–82.

KRUSPINSKI, J., BAIKIE, A. G., STOLLER, A., GRAVES, J., O'DAY, D. M., AND POLKE, P. (1967). 'A community mental health survey of Heyfield, Victoria', *Med. J. Austr.*, **1**, 1204–11.

KUMAR, R. AND ROBSON, K. (1978). 'Previous induced abortions and antenatal depression in primiparae: preliminary report of a survey of mental health in pregnancy', *Psychol. Med.*, **8**, 711–16.

KUSHLICK, A. AND BLUNDEN, R. (1974). 'The epidemiology of mental subnormality', in Clarke, A. D. and Clarke, A. D. B. (eds), *Mental Deficiency: The Changing Outlook, third edition* (London: Methuen).

LAMBERT, J. (1970). *Crime, Police and Race Relations* (London: Oxford University Press).

LAMBERT, L., ESSEN, J., AND HEAD, J. (1977). 'Variations in behaviour ratings of children who have been in care', *J. Child Psychol. Psychiat.*, **18**, 335–46.

LARSON, L. E. (1972). 'Influence of parents and peers during adolescence: the situation hypothesis revisited', *J. Marriage and the Family*, **34**, 67–74.

References

LASK, B (1979). 'Family therapy outcome research 1972-8', *J. Family therapy*, **1**, 87–92.

LAVIK, N. J. (1977). 'Urban-rural differences in rates of disorder. A comparative psychiatric population study of Norwegian adolescents', in Graham, P. J. (ed), *Epidemiological Approaches in Child Psychiatry*, pp 223–51 (London: Academic Press).

LEETE, R. (1976). 'Marriage and divorce', *Population Trends*, **3**, 3–8.

—— (1978a). 'One parent families: numbers and characteristics', Ibid., **13**, 4–9.

—— (1978b). 'Adoption trends and illegitimate births 1951–1977', Ibid., **14**, 9–16.

—— (1979). 'New directions in family life', Ibid., **15**, 4–9.

LEFKOWITZ, M. M., ERON, L. D., WALDER, L. O., AND HUESMANN, L. R.. (1977). *Growing Up to be Violent: A longitudinal study of aggression* (Oxford: Pergamon).

LESLIE, S. A. (1974). 'Psychiatric disorder in the young adolescents of an industrial town', *Brit. J. Psychiat.*, **125**, 113–24.

LEWIN, K., LIPPITT, R., AND WHITE, R. (1939). 'Patterns of aggressive behaviour in experimentally created social climates, *J. Soc. Psychol.*, **10**, 271–99.

LEWINE, R. R. J., WATT, N. F., PRENTKY, R. A., AND FRYER, J. H. (1978). 'Childhood behaviour in schizophrenia, personality disorder, depression and neurosis', *Brit. J. Psychiat.*, **133**, 347–57.

LEWIS, E. O. (1929). 'Report of an investigation into the incidence of mental deficiency in six areas, 1925–27', in *Report of the Mental Deficiency Committee*, part IV (London: HMSO).

LITTLE, A. (1965). 'The "prevalence" of recorded delinquency and recidivism in England and Wales', *Amer. Sociol. Rev.*, **30**, 260–63.

LITTLE, A. N. (1978). *Educational Policies for Multi-Racial Areas* (London: University of London, Goldsmiths' College).

LITTLEMORE, D., METCALFE, E., AND JOHNSON, A. L. (1974). 'Skeletal immaturity in psychiatrically disturbed adolescents', *J. Child Psychol. Psychiat.*, **15**, 133–38.

LOGAN, R. F. L. AND GOLDBERG, E. M. (1953). 'Rising eighteen in a London suburb: a study of some aspects of the life and health of young men', *Brit. J. Sociol.*, **4**, 323–45.

MCCANN-ERIKSON (1977). *You Don't Know Me: A survey of youth in Britain* (Cited by Thornes and Collard, op cit.).

MCCARTHY, D. (1974). 'The effects of emotional disturbance and deprivation on somatic growth', in Davis, J. A. and Dobbing, J. (eds). *Scientific Foundations of Paediatrics*, pp 56–67 (London: Heinemann Medical).

MCCLINTOCK, F. H. AND AVISON, N. H. (1968). *Crime in England and Wales* (London: Heinemann Educational).

References

McCord, W. and McCord, J. (1959). *Origins of Crime: a new evaluation of the Cambridge-Somerville study* (New York: Columbia University Press).

Macfarlane, J. W., Allen, L., and Honzik, M. P. (1954). *A Developmental Study of the Behavior Problems of Normal Children between 21 Months and 14 Years* (Berkeley: University of California Press).

McGregor, O. R. (1967). 'Towards divorce law reform', *Brit. J. Sociol.*, **18**, 91–9.

McIntosh, N. and Smith, D. J. (1974). *The Extent of Racial Discrimination*, Broadsheet No. 547 (London: PEP).

Mabey, C. (1974). *Social and ethnic mix in schools and the relationship with attainment of children aged 8 and 11*, Research Paper no. 9 (London: Centre for Environmental Studies).

Maccoby, E. E. (1951). 'Television: its impact on school children', *Public Opinion Quarterly*, **15**, 421–44.

Marks, I. M., *et al.* (1977). *Nursing in behavioural psychotherapy: an advanced clinical role for nurses* (London: Royal College of Nursing).

—— and Gelder, M. G. (1966). 'Different ages of onset in varieties of phobia', *Amer. J. Psychiat.*, **123**, 218–21.

Marland, M. (1975). *The Craft of the Classroom: A Survival Guide* (London: Heinemann Educational).

Marshall, W. A. and Tanner, J. M. (1974). 'Puberty', in Davis, J. A. and Dobbing, J. (eds), *Scientific Foundations of Paediatrics*, pp 124–51 (London: Heinemann Medical).

Martin, B. (1975). 'Parent-child relations', in Horowitz, F. D. (ed), *Review of Child Development Research*, vol. 4, pp 463–540 (Chicago: University of Chicago Press).

Masterson, J. F. (1967). *The Psychiatric Dilemma of Adolescence* (London: Churchill).

Mayall, B. and Petrie, P. (1977). *Minder, Mother and Child*. Studies in Education (new series), **5** (London: University of London Institute of Education).

Mayhew, P., Clarke, R. V. G., Sturman, A., and Hough, J. M. (1976). *Crime as Opportunity*. Home Office Research Study no. 34 (London: HMSO).

Meissner, W. W. (1965). 'Parental interaction of the adolescent boy', *J. genet. Psychol.*, **107**, 225–33.

Meyer, H. J., Borgatta, E. F., and Jones, W. C. (1965). *Girls at Vocational High: an experiment in social work intervention* (New York: Russell Sage Foundation).

Milgram, S. (1970). 'The experience of living in cities', *Science*, **167**, 1461–68.

Millham, S., Bullock, R., and Hosie, K. (1978). *Locking Up Children: Secure provision within the child care system* (Farnborough: Saxon House).

Money, J. (1961). 'Sex hormones and other variables in human eroticism', in Young, W. C. and Corner, G. W. (eds), *Sexual and Internal Secretions*, third edition, vol. 2 (Baltimore: Williams and Wilkins).

References

—— AND EHRHARDT, A. A. (1972). *Man and Woman: Boy and Girl. The differentiation and dimorphism of gender identity from conception to maturity.* (Baltimore: John Hopkins University Press).

MONGE, R. H. (1973). 'Developmental trends in factors of adolescent self-concept', *Develop. Psychol.*, **8**, 382–93.

MORRIS, A., GILLER, H., SZWED, E., AND GEACH, H. (1980). *Justice for Children* (London: Macmillan). (In press).

MOSS, P. AND PLEWIS, I. (1977). 'Mental distress in mothers of preschool children in Inner London', *Psychol. Med.*, **7**, 641–52.

MURCHISON, N. (1974). 'Illustrations of the difficulties of some children in one-parent families', in Finer, M., op. cit., vol. 2, pp 364–87.

MUSSEN, P. AND BOUTERLINE-YOUNG, H. (1964). 'Relationships between rate of physical maturing and personality among boys of Italian descent', *Vita Humana*, **7**, 186–200.

MUUSS, R. E. (1975). *Theories of Adolescence*, third edition (New York: Random House).

NATIONAL COMMISSION ON MARIHUANA AND DRUG ABUSE (1973). *Drug Use in America: Problems of perspective*, Second Report of the Commission (Washington, DC: U.S. Government Printing Office).

NEEDHAM, B. (1977). *How Cities Work: an introduction* (Oxford: Pergamon).

NESSELROADE, J. R. AND BALTES, P. B. (1974). Adolescent personality development and historical change: 1930–1972', *Monogr. Soc. Res. Child Develop.*, **39**, serial no. 154.

NEWMAN, O. (1973). *Defensible Space* (London: Architectural Press).

—— (1974). Unpublished paper presented to N.A.C.R.O. Conference on 'Architecture planning and urban crime'.

—— (1975). 'Reactions to the "Defensible Space" study and some further findings', *Int. J. Mental Health*, **4**, 48–70.

NEWTON, J., BARNES, G., CAMERON, C., GOLDMAN, P., AND ELIAS, J. (1976). 'Nurse specialists in family planning', *Brit. Med. J.*, **1**, 950–52.

——, ——, CAMERON, J., AND NEWTON, P. (1978). 'Nurse specialists in family planning; the results of a 2 year study', *Contraception*, **18**, 577–92.

NORTON, A. J. AND GLICK, P. C. (1976). 'Marital instability: past, present and future', *J. Social Issues*, **32**, 5–20.

NYLANDER, I. (1971). 'The feeling of being fat and dieting in a school population: an epidemiologic interview investigation', *Acta socio-med. Scand.*, **1**, 17–26.

OFFER, D. (1969). *The Psychological World of the Teenager* (London: Basic Books).

OFFICE OF POPULATION CENSUSES AND SURVEYS (1974). *Morbidity Statistics*

References

from General Practice, Studies on Medical and Population Subjects, no. 26 (London: HMSO).
—— (1978). *Trends in Mortality 1951–75* (London: HMSO).
—— (1979). *Population Trends* 15 (London: HMSO).
OFFORD, D. R. AND CROSS, L. A. (1969). 'Behavioural antecedents of adult schizophrenia', *Arch. gen. Psychiat.*, 21, 267–83.

PABLANT, P. AND BAXTER, J. C. (1975). 'Environmental correlates of school vandalism', *J. American Institute of Planners*, 241, 270–79.
PARNELL, R. W. (1951). 'Mortality and prolonged illness among Oxford undergraduates', *Lancet*, 1, 731–33.
PATTERSON, G. R. (1974). 'Interventions for boys with conduct problems: multiple settings, treatment and criteria', *J. Consult. Clin. Psychol.*, 42, 471–81.
—— (1977). 'Accelerating stimuli for two classes of coercive behaviors', *J. Abnorm. Child Psychol.*, 5, 335–50.
PEARCE, D. AND FARID, S. (1977). 'Illegitimate births: changing patterns', *Population Trends*, 9, 20–23.
PIAGET, J. (1970). 'Piaget's Theory', in Mussen, P. H. (ed), *Carmichael's Manual of Child Psychology*, third edition, vol. 1, pp 703–32 (New York: Wiley).
PILLING, D. AND PRINGLE, M. K. (1978). *Controversial Issues in Child Development* (London: Paul Elek).
POLLAK, M. (1972). *Today's Three Year Olds in London* (London: Heinemann/ SIMP).
POST OFFICE TELECOMMUNICATIONS (1979). Personal communication.
POWER, M. J., ALDERSON, M. R., PHILLIPSON, C. M., SCHOENBERG, E., AND MORRIS, J. N. (1967). 'Delinquent schools?' *New Society*, 10, 542–43.
——, ASH, P. M., SCHOENBERG, E., AND SOREY, E. C. (1974). 'Delinquency and the family', *Brit. J. Social Work*, 4, 13–38.
POWERS, E. AND WITMER, H. (1951). *An Experiment in the Prevention of Delinquency: The Cambridge-Somerville Youth Study* (New York: Columbia University Press).

QUINTON, D. (1979). 'Family life in the inner city: Myth and reality', in Marland, M. (ed), *Education for the Inner City* (London: Heinemann Educational). (In press).
—— AND RUTTER, M. (1976). 'Early hospital admissions and later disturbances of behaviour: An attempted replication of Douglas' findings', *Develop. Med. Child Neurol.*, 18, 447–59.
——, —— (1979). 'Parents with children In Care: I. Current circumstances and parenting skills, II. Intergenerational continuities'. (Submitted for publication).

References

RADLOFF, L. (1975). 'Sex differences in depression: the effects of occupation and marital status', *Sex Roles*, 1, 249–67.

RAPOPORT, J. L. (1979). 'Congenital anomalies, appearance and body build', in Rutter, M. (ed), *Scientific Foundations of Developmental Psychiatry* (London: Heinemann Medical). (In press).

REID, J. B. AND HENDRIKS, A. F. C. J. (1973). 'A preliminary analysis of the effectiveness of direct home intervention for treatment of predelinquent boys who steal', in Clark, F. W. and Hamerlynck, L. A. (eds), *Critical Issues in Research and Practice*. Proc. fourth Banff Int. Conf. on Behav. Modif. (Champaign, Ill.: Research Press).

—— AND PATTERSON, G. R. (1976). 'Follow-up analyses of behavioral treatment program for boys with conduct problems: a reply to Kent', *J. consult. clin. Psychol.*, 44, 299–302.

REID, W. J. AND SHYNE, A. W. (1969). *Brief and Extended Casework* (New York: Columbia University Press).

REINISCH, J. M. AND KAROW, W. G. (1977). 'Prenatal exposure to synthetic progestins and estrogens: effects on human development', *Arch. Sex. Behav.*, 6, 257–88.

REISS, I. L. (1976). *Family Systems in America*, second edition (Hinsdale, Ill.: The Dorsey Press).

REYNOLDS, D., JONES, D., AND ST. LEGER, S. (1976). 'Schools do make a difference', *New Society*, 37, 321.

—— AND MURGATROYD, S. (1977). 'The sociology of schooling and the absent pupil: the school as a factor in the generation of truancy', in Carroll, H. C. M. (ed), *Absenteeism in South Wales: Studies of Pupils, Their Homes and Their Secondary Schools* (Swansea: Faculty of Education, University of Swansea).

RICHARDSON, D. W. AND SHORT, R. V. (1978). 'Fertility in adolescence: time of onset of sperm production in boys', *J. biosoc. Sci.*, suppl. 5, 15–25.

RICHMOND, A. H. (1973). *Migration and Race Relations in an English City: a study in Bristol* (London: Oxford University Press/Institute of Race Relations).

RIESMAN, D. (1950). *The Lonely Crowd* (New Haven: Yale University Press).

ROBINS, L. (1972). 'Follow-up studies of behavior disorders in children', in Quay, H. C. and Werry, J. S. (eds), *Psychopathological Disorders in Childhood*, 414–50 (New York: Wiley).

—— (1973). 'Evaluation of psychiatric services for children in the United States', in Wing, J. K. and Häfner, H. (eds), *Roots of Evaluation: the epidemiological basis for planning psychiatric services*, pp 101–29 (London: Oxford University Press for the Nuffield Provincial Hospitals Trust).

—— (1978). 'Sturdy childhood predictors of adult antisocial behaviour: replications from longitudinal studies', *Psychol. Med.*, 8, 611–22.

—— (1979). 'Longitudinal methods in the study of normal and pathological development', in Kisker, K. P., Meyer, J.-E., Müller, C., and Stromgren, E. (eds), *Psychiatrie der Gegenwart. Band 1. 'Grundlagen und Methoden der Psychiatrie'*, 2 Auflage (Heidelberg: Springer-Verlag).

References

—— AND HILL, S. Y. (1966). 'Assessing the contributions of family structure, class and peer groups to juvenile delinquency', *J. crim. Law, Criminol. and Police Sci.*, **57**, 325–34.

——, WEST, P. A., AND HERJANIC, B. L. (1975). 'Arrests and delinquency in two generations: a study of black urban families and their children', *J. Child Psychol. Psychiat.*, **16**, 125–40.

ROFF, M., SELLS, S. B., AND GOLDEN, M. M. (1972). *Social Adjustment and Personality Development in Children* (Minneapolis: University of Minnesota Press).

ROLF, J. E. AND GARMEZY, N. (1974). 'The school performance of children vulnerable to behavior pathology', in Ricks, D. F., Alexander, T., and Roff, M. (eds), *Life History Research in Psychopathology*, vol. 3 (Minnesota: University of Minnesota Press).

ROSE, G. AND MARSHALL, T. F. (1974). *Counselling and School Social Work: An experimental study* (London: Wiley).

ROSE, R. M., GORDON, T. P., AND BERNSTEIN, I. S. (1972). 'Plasma testosterone levels in the male rhesus: influences of sexual and social stimuli', *Science*, **178**, 643–45.

ROSEN, B. M., BAHN, A. K., SHELLOW, R., AND BOWER, E. M. (1965). 'Adolescent patients served in outpatient psychiatric clinics', *Amer. J. publ. Hlth.*, **55**, 1563–77.

ROWNTREE, B. S. AND LAVERS, G. R. (1951). *English Life and Leisure: a social study* (London: Longmans Green).

ROY, A. (1978). 'Vulnerability factors and depression in women', *Brit. J. Psychiat.*, **133**, 106–10.

ROYAL COLLEGE OF PSYCHIATRISTS (1979). *Alcohol and Alcoholism* (London: Tavistock).

ROYAL COMMISSION ON THE DISTRIBUTION OF INCOME AND WEALTH (1978). *Report no. 6, Lower Incomes, Chairman: Lord Diamond* (London: HMSO).

RUTTER, M. (1966). *Children of Sick Parents: An environmental and psychiatric study*, Institute of Psychiatry Maudsley Monographs no. 16 (London: Oxford University Press).

—— (1970a). 'Autistic Children: Infancy to adulthood', *Semin. Psychiat.*, **2**, 435–50.

—— (1970b). 'Psychological development: predictions from infancy', *J. Child Psychol. Psychiat.*, **11**, 49–62.

—— (1970c). 'Sex differences in children's response to family stress', in Anthony, E. J. and Koupernik, C. (eds), *The Child in His Family*, 165–96 (New York: Wiley).

—— (1971a). 'Psychiatry', in Wortis, J. (ed), *Mental Retardation: An annual review III*, pp 186–221 (New York: Grune & Stratton).

—— (1971b). 'Parent-child separation: Psychological effects on the children', *J. Child Psychol. Psychiat.*, **12**, 233–60.

—— (1972a). 'Childhood schizophrenia reconsidered', *J. Autism Child. Schiz.*, **2**, 315–37.

References

—— (1972b). 'Relationships between child and adult psychiatric disorder', *Acta psychiat. Scand.*, **48**, 3–21.

—— (1972c). *Maternal Deprivation Reassessed* (Harmondsworth: Penguin).

—— (1974). 'The development of infantile autism', *Psychol. Med.*, **4**, 147–63.

—— (1975). *Helping Troubled Children* (Harmondsworth: Penguin).

—— (1977a). 'Individual differences', in Rutter, M. and Hersov, L. (eds), *Child Psychiatry: Modern Approaches*, pp 3–21 (Oxford: Blackwell Scientific).

—— (1977b). 'Separation, loss and family relationships', Ibid., pp 47–73.

—— (1977c). 'Other family influences', Ibid., pp 74–108.

—— (1977d). 'Prospective studies to investigate behavioral change', in Strauss, J. S., Babigian, H. M., and Roff, M. (eds), *The Origins and Course of Psychopathology* (New York: Plenum).

—— (1977e). 'Brain damage syndromes in childhood: concepts and findings', *J. Child Psychol. Psychiat.*, **18**, 1–21.

—— (1978). 'Communication deviance and diagnostic differences', in Wynne, L. C., Cromwell, R. L., and Matthysse, S. (eds), *The Nature of Schizophrenia: New Approaches to Research and Treatment*, pp 512–16 (New York: Wiley).

—— (1979a). 'Psychosexual development', in Rutter, M. (ed), *Scientific Foundations of Developmental Psychiatry* (London: Heinemann Medical). (In press).

—— (1979b). 'Emotional development', Ibid.

—— (1979c). 'Separation experiences: A new look at an old topic', *J. Pediatrics*, **95**, 147–54.

—— (1979d). 'Longitudinal studies: A psychiatric perspective', in Mednick, S. A. and Baert, A. E. (eds), *An Empirical Basis for Primary Prevention: Prospective Longitudinal Research in Europe* (London: Oxford University Press). (In press).

—— (1979e). 'Maternal deprivation 1972–1978: New findings, new concepts, new approaches', *Child Develop.* **50**, 283–305.

—— (1979f.) 'Protective factors in children's responses to stress and disadvantage', in Kent, M. W. and Rolf, J. E. (eds), *Primary Prevention of Psychopathology: vol. 3: Promoting Social Competence and Coping in Children*, 49–74 (Hanover, NH: University Press of New England).

—— (1979g). 'Raised lead levels and impaired cognitive/behavioural functioning: A review of the evidence', *Dev. Med. Child Neurol.* supplement. (In press).

—— (1979h). 'School influences on children's behaviour and development', *Paediatrics*. (In press).

—— AND CHADWICK, O. (1979). 'Neuro-behavioural associations and syndromes of "minimal brain dysfunction"', in Rose, F. C. (ed), *Clinical Neuro Epidemiology* (Tunbridge Wells: Pitman Medical). (In press).

——, COX, A., TUPLING, C., BERGER, M., AND YULE, W. (1975a). 'Attainment and adjustment in two geographical areas. I. The prevalence of psychiatric disorder', *Brit. J. Psychiat.*, **126**, 493–509.

References

——, GRAHAM, P., CHADWICK, O. F. D., AND YULE, W. (1976). 'Adolescent turmoil: fact or fiction?' *J. Child Psychol. Psychiat.*, **17**, 35–56.

——, GREENFELD, D., AND LOCKYER, L. (1967). 'A five to fifteen year follow-up study of infantile psychosis. II. Social and behavioural outcome', *Brit. J. Psychiat.*, **113**, 1183–99.

—— AND MADGE, N. (1976). *Cycles of Disadvantage* (London: Heinemann Educ.).

——, MAUGHAN, B., MORTIMORE, P., OUSTON, J., WITH SMITH, A. (1979). *Fifteen Thousand Hours: Secondary Schools and their effects on Children* (London: Open Books).

—— AND QUINTON, D. (1977). 'Psychiatric disorder—Ecological factors and concepts of causation', in McGurk, H. (ed), *Ecological Factors in Human Development* (Amsterdam: North-Holland).

——, TIZARD, J., AND WHITMORE, K. (eds) (1970). *Education, Health and Behaviour* (London: Longmans).

——, YULE, B., MORTON, J., AND BAGLEY, C. (1975b). 'Children of West Indian immigrants. III. Home circumstances and family patterns', *J. Child Psychol. Psychiat.*, **16**, 105–23.

——, ——, QUINTON, D., ROWLANDS, O., YULE, W., AND BERGER, M. (1975c). 'Attainment and adjustment in two geographical areas: III. Some factors accounting for area differences', *Brit. J. Psychiat.*, **126**, 520–33.

—— AND YULE, W. (1973). 'Specific Reading Retardation'. In Mann, L. and Sabatino, D. A. (eds), *The First Review of Special Education* (Philadelphia: Butterwood Farms Inc).

——, ——, BERGER, M., YULE, B., MORTON, J., AND BAGLEY, C. (1974). 'Children of West Indian Immigrants. I. Rates of behavioural deviance and of psychiatric disorder', *J. Child Psychol. Psychiat.*, **15**, 241–62.

RYDE-BLOMQVIST, E. (1978). 'Contraception in adolescence—a review of the literature', in Parkes, A. S., Short, R. V., Potts, M., and Herbertson, M. A. (eds), *Fertility in adolescence, J. biosoc. Sci., suppl.* 5, pp 129–59 (Cambridge: Galton Foundation).

SAINSBURY, P. (1955). *Suicide in London* (London: Chapman & Hall).

SANDBERG, S. T., RUTTER, M., AND TAYLOR, E. (1978). 'Hyperkinetic disorder in psychiatric clinic attenders', *Develop. Med. Child Neurol.*, **20**, 279–99.

SCARR, S. AND WEINBERG, R. A. (1976). 'IQ test performance of black children adopted by white families', *Amer. Psychol.*, **31**, 726–39.

SCHACHAR, R., RUTTER, M., AND SMITH, A. (1979). 'The characteristics of situationally and pervasively overactive children: implications for syndrome definition'. (Submitted for publication).

SCHOFIELD, M. (1965). *The Sexual Behaviour of Young People* (London: Longmans).

—— (1973). *The Sexual Behaviour of Young Adults* (London: Allen Lane).

References

SCHOOF-TAMS, K., SCHLAEGEL, J., AND WALCZAK, L. (1976). 'Differentiation of sexual morality between 11 and 16 years', *Arch. Sex. Behav.*, **5**, 353–70.

SCOTT, J. A. (1962). 'Intelligence, physique and family size', *Brit. J. prev. soc. Med.*, **16**, 165–73.

SELIGMAN, M. E. P. (1975). *Helplessness: On Depression, Development and Death* (San Francisco: W. H. Freeman).

—— (1976). 'Depression and learned helplessness', in Van Praag, H. M. (ed), *Research in Neurosis*, pp 72–107 (Utrecht: Bohn, Scheltema & Holkema).

SHAFFER, D. (1974). 'Suicide in childhood and early adolescence', *J. Child Psychol. Psychiat.*, **15**, 275–92.

—— (1977). 'Drug treatment', in Rutter, M. and Hersov, L. (eds), *Child Psychiatry: Modern Approaches*, pp 901–22 (Oxford: Blackwell Scientific).

—— (1978). 'Longitudinal research and the minimal brain damage syndrome', in Kalverboer, A. F., van Praag, H. M., and Mendlewicz, J. (eds), *Minimal Brain Dysfunction: Fact or Fiction?* Advances in Biological Psychiatry, vol. 1 (Basel: Karger).

——, PETTIGREW, A., WOLKIND, S., AND ZAJICEK, E. (1978). 'Psychiatric aspects of pregnancy in schoolgirls: a review', *Psychol. Med.*, **8**, 119–30.

SHAW, C. R. AND McKAY, H. D. (1942). *Juvenile Delinquency and Urban Areas* (Chicago: University of Chicago Press).

SHEPHERD, M., OPPENHEIM, B., AND MITCHELL, S. (1971). *Childhood Behaviour and Mental Health* (London: University of London Press).

SHERIF, M., HARVEY, O. J., WHITE, B. J., HOOD, W. R., AND SHERIF, C. W. (1961). *Intergroup Conflict and Cooperation: The Robbers' Cave Experiment* (Norman, Oklahoma: University of Oklahoma Press).

SHIELDS, J. (1977). 'Polygenic influences', in Rutter, M. and Hersov, L. (eds), *Child Psychiatry: Modern Approaches*, pp 22–46 (Oxford: Blackwell Scientific).

—— (1979). 'Genetics and mental development', in Rutter, M. (ed), *Scientific Foundations of Developmental Psychiatry* (London: Heinemann Medical). (In press).

SIMMONS, R. G., ROSENBERG, F., AND ROSENBERG, M. (1973). 'Disturbance in the self-image at adolescence', *Amer. Sociol. Rev.*, **38**, 553–68.

SINCLAIR, I. A. C. (1971). *Hostels for Probationers* (London: HMSO).

—— AND CLARKE, R. V. G. (1973). 'Acting-out behaviour and its significance for the residential treatment of delinquents', *J. Child Psychol. Psychiat.*, **14**, 283–91.

SMART, C. (1979). 'The new female criminal: reality or myth?' *Brit. J. Criminol.*, **19**, 50–9.

SMITH, S. M. (ed) (1978). *The Maltreatment of children* (Lancaster: MTP Press).

SMITH, C. S., FARRANT, M. R., AND MARCHANT, H. J. (1972). *The Wincroft Youth Project—a social work programme in a slum area* (London: Tavistock).

SOMMER, B. B. (1978a). *Puberty and Adolescence.* (New York: Oxford University Press).

—— (1978b). 'Stress and menstrual distress', *J. Human Stress*, **4**, 5–10 and 41–47.

References

SORENSON, R. C. (1973). *Adolescent Sexuality in Contemporary America: personal values and sexual behaviour ages thirteen to nineteen* (New York: World Publishing).

STACEY, M., DEARDEN, R., PILL, R., AND ROBINSON, D. (1970). *Hospitals, Children and Their Families: The report of a pilot study* (London: Routledge & Kegan Paul).

STANLEY, E. J. AND BARTER, J. T. (1970). 'Adolescent suicidal behaviour', *Amer. J. Orthopsychiat.*, 40, 87–96.

STARR, J. M. (1974). 'The peace and love generation: changing attitudes toward sex and violence among college youth', *J. Social Issues.*, 30, 73–106.

START, K. B. AND WELLS, B. K. (1972). *The Trend of Reading Standards* (Slough: NFER).

STEFFENSMEIER, D. J. (1978). 'Crime and the contemporary woman: An analysis of changing levels of female property crime, 1960–75', *Social Forces*, 57, 566–84.

STEWART, A. L. (1977). 'The survival of low birth weight infants', *Brit. J. Hosp. Med.*, 18, 182–90.

STONE, J. AND TAYLOR, F. (1977). *Vandalism in Schools* (London: Save the Children Fund).

SURGEON-GENERAL (1972). *Television and Growing Up: The impact of televised violence* (Washington, DC: Supt. of Documents, U.S. Government Printing Office).

SUSSENWEIN, F. (1977). 'Psychiatric social work', in Rutter, M. and Hersov, L. (eds), *Child Psychiatry: Modern Approaches*, pp 967–91 (Oxford: Blackwell Scientific).

SUTER, L. E. AND MILLER, H. P. (1973). 'Income differences between men and career women', in Huber, J. (ed), *Changing Women in A Changing Society* (Chicago: University of Chicago Press).

TAIT, C. D., AND HODGES, E. F. (1962). *Delinquents, Their Families and the Community* (Springfield, Ill.: Charles C. Thomas).

TANNER, J. M. (1966). 'Galtonian eugenics and the study of growth. The relation of body size, intelligence test score, and social circumstances in children and adults', *Eugen. Rev.*, 58, 122–35.

—— (1970). 'Physical growth', in Mussen, P. H. (ed), *Carmichael's Manual of Child Psychology*, third edition, vol. 1, pp 77–155 (New York: Wiley).

—— (1971). 'Sequence, tempo and individual variation in the growth and development of boys and girls aged twelve to sixteen', *Daedalus*, 907–30.

——, WHITEHOUSE, R. H., AND TAKAISHI, M. (1966). 'Standards from birth to maturity for height, weight, height velocity, and weight velocity: British children 1965', *Arch. Dis. Childh.*, 41, 454–71; 613–35.

TAYLOR, F. (1978). 'How the graffiti disappeared from the ladies' loos', *Education*, 27 September.

TAYLOR, J. H. (1976). *The Half-Way Generation: A study of Asian Youths in Newcastle upon Tyne* (Slough: NFER).

References

TENNANT, T. G. (1970). 'Truancy and stealing. A comparative study of Education Act cases and property offenders', *Brit. J. Psychiat.*, **116**, 587–92.

THEANDER, S. (1970). 'Anorexia nervosa. A psychiatric investigation of 94 female patients', *Acta Psychiat Scand.* suppl. 214.

THOMPSON, J. (1976). 'Fertility and abortion inside and outside marriage', *Population Trends*, **5**, 3–8.

THORNES, B., AND COLLARD, J. (1979). *Who Divorces?* (London: Routledge & Kegan Paul).

TIZARD, J. (1964). *Community Services for the Mentally Handicapped* (London: Oxford University Press).

——, MOSS, P., AND PERRY, J. (1976). *All Our Children: Preschool services in a changing society* (London: Temple Smith).

TOOLAN, J. M. (1962). 'Suicide and suicidal attempts in children and adolescents', *Amer. J. Psychiat.*, **118**, 719–24.

TOWNSEND, H. E. R., AND BRITTAN, E. M. (1972). *Organization in Multiracial Schools* (Slough: NFER).

TRISELIOTIS, J. (1978). 'Growing up Fostered', *Adoption and Fostering*, **94**, 11–23.

TUTT, N. (1976). 'Recommittals of juvenile delinquents', *Brit. J. Criminol.*, **16**, 385–88.

U.S. BUREAU OF THE CENSUS (1977). *Statistical Abstract of the United States* (Washington, D.C.: Government Printing Office).

U.S. DEPARTMENT OF HEALTH, EDUCATION AND WELFARE (1966). *Patients in Mental Hospitals.* Chevy Chase, Md: Public Service Publication no. 1818.

VAILLANT, G. E. (1977). *Adaptation to Life: how the best and brightest came of age* (Boston: Little, Brown).

VARLAAM, A. (1974). 'Educational attainment and behaviour at school', *Greater London Intelligence Quarterly*, no. 29, December 1974, 29–37.

VEREKER, C., MAYS, J. B., GITTUS, E., AND BROADY, M. (1961). *Urban Redevelopment and Social Changes: a study of social conditions in Central Liverpool, 1955-6* (Liverpool: Liverpool University Press).

WADSWORTH, M. (1979). *Roots of Delinquency: infancy, adolescence and crime* (Oxford: Martin Robertson).

WALDRON, S. (1976). 'The significance of childhood neurosis for adult mental health: a follow-up study', *Amer. J. Psychiat.*, **133**, 532–38.

WALLERSTEIN, J., AND KELLY, J. (1979). 'Children and divorce', in J. Noshpitz (ed), *Basic Handbook of Child Psychiatry,* vol. 4 (New York: Basic Books). In press.

321

References

WALLIS, C. P., AND MALIPHANT, R. (1967). 'Delinquent areas in the County of London: ecological factors', *Brit. J. Criminol.*, **7**, 250–84.

WALTERS, G. C., AND GRUSEC, J. E. (1977). *Punishment* (San Francisco: Freeman).

WARNOCK, H. M. (1978). See DEPARTMENT OF EDUCATION AND SCIENCE, 1978b.

WARREN, W. (1965a). 'A study of adolescent psychiatric in-patients and the outcome six or more years later. I. Clinical histories and hospital findings', *J. Child Psychol. Psychiat.*, **6**, 1–17.

—— (1965b). Ibid. II. The follow-up study, **6**, 141–60.

—— (1968). 'A study of anorexia nervosa in young girls', Ibid., **9**, 27–40.

WATT, N. F. (1976). 'Longitudinal changes in the social behavior of children hospitalized for schizophrenia as adults', *J. nerv. ment. Dis.*, **155**, 42–54.

—— AND LUBENSKY, A. W. (1976). 'Childhood roots of schizophrenia', *J. consult. clin. Psychol.*, **44**, 353–75.

——, STOLOROW, R. D., LUBENSKY, A. W., AND McCLELLAND, D. C. (1970). 'School adjustment and behavior of children hospitalized for schizophrenia as adults', *Amer. J. Orthopsychiat.*, **40**, 637–57.

WEDGE, P., AND PROSSER, N. (1973). *Born to Fail?* (London: Arrow Books).

WEINER, I. B. (1970). *Psychological Disturbance in Adolescence* (New York: Wiley Inter Science).

—— AND DEL GAUDIO, A. C. D. (1976). 'Psychopathology in adolescence: an epidemiological study', *Arch. gen. Psychiat.*, **33**, 187–93.

WEINTRAUB, S., NEALE, J. B., AND LIEBERT, D. E. (1975). 'Teacher ratings of children vulnerable to psychopathology', *Amer. J. Orthopsychiat.*, **45**, 839–45.

——, PRINZ, R. J., AND NEALE, J. B. (1978). 'Peer evaluations of the competence of children vulnerable to psychopathology', *J. abn. Child Psychol.*, **6**, 461–74.

WEISSMAN, M. M., AND KLERMAN, G. L. (1977). 'Sex differences and the epidemiology of depression', *Arch. gen. Psychiat.*, **34**, 98–111.

WELLS, R., AND DEZEN, A. (1978). 'The results of family therapy revisited: The nonbehavioral methods', *Family Process*, **17**, 251–74.

WELNER, A., WELNER, A., McCRARY, D. P., AND LEONARD, M. A. (1977). 'Psycholopathology in children of in-patients with depression: a controlled study', *J. Nerv. ment. Dis.*, **164**, 408–13.

WERNER, E. E., AND SMITH, R. S. (1977). *Kauai's Children Come of Age* (Honolulu: University Press of Hawaii).

WEST, D. J. (1967). *The Young Offender* (Harmondsworth: Penguin).

—— AND FARRINGTON, D. P. (1973). *Who Becomes Delinquent?* (London: Heinemann Educational).

——, —— (1977). *The Delinquent Way of Life* (London: Heinemann Educational).

WHITE, R. K., AND LIPPITT, R. (1960). *Autocracy and Democracy: An experimental enquiry* (New York: Harper & Row).

WILMOTT, A. S. (1977). *CSE and GCE Grading Standards. The 1973 Comparability Study*. Schools Council Research Studies (London: Macmillan Education).

WILSON, C. W. M. (1972). 'Amphetamine abuse and government legislation', *Brit. J. Addict.*, **67**, 107–12.

References

Wing, J. K., and Fryers, T. (1976). *Psychiatric Services in Camberwell and Salford: Statistics from the Camberwell and Salford Psychiatric Registers 1954–1974* (London: Institute of Psychiatry).

Wolf, M. M., Phillips, E. L., and Fixsen, D. L. (1975). *Achievement Place Phase II: Final Report* (Dept. of Human Development, University of Kansas).

World Health Organization (1976). *New Trends and Approaches in the Delivery of Maternal and Child Care in Health Services: report of a WHO Expert Committee.* WHO Technical Report Series no. 600 (Geneva: WHO).

—— (1977). *Child Mental Health and Psychosocial Development: report of a WHO Expert Committee.* WHO Technical Report Series no. 613 (Geneva: WHO).

Wynne, J. and Hull, D. (1977). 'Why are children admitted to hospitals?' *Brit. Med. J.* **2**, 1140–42.

Yankelovich, D. (1972). *The Changing Values on Campus* (New York: Washington Square Press).

—— (1974). *The New Morality: a profile of American youth in the 70s* (New York: McGraw Hill).

Yarrow, M. R., Scott, P., de Loeuw, L., and Hernig, C. (1962). 'Child-rearing in families of working and non-working mothers', *Sociometry*, **25**, 122–40.

Yudkin, S. (1967). *0–5: a report on the care of pre-school children* (London: National Society Children's Nurseries).

Yule, W. (1977). 'Behavioural approaches', in Rutter, M. and Hersov, L. (eds), *Child Psychiatry: Modern Approaches*, pp 923–48 (Oxford: Blackwell Scientific).

—— (1978). 'Behavioural treatment of children and adolescents with conduct disorders', in Hersov, L. A., Berger, M., and Shaffer, D. (eds), *Aggression and Anti-social Behaviour in Childhood and Adolescence*, pp 115–41 (Oxford: Pergamon).

——, Berger, M., Rutter, M., and Yule, B. (1975). 'Children of West Indian Immigrants: II. Intellectual performance and reading attainment', *J. Child Psychol. Psychiat.*, **16**, 1–17.

——, ——, and Wigley, V. (1977). 'The teacher-child interaction project', *Bull. Brit. Assoc. Behav. Psychother.*, **5**, 42–7.

Zimbardo, P. G. (1969). 'The human choice: individuation, reason and order versus deindividuation, impulse and chaos', in Arnold, W. J., and Page, M. M. (eds), *Nebraska Symposium on Motivation* (Lincoln: University of Nebraska).

—— (1973). 'A field experiment in auto-shaping', in Ward, C. (ed), *Vandalism* (London: Architectural Press).